HEGEL AND THE TRANSFORMATION OF PHILOSOPHICAL CRITIQUE

Hegel and the Transformation of Philosophical Critique

WILLIAM F. BRISTOW

CLARENDON PRESS · OXFORD

OXFORD

UNIVERSITY PRESS

Great Clarendon Street, Oxford OX2 6DP

Oxford University Press is a department of the University of Oxford.
It furthers the University's objective of excellence in research, scholarship,
and education by publishing worldwide in

Oxford New York

Auckland Cape Town Dar es Salaam Hong Kong Karachi
Kuala Lumpur Madrid Melbourne Mexico City Nairobi
New Delhi Shanghai Taipei Toronto

With offices in

Argentina Austria Brazil Chile Czech Republic France Greece
Guatemala Hungary Italy Japan Poland Portugal Singapore
South Korea Switzerland Thailand Turkey Ukraine Vietnam

Oxford is a registered trade mark of Oxford University Press
in the UK and in certain other countries

Published in the United States
by Oxford University Press Inc., New York

British Library Cataloguing in Publication Data

Data available

Library of Congress Cataloging in Publication Data
Bristow, William F.
Hegel and the transformation of philosophical critique / William F. Bristow.
p. cm.
Includes bibliographical references and index.
ISBN-13: 978–0–19–929064–2 (alk. paper)
ISBN-10: 0–19–929064–4 (alk. paper)
1. Hegel, Georg Wilhelm Friedrich, 1770–1831. 2. Kant, Immanuel, 1724–1804.
Kritik der reinen Vernunft. 3. Reason–History. I. Title.
B2949.R25B75 2007 193–dc22 2006037200

Typeset by Laserwords Private Limited, Chennai, India
Printed in Great Britain
on acid-free paper by
Biddles Ltd, King's Lynn, Norfolk

ISBN 978–0–19–929064–2

1 3 5 7 9 10 8 6 4 2

To Frederick Neuhouser

Acknowledgments

I gratefully acknowledge the considerable help and support I have received during the writing of this book. Fred Neuhouser's widely admired lectures on Fichte and Hegel at Harvard in the early 1990s first drew me to become a student of their systems of philosophy and shaped my understanding of them immeasurably. His support has been not only philosophical and intellectual but also moral. I have drawn on his unwavering belief in this project in periods of self-doubt. In acknowledgment that without Fred's support the book would not have appeared, and in deeply felt gratitude for that support, I am pleased to dedicate the work to him.

I have benefited from and been influenced by Charles Parsons's lectures on Kant's *Critique of Pure Reason* to a degree similar to the benefit and influence of Fred Neuhouser's lectures on Fichte and Hegel. Moreover, the exposure to Charles Parsons's extraordinary standards of care and charity in the interpretation of Kant has disciplined this work and made it better than it otherwise would have been.

The extraordinary teaching of Stanley Cavell, as presented both in his writings and in his seminars, has strongly influenced and inspired me, both in general and in relation to the development of this project in particular. Cavell's work contains rich investigations into the ways and byways of philosophical criticism and of our hopes for and disappointments in it, in relation to some of our basic aspirations as human beings. This book, which foregrounds and motivates the self-transformational ambition of Hegel's philosophical criticism, is beholden to Cavell's work and teaching in various, sometimes subterranean ways.

During the formative period of this project, I had the benefit of reading some of Paul Franks's exciting work on the thought of the German idealists and of gestalt-changing conversations with him about their philosophies. These encounters stimulated and shaped my thinking as it relates to this project. I also had the benefit during this same period of countless long philosophical conversations with Arata Hamawaki, about everything really, but often revolving around or returning to the thought of Kant and that of post-Kantian philosophers. Beyond the immense amount that I learned from them in terms of content, these treasured conversations did much to shape me philosophically, and I feel fortunate to have the opportunity here to acknowledge their influence and express my thankfulness for them.

During later stages of this project, transplanted to Southern California, I profited greatly from enjoyable, stimulating, and instructive philosophical conversations on relevant topics with Wayne Martin. In addition, Wayne generously read drafts of portions of the work and provided very useful comments. His support has helped to sustain and improve the project significantly. Sally Sedgwick has also had a beneficial influence on this project, ever since I had the good fortune of meeting her when she was a visiting professor at Harvard in the late 1990s. The happy discovery that we shared a general interpretive orientation to Hegel's critique of Kant encouraged me in my then still tentative inquiries in this direction. Sally generously read and provided very helpful comments on portions of the work that have led to improvements.

Ian Duckles, John H. Smith, and Nick White have also generously read portions of this work and provided helpful comments. I would also like to thank the anonymous referees of the manuscript, whose comments, besides leading to significant improvements in the work, have also taught me to see more clearly its permanent limitations. And sincere thanks to Jess Smith, Carolyn McAndrew and my production editor, Jenni Craig, for their work in bringing the book through the production process at OUP.

I owe an inestimable personal debt to my wife Miren Boehm, whose love and support has nourished and sustained me through the later stages of this project.

I thank the School of Humanities, University of California, Irvine, for a Faculty Development Award, which enabled one term of course relief devoted to this project, and for sabbatical leave, which enabled another.

I am grateful for the permission to reproduce material in Chapter One from the following copyrighted material: 'Are Kant's Categories Subjective?' *The Review of Metaphysics*, vol. LV, No. 3, March 2002, 551–80. Copyright (2002) by *The Review of Metaphysics*.

Contents

Abbreviations

Immanuel Kant

References to Kant's texts are given by volume and page number of the Academy edition, *Kants gesammelte Schriften* (29 volumes; Deutschen Akademie der Wissenschaften, Berlin, Walter de Gruyter, 1900–1942). The exception is the *Critique of Pure Reason*, which I cite using the standard A and B pagination of the first and second editions respectively. Below I indicate the abbreviations I use for individual works and the English translations of these works to which I refer.

Ak   *Kants gesammelte Schriften* (29 volumes; Deutschen Akademie der Wissenschaften, Berlin, Walter de Gruyter, 1900–1942). Cited by volume and page number.

GMS   *Die Grundlegung zur Metaphysik der Sitten* (1785). In volume 4 of Academy edition (Ak).
          Groundwork of the Metaphysics of Morals, translated and edited by Mary Gregor (Cambridge: Cambridge University Press, 1998).

InDiss   *De mundi sensibilis atque intelligibilis forma et principiis* (commonly referred to as Inaugural Dissertation), (1770). In volume 2 of the Academy edition (Ak).
          On the Form and Principles of the Sensible and Intelligible World, translated by David Wolford in Immanuel Kant, *Theoretical Philosophy: 1755-1770* (Cambridge: Cambridge University Press, 1992), 373–416.

KU   *Kritik der Urteilskraft* (1790). In volume 5 of the Academy edition (Ak).
          Critique of Judgment, translated by Werner Pluhar (Indianapolis: Hackett, 1987).

KpV   *Kritik der praktischen Vernunft* (1788). In volume 5 of the Academy edition (Ak).

      Critique of Practical Reason, translated and edited by Mary Gregor (Cambridge: Cambridge University Press, 1997).

KrV *Kritik der reinen Vernunft* (1781; 2nd edn., 1787).
      Critique of Pure Reason, translated and edited by Paul Guyer and Allen W. Wood (Cambridge: Cambridge University Press, 1998). I also use the translation of Norman Kemp Smith (New York: St Martin's, 1965).

MS *Metaphysik der Sitten* (1797). In volume 6 of Academy edition (Ak).
      Metaphysics of Morals, in Immanuel Kant *Practical Philosophy*, translated and edited by Mary J. Gregor (Cambridge: Cambridge University Press, 1996), 353–603.

Prol *Prolegomena zu einer jeden künftigen Metaphysik, die als Wissenschaft wird auftreten können* (1783). In volume 4 of Academy edition (Ak).
      Prolegomena to any Future Metaphysics, translated by Paul Carus, revised by James W. Ellington (Indianapolis: Hackett, 1977).

Rel *Die Religion innerhalb der Grenzen der bloßen Vernunft* (1792–1793). In volume 6 of Academy edition (Ak).
      Religion Within the Boundaries of Mere Reason, and Other Writings, translated and edited by Allen Wood and George di Giovanni (Cambridge: Cambridge University Press, 1998).

Georg Wilhelm Friedrich Hegel

I cite Hegel's works using the edition usually cited: *Werke im zwanzig Bänden*, edited by Eva Moldenhauer and Karl Markus Michel (Frankfurt am Main: Suhrkamp, 1970). In referring to his individual works, I have employed the abbreviations below. Where an abbreviation refers to both the German original and an English translation, I give page references to both, with the German first and the English second, separated by an oblique (/). In those cases in which the text is divided into relatively brief sections (for example, the *Encyclopedia Logic* and the *Philosophy of Right*) I cite using section rather than page number, which eliminates the need for two citations.

BKH *Between Kant and Hegel: Texts in the Development of Post-Kantian Idealism*, translated and annotated by George di Giovanni and H. S. Harris (Albany, NY: SUNY Press, 1985). I use this text when citing the English translation of Hegel's essays *On the Essence of Philosophical Critique* (WdpK) and *On the Relation of Skepticism to Philosophy* (VSP), as well as writings by Karl Leonhard Reinhold and G. E. Schulze.

Diff *Differenz der fichte'schen und schelling'schen Systems der Philosophie* (1801). In *Werke*, volume 2.
The Difference Between Fichte's and Schelling's System of Philosophy, translated by H. S. Harris and W. Cerf (Albany: SUNY Press, 1977).

EL *Die Enzyklopädie des philosophischen Wissenschaften, erster Teil: Logik* (1817/1827). In *Werke*, volume 8. (Known as the *Encyclopedia Logic*). I cite this text by section number. Some of the sections are supplemented by Hegel's elucidatory remarks and by additions derived from student notes to Hegel's lectures. Following convention, I append 'A' (for *Anmerkung*) to the section number when citing Hegel's remarks to a section, and I append 'Z' (for *Zusatz*) to the section number when citing the student additions.
Hegel's Logic, translated by William Wallace (Oxford: Clarendon Press, 1975).

GW *Glauben und Wissen* (1802). In *Werke*, volume 2.
Faith and Knowledge, translated and edited by W. Cerf and H. S. Harris (Albany, NY: State University of New York Press, 1977).

PhG *Die Phänomenologie des Geistes* (1807). In *Werke*, volume 3.
Phenomenology of Spirit, translated by A. V. Miller (Oxford: Oxford University Press, 1977). I cite the English translation by numbered paragraph.

PhR *Grundlinien der Philosophie des Rechts* (1820). In *Werke*, volume 7.
Elements of the Philosophy of Right, edited by Allen Wood, translated by H. B. Nisbet (Cambridge: Cambridge University Press, 1991). I cite this text by section number. Some of the sections are supplemented by Hegel's elucidatory remarks and by additions compiled by Eduard Gans from lecture notes of students at Hegel's lectures. Following convention, I append 'A' (for *Anmerkung*) to the section number when citing Hegel's remarks to a section and I append 'Z' (for *Zusatz*) to the section number when citing the student additions.

VGP   *Vorlesungen über die Geschichte der Philosophie.* In *Werke*, volumes 18–20.

       Hegel's Lectures on the History of Philosophy, 3 volumes, translated by E. S. Haldane and Frances H. Simson (London: Routledge and Kegan Paul, 1896, reprinted 1955).

VSP   *Verhältnis des Skeptizismus zur Philosophie. Darstellung seiner verschiedenen Modifikationen und Vergleichung des neuesten mit dem alten* (1802). In *Werke*, volume 2.

       On the Relation of Skepticism to Philosophy, Exposition of its Different Modifications and Comparison of the Latest Form with the Ancient One, translated with notes by H. S. Harris in BKH, 311–62.

WL   *Wissenschaft der Logik* (1812–1816). In *Werke*, volumes 5 and 6.

       Science of Logic, translated by A. V. Miller (Amherst, NY: Prometheus Books, 1999).

WdpK   *Einleitung. Über das Wesen der philosophischen Kritik überhaupt und ihr Verhältnis zum gegenwärtigen Zustand der Philosophie insbesondere* (1802). In *Werke*, volume 2.

       The Critical Journal, Introduction: On the Essence of Philosophical Criticism Generally, and its Relationship to the Present State of Philosophy in Particular, translated with notes by H. S. Harris in BKH, 272–91.

Werke *Werke im zwanzig Bänden*, edited by Eva Moldenhauer and Karl Markus Michel (Frankfurt am Main: Suhrkamp, 1970).

Introduction

Whether, or to what extent, Hegel's system of philosophy regresses to the dogmatic rational metaphysics that Kant had effectively criticized in his *Critique of Pure Reason* is one of the central perennial issues about Hegel's thought. Undeniably, Hegel makes bold claims on behalf of reason, in conscious defiance of the limits Kant famously draws. According to Kant's critical limits, human reason cannot achieve knowledge beyond the bounds of possible experience, and hence knowledge of reason's special objects in metaphysics (of God, of the soul, of the size, age, or causal ground of the world as a whole) is impossible for us. Kantian criticism consists in the self-limitation of human reason. Hegel, in contrast, claims for his system what he calls 'absolute' knowledge, (or also 'knowledge of the absolute'). Instead of limiting itself, reason finally attains in Hegel's system of thought perfectly adequate knowledge of that which it has in the history of metaphysics forever been attempting to know. Hegel presents his system as the complete fulfillment of reason's age-old ambitions.[1] While so much is undeniable, readers are sharply divided in their responses to Hegel's apparently transgressive metaphysics.

If Hegel's thought has been largely absent in the tradition of Anglo-American analytic philosophy over the last century, this is to a great extent due to the widespread perception that his thought is 'extravagantly' metaphysical. In a tradition of philosophy marked by its hostility to metaphysics in general, Hegel's talk of 'the Absolute', 'Spirit', 'the Subject', 'the Negative', etc.—all usually capitalized in English translations—has been read as so untied to epistemological constraints as to be nonsense. Hegel acquired the reputation as an unregenerate speculative metaphysician, complacently unconcerned with issues of epistemological justification. Consequently Hegel's thought

---

[1] Hegel writes in the Introduction to his *Science of Logic* that its 'content is the exposition of God as he is in his eternal essence before the creation of nature and the finite mind' (Hegel, WL, vol. 5, 44/50). (For the manner in which I refer to the texts of Hegel and of Kant, please see the section entitled 'Abbreviations'.)

was supposed worthy of serious consideration (if at all) mostly only in the domain of social and political philosophy, not in the domain of metaphysics or epistemology.[2]

Things have changed recently. In the past generation or so, Hegel studies have enjoyed a renaissance in English language scholarship.[3] Partly this renaissance has been fueled by formidable recent work combating the misconception of Hegel as a retrograde metaphysician, simply unconcerned with the epistemological grounding of his bold metaphysical claims.[4] Recent studies have convincingly made the case, not only that Hegel has an epistemology, but that Hegel is *intensely* concerned with the epistemological justification of his metaphysical system. However, there is fundamental disagreement among recent commentators regarding how to understand the shape and direction of Hegel's epistemology.[5] This study offers a new interpretation of the shape of Hegel's epistemology, one that takes advantage of recent work, but which goes beyond that work as well, in part through bringing together disparate, apparently contradictory strands of recent scholarship.

Granted Hegel's intense concern with epistemological justification, how could sensitive readers have missed his epistemology? Prominent among the many tasks of Hegel's *Phenomenology of Spirit* is its epistemological task: to demonstrate exhaustively and thoroughly the possibility of absolute knowledge, the possibility of the metaphysical system he subsequently propounds

---

[2] Michael Forster documents nicely the traditional blindness to Hegel's epistemology—not only among casual readers of Hegel's work, but among Hegel scholars as well—in a chapter entitled 'Hegel's Epistemology?' of his book *Hegel and Skepticism*.

[3] Charles Taylor's *Hegel* is often cited as marking a turning point.

[4] Recent work in English expounding and defending Hegel as an epistemologist includes: Michael Forster, *Hegel and Skepticism* and *Hegel's Idea of a Phenomenology of Spirit*; Paul Franks, *All or Nothing*; William Maker, *Philosophy Without Foundations: Rethinking Hegel*; Robert Pippin, *Hegel's Idealism: The Satisfactions of Self-Consciousness*; Tom Rockmore, *Hegel's Circular Epistemology* and *On Hegel's Epistemology and Contemporary Philosophy*; Kenneth Westphal, *Hegel's Epistemological Realism* and *Hegel's Epistemology: A Philosophical Introduction to the* Phenomenology of Spirit. Karl Ameriks surveys and discusses much of this work in his article 'Recent Work on Hegel: The Rehabilitation of an Epistemologist?' For recent work on Hegel's epistemology by German scholars, see *Skeptizismus und spekulatives Denken in der Philosophie Hegels*, edited by Hans-Friedrich Fulda and Rolf-Peter Horstmann.

[5] Two fundamental disagreements are worth mentioning here: (i) Kenneth Westphal's attention to Hegel's epistemology has led him to the view 'that Hegel's "idealism" is in fact a realist form of holism' (*Hegel's Epistemology*, xi), whereas Pippin's perception that Hegel continues Kant's critical programme has led him to view Hegel's position as inscribed into a broadly idealist framework; (ii) Michael Forster's attention to the relatively neglected early work by Hegel on the difference between ancient and modern skepticism has led him to interpret Hegel's epistemological procedure as an adaptation of ancient skeptical procedure (and to recommend it to us as such), whereas Pippin interprets (and recommends to our attention) Hegel's epistemological procedure as an adaptation of Kant's.

(in his *Science of Logic* and in his *Encyclopedia of Philosophical Sciences*). Given that Hegel's most famous work is a systematic epistemological grounding of his metaphysics, how could readers find Hegel indifferent to epistemological questions and content dogmatically to assert metaphysical claims?

Ironically, the answer lies in the very intensity of Hegel's reflection on, and experimentation with, epistemological procedure in his Jena period (1800–1806). Hegel's engagement with epistemological procedure arises in the context of controversies surrounding Kant's epistemological project of critique. Naturally enough, one effect of Kant's 'revolution in methodology', of his celebrated project of philosophical critique, is to concentrate philosophers' attention on the question of how metaphysical knowledge can be justified. In the immediate aftermath of the publication of Kant's *Critique of Pure Reason*, there is much controversy regarding Kant's critical project. Hegel cuts his philosophical teeth, so to speak, in an environment in which the so-called 'meta-critical' challenges to Kant's criticism are salient. His earliest published writings show him concerned from the beginning with how to establish metaphysics as a science, as Kant's criticism promises to do, against the background of the assumption (shared by many of Hegel's contemporaries) that Kant's critique fails to fulfill its promise to do so. The ultimate result of Hegel's early reflection on epistemological procedure is his *Phenomenology of Spirit*. But the *Phenomenology of Spirit* is such a multifaceted work, and its epistemological method has such an unusual form, that one easily overlooks altogether the respects in which it dispatches an epistemological task. Ironically, Hegel's intense early reflection on the question of *how* to ground our metaphysical knowledge in the face of skeptical challenges ultimately yields a method so unfamiliar that we miss the epistemology altogether and judge that he complacently propounds dogmatic metaphysics, oblivious to Kant's trenchant challenges to the possibility of such knowledge.

This study argues that Hegel's *Phenomenology of Spirit* is, in its epistemological aims and methodology, thoroughly shaped by Hegel's response to the event of Kant's philosophical criticism. The story of Hegel's response to the event of Kant's criticism has a few very important plot twists. The story begins with a fundamental objection that Hegel directs against Kant's critical project. The main work of Part I of this two-part study is to develop (and provide limited defense for) Hegel's objection. The basic outline of the objection is as follows. The task of Kant's philosophical criticism is to determine, in a subjective reflection on our cognitive capacities, how and whether metaphysics (rational knowledge) is possible for us. The critical inquiry is (I argue) an attempt to establish the content and authority of the highest norms of reason as a pro-paedeutic to the subsequent construction of a science of metaphysics on the basis of these norms. Though Hegel nowhere develops his objection fully and thoroughly, he expresses the view at several places that Kant's project of philo-sophical critique begs the question *against* the possibility of metaphysics for us; Hegel expresses the view, moreover, that the attempt to establish the content and authority of reason's highest principles in a prior, self-reflective inquiry implicitly *confines* us cognitively to a subjectively constituted domain, that is, to knowledge of mere appearances. Thus, Hegel objects that the subjectivism at which Kant's critical inquiry arrives—meaning by 'subjectivism' merely the general claim that knowledge of objects is relativized to the standpoint of the knowing subject—is implicit from the beginning in Kant's critical procedure. Though Hegel's usually rather summary dismissals of Kant's criticism have tended either to be uncritically embraced (by commentators already sym-pathetic to Hegel) or quickly dismissed as based on a crude reading of Kant's doctrines (by philosophers already sympathetic to Kant), few have under-taken to develop and construct Hegel's objection carefully and critically. Part I develops a case on behalf of Hegel's contention against Kant's critical project, responsive to the complexity and philosophical richness of Kant's project.

The context of analytic philosophy poses obstacles to gaining a fair hearing for Hegel's objection against Kant's criticism. The obstacles derive from the way in which prominent preoccupations of analytic epistemology have shaped the analytic reception of Kant's epistemology. So I comment here briefly on the shape of this reception in order to explain how I attempt to overcome the obstacles in presenting Hegel's objection in Part I. However, we get there by way of a brief comment on the way in which Hegel's epistemology finds itself on the agenda of contemporary analytic epistemologists.

Surprisingly, the recent wave of interest in Hegel's epistemology is not limited to scholars of Hegel's thought but extends also to a smattering of prom-inent analytic epistemologists themselves.[6] It's one thing for Hegel's epistem-ology to be taken seriously by analytic philosophers interested in the history of philosophy; but it is quite another for it to be drawn upon by contemporary analytic epistemologists, as if it might actually be (at least partly) right! What

---

[6] John McDowell remarks in the preface to his Locke lectures, published as *Mind and World*, that he would like to conceive those lectures as a 'prolegomenon to a reading of [Hegel's *Phenomenology of Spirit*]' (ix). Robert Brandom also points in recent work towards Hegel's thought as containing lessons for us in how to understand knowledge. See, in particular, *Making It Explicit: Reasoning, Representing and Discursive Content* and *Articulating Reasons: An Introduction to Inferentialism*.

explains this surprising development? Speaking quite generally, of course, analytic philosophy—over the last five decades or so—has been oriented against the Cartesian dualism of mind and world and against the conception of the epistemological task associated with this dualism. In general, analytic philosophers have wanted to reject or get beyond the Cartesian conception of knowledge as achieved through bridging an ontological and epistemological gulf across which the subjective and the objective are supposed to face each other.[7] Such a conception seems destined to deposit us either in external world skepticism or in subjectivism. Hegel is one of the first philosophers in the tradition to conceive what is distinctively modern in philosophy in terms of this ontological and epistemological gulf. Moreover, Hegel explicitly turns against the modern in philosophy, on this conception of what the modern in philosophy consists in. Now that certain strands of analytic epistemology, worked out independently of Hegel, have arrived at a similar conception of our struggle to understand human knowledge correctly, some analytic philosophers are discovering Hegel's thought as a resource in their own work.

However, we need to say slightly more in order to explain how Hegel's thought finds itself on the agenda of contemporary epistemologists. It gets there by way of dissatisfaction with naturalized epistemology. Naturalizing epistemologists also would transcend the Cartesian conception of the epistemological task. But the naturalization strategy does not lead thinkers in the direction of Hegel's thought. The naturalization of epistemology consists—in one classic characterization, anyway—in construing epistemological inquiry as contained within the (empirical) science of nature. According to naturalizing epistemologists, the task of epistemology should not be construed as that of *justifying* the possibility of knowledge of objects (objects conceived, initially anyway, as 'external') from a standpoint of epistemological reflection situated (somehow) outside or before our actual knowledge. Instead, the task should be conceived as the natural-scientific task of *explaining* (empirically, of course) how 'the human subject ... posits bodies and projects his physics from his data ... ' from a position situated *within* the ongoing concern of natural science.[8] However, epistemology so construed may seem to elide something essential to epistemology, namely, the moment of the epistemic subject's recognition of (or failure to recognize) the *reasons* for judgment. One important source of dissatisfaction with the strategy of naturalizing

---

[7] I take this characterization of the modern epistemological situation from John McDowell's 'Knowledge and the Internal', 889.

[8] Willard Van Orman Quine, 'Epistemology Naturalized', 83.

epistemology is that it can seem either to ignore rational relations (and the capacities necessary for us to recognize them) or to reduce them to natural causal relations. Accordingly there arises the ambition within contemporary analytic epistemology to exorcize the spectre of an ontological and epistemological gulf to be bridged, but without reducing rational norms or our human capacity to respond to rational norms to natural causal relations fully explicated in the terms of empirical science. This task has led some such thinkers back to Hegel, since Hegel undertakes to understand human knowers *both* as rational beings, who as such are responsive to—and responsible for their adherence to—norms of reason, *and* as fully at home in nature.

At this point we must take brief notice of the Kantian background. The background to the perceived tension between seeing ourselves as responsive to reasons in knowledge, on the one hand, and seeing ourselves as fully integrated into the natural world on the other, lies more immediately in Kant's philosophy than in Descartes's. We owe to Kant, more than to any other modern philosopher, the articulated conception of the human subject as self-consciously responsive to norms in its activity of knowledge. However, in Kant's philosophy, this conception is bound up with a version of the modern dualism that contemporary epistemologists would transcend. According to Kant, we place ourselves, by virtue of our self-conscious capacity to recognize reasons (or fail to), in what he calls a 'realm of freedom', a realm structured by normative laws (reasons), over against what he calls 'the realm of nature', which is structured in a thoroughgoing way by natural causal laws. As Hegel is interpreted in this study, he attempts to transcend Kant's version of the modern dualism, but while maintaining hold of Kant's conception of the human subject as responsive to reasons in its epistemic activity. The recent interest in Hegel's epistemology among analytic philosophers is funded, to a significant degree, by the perception of his thought as undertaking this needed task.

But this raises a question. If analytic epistemology has been turned against what we might call the 'Cartesian paradigm', and if Hegel's thought is proving useful now in the conceptual struggle against that paradigm, in opposition to Kant's thought, which is still structured by it, then why has Kant's epistemology enjoyed such sustained and significant influence within the tradition of analytic epistemology, whereas Hegel's has been virtually completely absent? The answer lies in the way in which Kant's epistemology has been received within analytic epistemology. Though Kant's epistemology has indeed enjoyed a significant place in the tradition of analytic epistemology, the *interpretations* of Kant's epistemology by virtue of which it has enjoyed this place have tended either simply to excise, or at least to soft-pedal, Kant's subjectivism. So, for example, Peter Strawson interprets Kant's epistemology in his *Bounds of Sense* in such a way that the idealism and subjectivism can be (and ought to be) more or less cleanly excised from his thought. According to Strawson's interpretation, the subjectivism follows only from the 'misleading' and 'disastrous' psychological model in terms of which Kant chooses to present his epistemological investigation. Though Kant presents his epistemological investigation 'as an investigation into the structure and workings of the cognitive capacities of beings such as ourselves', the philosophical heart of the work is best distilled from Kant's arbitrary psychological idiom.[9] The Strawsonian process of distillation yields a philosophical project that looks suspiciously like that of the logical positivists. Against the background of the attack on the possibility of traditional rationalist metaphysics, Kant's positive contribution to the discipline of epistemology, on this interpretation, is to undertake to articulate 'the conceptual structure which is presupposed in all empirical inquiries'.[10] Moreover, Kant's epistemological procedure shows, as against the Cartesian tradition, the bankruptcy of any attempt 'to justify our belief in the objective world by working outwards, as it were, from the private data of individual consciousness'.[11] Thus, on Strawson's interpretation of Kant's epistemology, far from it being the case that Kant's epistemology belongs to the Cartesian paradigm, Kant provides us both powerful arguments against the procedure of that paradigm and a model for a new epistemological procedure that escapes that paradigm.

Though Strawson's interpretation of Kant's epistemology has been tremendously influential in the context of analytic Kant studies (even among scholars of Kant's thought who aspire to greater historical sensitivity than Strawson himself does),[12] there have of course been opposing interpretations which have also enjoyed great influence. Here I mention only one other, in

---

[9] P. F. Strawson, *Bounds of Sense*, 19. But see all of part one.   [10] *Ibid.*, 18.

[11] *Ibid.*, 19. According to Strawson's reading of Kant's transcendental deduction of the categories and of his refutation of idealism, both arguments contain centrally the claim 'that the fundamental condition of the possibility of empirical self-consciousness is that experience should contain at least the seeds of the idea of one experiential or subjective route through an objective world' (127–8). Thus, if Kant's arguments work, on this interpretation, there could be no Cartesian epistemological gulf as defined by doubt regarding the existence of the *external objects* of the inner representations of which we are immediately certain in empirical self-consciousness.

[12] Paul Guyer's work shares with Strawson's a general orientation to what is philosophically productive in Kant's *Critique of Pure Reason*. Guyer provides thorough (and ultimately damning) criticism of Kant's various versions of his transcendental deduction of the categories. According to Guyer, if we look to Kant's text for something of contemporary philosophical import, then we ought to look away from his transcendental deduction (hence away from the principle of apperception)

order to round out the sketch of the scene in which it has been difficult for Hegel's objection to Kant's epistemology to gain a fair hearing. Henry Allison has strongly *defended* Kant's idealism in opposition to readings such as Strawson's.[13] But, Allison's defense consists largely in a battle against what he calls the prevailing 'subjectivistic, psychologistic, phenomenalistic reading' of Kant's idealism. According to Allison, Strawson's resistance to Kant's idealism is emblematic of the resistance of generations of readers, in the respect that it is founded on a *misunderstanding* of that idealism, in particular, a misunderstanding of it as *subjectivist*. Readers typically fail to appreciate the specific differences between Kant's idealism (as *transcendental* idealism) and Berkeleyan idealism. Allison attempts to rehabilitate Kant's idealism as a philosophically powerful and well-motivated position by teaching us to see his idealism as specifically transcendental, not subjectivist.[14]

Reserving details for Chapter 1, here I make only the following general point: in its reception in analytic philosophy, philosophical interest in Kant's epistemology has had to be won either by finding the idealism (subjectivism) extraneous to the philosophically interesting core of Kant's position, or by fighting a battle of interpretation against a 'subjectivistic' reading of Kant's idealism. In such a context, it was inevitable that Hegel's reading of Kant's idealism as subjectivism would be, as it has been, largely misheard. In such a context, it was inevitable that those sympathetic to Kant's project would dismiss Hegel's interpretation and objection either as failing to acknowledge what is philosophically innovative and promising in Kant's critical epistemology or as conflating Kant's idealism with Berkeley's. I attempt to gain a hearing for Hegel's objection in this study in full consciousness of the obstacles presented by the shape of the analytic reception of Kant's epistemology. I attempt to show in Chapter 1 specifically how the interpretation of Kant on which Hegel bases his objection acknowledges sharp specific differences between Kant's idealism and Berkeley's and between Kant's epistemological project and Descartes's. I also attempt to show how Hegel's interpretation responds to what is philosophically innovative in Kant's criticism, though on a different interpretation of Kant's philosophical innovation than that prevailing in analytic commentary.

and toward his accounts of the necessary conditions of empirical time-determination in the Analytic of Principles. (See Paul Guyer, *Kant and the Claims of Knowledge*.)

[13] Henry Allison, *Kant's Transcendental Idealism: An Interpretation and Defense*.

[14] Others who have urged the importance of understanding the transcendental standpoint from which Kant's idealism is asserted, in order to see the difference between Kant's idealism and subjectivism, are Graham Bird and Gerold Prauss. See Graham Bird, *Kant's Theory of Knowledge* and Gerold Prauss, *Erscheinung bei Kant* and *Kant und das Problem der Dinge an Sich*.

According to Hegel's reading, the heart of the Kantian philosophy is his articulation of a structure of subjectivity, according to which the subject is autonomous in relation to the norms under which it stands. In Chapter 1, I undertake to show on behalf of Hegel's interpretation the role of Kant's articulation of what I (not Kant) call the structure of epistemic subjectivity or agency in his transcendental deduction of the categories. According to my interpretation, Kant solves the epistemological problem to which the deduction is addressed by showing that our responsible agency in epistemic judgment implies that the ultimate source of the norms is necessarily our self-constituting activity itself. But the price of his solution is subjectivism. I defend Hegel's interpretation, according to which Kant's subjectivism follows not primarily from Kant's account of the status of space and time as subjective conditions of human sensibility (as indispensable as that may be for Kant's full account), but essentially from Kant's articulation of the structure of epistemic agency in judgment. Though Hegel's reading of Kant's idealism is tendentious in various respects, it is very far from conflating Kant's epistemological project with Descartes's or Kant's idealism with Berkeley's.

The reading I offer on behalf of Hegel builds on recent work on Kant's thought. Kant's philosophy has been receiving a significant reinterpretation—slowly and in fits and starts, as these things go—corresponding to changes in dominant contemporary philosophical questions and concerns. A generation ago, interpreters tended to emphasize the positivist Kant, the Kant who attacks the possibility of metaphysics and who sees the distinctive task of epistemology instead in the task of articulating the conceptual framework against which alone emphatically empirical knowledge and natural science are possible. From the standpoint of this perspective on Kant's system, one perceives a large gulf between Kant and the post-Kantian tradition, since, from this perspective, one naturally perceives the post-Kantian thinkers, in stark contrast to Kant, to be unscrupulously metaphysical and not particularly helpful in interpreting philosophy's tasks relative to natural science. This approach to Kant's epistemology also isolates it (relatively, anyway) from Kant's own practical writings and from the rest of his critical system. Though the positivist orientation to Kant's epistemology is alive and well, contemporary interest in making intelligible the place of rational norms and agency within nature (both epistemic and practical norms and agency) has given rise to a different orientation. From this new perspective, emphasis is placed rather on Kant's articulation, both in his theoretical and in his practical philosophy, of a structure of subjectivity or of rational agency according to which the highest laws or norms under which the agent stands in his activity are derived from (are indeed formal expressions of) that agency itself. Since the post-Kantian philosophers (still speaking quite generally of course) proceed from Kant's critical philosophy on an interpretation of it according to which autonomy is its core, unifying concept, there is an obvious continuity, not a gulf, between Kant and these thinkers on this new orientation. I attempt to show in this study that the central background of Hegel's response to Kant's critical philosophy is not an uncharitable reading of Kant's idealism as subjectivism, as is apt to seem the case from a traditional orientation to Kant's thought, but rather an interpretation of Kant's thought as proceeding from an exciting new articulation of the knowing subject as essentially autonomous.[15]

---

[15] In this respect I take myself to build on the work of Robert Pippin's important book *Hegel's Idealism: The Satisfactions of Self-Consciousness.* Pippin argues that Hegel's philosophical system in general ought to be read as expressing Hegel's ambition to 'complete' Kant's critical project. According to Pippin, the core of the Hegelian enterprise is Kant's insight that our knowledge is ineliminably apperceptive. As Pippin puts it, 'the subject must be able to make certain basic discriminations in any experience in order for there to be experience at all' (7–8). The most fundamental discrimination on which experience depends is the self-reflective discrimination: being conscious of the experience (or the representation) *as one's own thought.* Since the philosophical project consists largely in the task of articulating this fundamental condition on the possibility of experience into a system of conceptual discriminations, Hegel's system is, like Kant's, both anti-empiricist and anti-rationalist: the former by virtue of the fact that the conceptual conditions make experience possible, and so cannot be derived from experience; and the latter because 'human reason can attain non-empirical knowledge only *about itself*, about what has come to be called recently our "conceptual scheme"' (8). Hegel's *difference* from Kant, according to Pippin, consists primarily in his doctrine that the strict Kantian duality between intuitional and conceptual elements in knowledge cannot be maintained; this duality does not itself sustain critical investigation. Hegel's rejection of Kant's 'phenomenality restriction', the doctrine that we can know things only as they appear, not as they are in themselves, follows from his rejection of this strict duality. Hence Pippin sees Hegel's difference from Kant's system as a consequence primarily of his prosecuting the Kantian critical inquiry more thoroughly and completely.

Though I have been influenced by Pippin's demonstration of the significance for Hegel's project of Kant's interpretation of the knowing subject as essentially apperceptive and by Pippin's construal of Hegel's project as completing, not rejecting, Kant's, my reading diverges sharply from Pippin's in some important respects. I find that Pippin underestimates the extent to which Hegel transforms Kant's project. Pippin's interpretation of Hegel's thought retains and employs (uncritically) the dualistic structure that Hegel means exactly to overcome through his intensification of Kant's criticism. Though Pippin's Hegel criticizes the finality of the dualism between appearances and things in themselves, because Pippin wants a non-metaphysical reading of Hegel, he takes Hegel to agree with Kant that human reason can attain non-empirical knowledge *only about itself*. Pippin's reinterpretation of Hegel as adopting the Kantian method has the consequence that Hegel's claims are reinterpreted as respecting critical boundaries to our knowledge. This means, in particular, that Hegel's seemingly transgressive claims are taken to express merely the self-knowledge of human reason or knowledge only of 'our conceptual scheme'. I argue that Hegel's main effort in redesigning Kant's critical method in his *Phenomenology of Spirit* is to free the critical procedure from the implicit presupposition of subjectivism. On Pippin's interpretation, Hegel is so far Kantian that he remains a sort of subjectivist.

The main case of Chapter 2—the second main contention of Part I of this study—is that Kant's articulation of norm-governed agency that we find nearly explicit in the transcendental deduction of the categories and more fully explicit in his account of the structure of human practical reason in his practical writings is already implicit in the epistemological project of a critique of pure reason. Hence, Kant's subjectivism is but an expression of his revolution in philosophical methodology. The epistemological demand expressed in Kant's critical project is to validate the authority of the norms of reason in a process of reflection on our cognitive faculties. This demand already implies (unconsciously, as it were) a highest principle of reason, namely, the conformity of externally given content to the principle expressing the formal self-relating activity of the subject. Hence, according to Hegel's reading, Kant's subjectivism is not merely the product of an arbitrary and disastrous choice of metaphor on Kant's part, nor is it simply the consequence of the subjective status of the forms of sensibility, space and time; rather, Kant's subjectivism expresses his innovative articulation of the basic structure of the norm-governed activity of the subject who must responsibly conform its own activity to its norms; this structure is expressed in one way in Kant's account of epistemic agency in his transcendental deduction of the categories and in another way already in his articulation of a new epistemological project of critique.

Part II then tells the story of Hegel's development of the epistemological project and method of his *Phenomenology* in response to the objection to Kant's philosophical criticism elaborated in Part I. A major claim of Part II is that Hegel radically changes his orientation to Kant's project of critique while at Jena, and that his project in the *Phenomenology* is a product of this change.[16] In his early Jena writings, Hegel rejects the epistemological project of critique altogether, on the basis of his perception of it as inherently subjectivist, in favor of an epistemological procedure adapted from the ancient skeptics.[17] According to the view expressed in Hegel's early Jena writings,

[16] Hyppolite writes, at the beginning of his commentary on the *Phenomenology of Spirit*, that 'all commentators have noted, [that] in some respects the *Phenomenology* clearly marks a return to the point of view of Kant and Fichte' (*Genesis and Structure of Hegel's* Phenomenology of Spirit, 5–6). Against the background of this general agreement among commentators, my contribution consists in the particular interpretation I offer of the nature and significance of Hegel's return to the standpoint of Kant's criticism.

[17] Michael Forster's work performs an important service in showing the significance of Hegel's early Jena article on the difference between ancient and modern skepticism for understanding Hegel's epistemology. (See especially his *Hegel and Skepticism*.) I believe that Forster's work functions as a corrective to Pippin's relative neglect of Hegel's *opposition* to the trajectory of modern (Cartesian, dualistic) epistemology. However, I also maintain that Forster's interpretation fails to

since the distinctively modern dualisms and subjectivism are implicit in the epistemological procedure of critique, criticism cannot overcome them. To escape these plagues of modern philosophy we must reach back to ancient epistemology, which is yet innocent of them. In this way, modern dualisms are not so much overcome as forbidden entry into the structure of epistemological questioning in the first place. In articulating Hegel's orientation to Kant's criticism in the early Jena writings, I aim to show that his rejection of Kant's epistemological project in this period is bound up with a rejection of the distinctively modern in philosophy and in culture in general.

However, when one compares the early Jena writings with the prefatory material to the *Phenomenology*, one finds a significant change in Hegel's relation to Kant's critical programme. Hegel comes to see the Kantian epistemological project as necessary; indeed Hegel's late Jena work, his *Phenomenology*, is his attempt to carry out that project; the *Phenomenology* is a version of Kant's critical project, though a version that has been significantly transformed. I argue in Chapter 4 that Hegel's return to the standpoint of Kantian criticism turns on his belated recognition that the epistemological demand expressed in that project—namely, that we establish the possibility of metaphysical knowledge in a subjective reflection on our cognitive criteria as a condition of the possibility of metaphysics itself—is grounded in the independence (*Selbständigkeit*) of the knowing subject. Whereas Hegel earlier rejects distinctively modern epistemological projects—prominently Kant's criticism—as inherently subjectivistic, he comes to recognize that the epistemological demand expressed in these projects cannot be dismissed, insofar as it is backed by a distinctively modern *self-discovery*, the discovery of the individual subject as self-standing. Kant contributes essentially to this discovery with his articulation of the knowing and acting subject as the author of the highest principles of its epistemic and practical activity. With this recognition, Hegel comes to see that modern dualisms and subjectivism cannot be evaded by returning to an ancient model of epistemology that is yet innocent of these. Modern subjectivism expresses the discovery in the modern era of the structure (what he sometimes calls 'the principle') of subjectivity. A sea change in Hegel's philosophical orientation follows from this recognition—a sea change through which Hegel becomes Hegel, as it were. In consequence

account sufficiently for the respects in which Hegel comes to recognize the modern epistemological project—in the form, particularly, of Kant's project of critique—as necessary. According to my account, this recognition transforms Hegel's conception of the epistemological task relative to his position in the early Jena article.

of this recognition, Hegel must change his conception of the way in which philosophy is related, not only to its own history, but to the history of culture in general. The expression of this change in Hegel's conception of the object of philosophy, in his ontology, is the famous claim from the Preface to the *Phenomenology* that 'the True must be grasped and expressed not only as Substance, but equally as subject'.[18] However, I concentrate here (more modestly) on the expression of this change in Hegel's epistemological procedure. The epistemological expression of Hegel's recognition is that Kant's project of philosophical critique cannot be dismissed or evaded; validation of the possibility of metaphysics in a prior, reflective inquiry is necessary.

However, the problem arises immediately regarding the *possibility* of the critical enterprise. Hegel still maintains the objection that motivated him to reject Kant's epistemological project in the first place: criticism implicitly presupposes subjectivism, and hence begs the question against the possibility of the (metaphysical) knowledge that it pretends to test in open inquiry. In Chapter 5 I argue that the method of the *Phenomenology* (the many contortions of that method) is determined by the effort to meet the epistemological demand of Kantian critique without implicitly presupposing subjectivism. This project turns out to require, I argue, *self-transformational* criticism.

In my treatment of Hegel's epistemological method, I emphasize what we might call its self-transformational dimension. In a passage in the Introduction in which Hegel characterizes what is distinctive about his approach to skeptical challenges in the work, he describes the path of the investigation as a 'pathway of despair' (PhG, 22–3/¶ 78). Hegel's *Phenomenology* consists in a sequence of stages on the journey of the knowing subject that begins at the standpoint of 'natural' or ordinary consciousness and ends at the standpoint of philosophy, with knowledge of the absolute. The knowing subject reflects on its knowledge and compares its claims to knowledge with its criteria for knowledge claims. The conflict between them forces reconception of both. Each successive configuration of consciousness, which emerges from the internal criticism of the preceding configuration, is another step in the journey (or, to use another of Hegel's figures: another rung up the ladder) from ordinary consciousness to philosophical consciousness. This journey is Hegel's justification of philosophy's principle, or (what comes to the same) his justification of the possibility of metaphysics, against all manner of skeptical

---

[18] Hegel, PhG, 22–3/¶ 17. (Please see 'Abbreviations' for the manner in which I refer to this and other texts by Hegel and Kant.)

threat. In order to appreciate the force of Hegel's demonstration, we students of the book must ourselves travel the journey according to the prescribed itinerary. We must submit our own claims to know to the self-criticism that generates the movement of consciousness along the path.

The path of critical reflection is self-transformational in the sense that our self-conception and our conception of the ultimate rational norms change radically through the inquiry. Hegel's description of the journey as a pathway of despair marks the fact that the ordinary natural consciousness only achieves the standpoint of philosophy through submission to self-criticism, a process that turns out to require the 'loss of its truth'. The reflecting subject comes to be constituted differently through coming to recognize (and, to some extent, *constitute*) different fundamental norms or laws for its activity. Thus, the path 'counts for [the reflecting subject] as the loss of its own self'. Hegel's procedure of critical self-examination is Socratic in the respect that the self must be willing to stake itself, in staking its own truth, its own conception of the most fundamental norms of its existence, in the inquiry. The critical self-examination has immediate existential stakes. It follows from this, as Plato illustrates in his famous allegory of philosophical education in the *Republic*, the allegory of what he calls 'the upward journey of the soul to the intelligible realm', that we naturally *resist* philosophical education, out of a misplaced sense of self-preservation. Hegel presents with his *Phenomenology* his own version of Plato's upward journey of the soul to the intelligible realm, a journey requiring, for him as for Plato, a self-transformation (what Plato calls a turning of the whole soul around).[19]

Though commentators have not wholly neglected the self-transformational dimension of Hegel's *Phenomenology*, I believe that its significance has not been fully appreciated. It is easy to dismiss the self-transformational ambition of the text as melodramatic ornamentation or as symptomatic of Hegel's romantic extravagance or enthusiasm. I show that—much to the contrary—the self-transformational ambition of Hegel's method is motivated by his attempt fully to meet the epistemological demand expressed in Kant's criticism, against the background of Hegel's objection that Kant's own prosecution of criticism fails fully to meet that demand. Kant's criticism implicitly presupposes subjectivism—thereby begs its own question and fails to fulfill its own epistemological demand—exactly because the criticizing subject occupies a fixed and immovable stance, over against the standpoint

---

[19] Plato, *Republic*, 514a–521c.

of metaphysics. That objects must conform to our knowing rather than our knowing to objects, hence that we can know things only as they are *for us*, not as they are in themselves, is a conclusion implicitly presupposed in the structure of Kant's critical reflection. Kant's subjectivism is an expression of the failure of the method to put the standpoint of the reflecting subject equally at stake in the critical procedure with the possibility of metaphysics. If my argument succeeds, it establishes, then, that this dimension of Hegel's project that we are apt to dismiss as romantic excess or melodramatic orientation is, far from being symptomatic of Hegel's notorious epistemological lassitude or complacency, an expression of his epistemological seriousness and rigor.

PART I

HEGEL'S OBJECTION

1

Is Kant's Idealism Subjective?

Hegel consistently characterizes Kant's transcendental idealism as 'subjectivism'. In this chapter I develop Hegel's interpretation of Kant's idealism as subjectivism and provide a limited defense of it. In one sense Kant's idealism is indisputably subjectivist. According to Kant's doctrine of transcendental idealism, we can know objects only as they appear to us, not as they are in themselves. We can know objects only as relativized to our human standpoint. The distinctiveness of Hegel's reading emerges in response to the nature or the source of the Kantian relativization to our standpoint. Does this relativization have a source in Kant's conception of the nature of thinking (or of the role of our activity in knowledge), or is it, as some maintain, strictly a function of the ideality of space and time as forms of our sensibility (hence, strictly a function of our passivity in knowledge)?

According to the view developed here, Kant's relativization (and corresponding restriction) of our knowledge is primarily a consequence of Kant's principle of apperception and of the role it plays in the transcendental deduction of the categories. The principle of apperception articulates the essential role of our epistemic agency in cognition. The identification of the essential role of our epistemic agency in cognition enables Kant to solve his main epistemological problem (the problem of the possibility of synthetic, *a priori* knowledge), but only at the cost of subjectivism, of the relativization of our knowledge to our standpoint. I aim in this chapter to show that Kant's relativization of knowledge to our human standpoint follows from his articulation in the transcendental deduction of a normative structure according to which we, *as knowing subjects*, can understand ourselves to be bound by norms in the norm-governed activity of knowing only to the extent that the highest order norms of the activity have their source ultimately in us.

1.1 AN AMBIGUITY IN 'SUBJECTIVISM'

Before turning to the transcendental deduction, it is necessary to distinguish
Hegel's interpretation of Kant's idealism as subjectivism from another with
which it is sometimes confused. We are likely to hear in the characterization
of Kant's idealism as 'subjectivism' an objection or an accusation. Clearly
Kant *intends*, in his attempt to distinguish and to specify a *transcendental*
idealism, to redeem our knowing as genuinely objective. It is no doubt a
debatable—and much debated—question whether he succeeds. To say that
Kant's idealism is subjectivism will likely say to us that he fails. Accordingly,
those who would defend Kant's epistemology often find it necessary to
proceed by way of defending it against what one prominent Kant interpreter
calls '[t]he subjectivistic, psychologistic, phenomenalistic reading of Kant'.[1]
I want to show first that Hegel is not guilty of the subjectivistic reading of
Kant that apologists of Kant's epistemology are concerned to refute.

This other subjectivist reading has many facets, but it is primarily distinguished by its interpretation of Kant's claim that we can know only
appearances. Proponents of this reading take Kant to mean by this claim that
we can know only representations, which are, in turn, taken to be mental
items or 'ideas' in Berkeley's sense. The 'objects' of our knowledge, on this
reading of Kant's view, reduce to these mental items, to ideas in Berkeley's
sense. This subjectivist reading, according to which Kant's transcendental
idealism is, in Peter Strawson's oft-repeated words, 'closer to Berkeley than
[Kant] acknowledges', underwrites several objections to Kant's idealism, the
most fundamental being that Kant fails on this interpretation in his pro-
fessed aim to redeem our claim to genuine objectivity in our knowledge.[2]
If Kant redeems only knowledge of the contents of our own minds (that is,
only knowledge of these mind-dependent or 'subjective' contents), then the
insistence that this is knowledge *of objects* at all seems strained, and seems to
depend on the same considerations as Berkeley's similar insistence.

Recent commentary makes the compelling case that the proponents of the
subjectivist reading fail to let the Kantian distinction between the transcendental and the empirical standpoints—which is, of course, distinctive to Kant's

    [1] Allison, *Kant's Transcendental Idealism*, (1983), 13.
    [2] Strawson, *The Bounds of Sense*, 22. For an account of the objections to Kant's idealism
underwritten by this subjectivist interpretation of him, see Allison, *Kant's Transcendental Idealism*,
(1983), 5–6.

procedure, and foreign to the thought of Berkeley or of Descartes—inflect their interpretation of Kant's idealism, in particular of his claim that our knowledge is only of appearances.[3] Roughly, the empirical standpoint is the standpoint from which we make knowledge claims about empirical objects, whereas the transcendental standpoint is that philosophical standpoint from which we reflect *a priori on the possibility of our knowledge of objects*. This duality in standpoints implies an ambiguity in the idealism/realism opposition, as well as a corresponding ambiguity in the claim that we know only appearances. The sense of the claim that we know only appearances depends on the standpoint from which it is made. Proponents of the subjectivist reading, in their failure to be sensitive to the significance of this duality and consequent ambiguity, interpret the claim as asserting that we can know only the modifications of the (empirical) subject. The claim, so taken, denies the possibility of knowledge of mind-independent objects at all. The defenders of Kant against this subjectivist reading argue, on the contrary, that we should understand Kant's claim that we know only appearances as made from the *transcendental* standpoint. Moreover, this claim as made from the transcendental standpoint is part of an account of the possibility of knowledge of (mind-independent) objects from the empirical standpoint. That is, the possibility of *empirical* realism *requires*, according to Kant, *transcendental* idealism.

Henry Allison's account is explicit on this point. Kant finds in reflecting on the possibility of our knowledge that empirical knowledge—knowledge of objects that are mind-independent from the empirical standpoint—has certain *a priori* conditions. Allison describes such conditions as epistemic conditions, in part to mark them off both from psychological and from ontological conditions.[4] A psychological condition would be merely a condition we need in order to know the object, rather than a condition through which alone the object, as object of knowledge, is possible for us at all. (As Allison puts it, an epistemic condition has an 'objectivating' function.) Nevertheless, such conditions are not ontological, since they do not condition things themselves, but only objects *qua* objects of knowledge or experience. Allison holds that the mere fact of such *a priori* conditions *of knowledge*, which do not likewise condition things themselves, necessitates the distinction *at the level of transcendental reflection* between appearances and things

---

[3] Significant works which precede Allison's in offering an interpretation of Kant's epistemology constructed in opposition to the subjectivist reading are Bird, *Kant's Theory of Knowledge*, and Prauss, *Erscheinung bei Kant* and *Kant und das Problem der Dinge an sich*.

[4] Allison, *Kant's Transcendental Idealism*, (1983), 10–13.

as they are in themselves.[5] Hence, the fact of such epistemic conditions
necessitates *transcendental* idealism, understood, however, not ontologically,
but epistemologically. Taken ontologically, transcendental idealism implies
that there are two sets of things, the set of things in themselves, which we
cannot know, and the set of appearances/representations/ideas, which we can.
Understood epistemologically, transcendental idealism is the claim, simply,
that human knowledge is governed by these conditions.[6] On the subjectivist
reading, Kant is taken to claim flatly that we can have no knowledge of mind-
independent objects. If we interpret Kant instead according to the specific
dimensionality of transcendental philosophy, then we take his idealism to
consist in the claim that the possibility of knowledge of mind-independent
objects from the empirical standpoint depends on *a priori*, transcendental
conditions. These conditions, which are 'subjective' only from the standpoint
of transcendental reflection, are necessary conditions of the possibility of our
knowledge *of objects* from the empirical standpoint.

In the context in which philosophical interest in Kant's epistemological
idealism is won in a battle against a subjectivist reading of it, Hegel's
repeated insistence that Kant's idealism is 'subjectivism' is perhaps bound
to be misheard. In this context, a fairly common objection against Hegel's
interpretation of Kant's epistemology is that Hegel conceives Kant's idealism
'in terms of a simple subjectivity as against objectivity', to use Graham
Bird's phrase. It is objected that Hegel fails to appreciate this very ambiguity
or dimensionality of the subjective/objective opposition specific to Kant's
transcendental philosophy, and for this reason misperceives Kant's idealism
in empirical or psychological terms.[7]

However, it is clear from several passages that Hegel does not fail to appreciate the complexity of the subjective/objective opposition inherent in Kant's

---

[5] *Ibid.*, 13. Allison has amended his view in recent work. While he still maintains that 'the
generic notion of an epistemic condition brings with it a certain idealistic commitment of a
non-phenomenalistic sort', he no longer thinks that it grounds the transcendental distinction
between appearances and things as they are in themselves in the distinctive way in which Kant
draws it. The transcendental distinction and Kant's distinctive idealism follow from the claim that
sensibility has its own *a priori* forms, not from the generic notion of an epistemic condition. (See
Allison, Idealism and Freedom, 5–8.) I do not see that Allison can amend his view in this way
without amending it more substantially. Moreover, I see no need to amend the view. I discuss
this issue, though not in connection with Allison's reading in particular, in the latter part of the
chapter.
[6] Allison, *Kant's Transcendental Idealism*, (1983), 13.
[7] This charge against Hegel is developed by Graham Bird in his article 'Hegel's Account of
Kant's Epistemology in the *Lectures on the History of Philosophy*'; and by J. E. Smith in his article,
'Hegel's Critique of Kant'. (The quotation from Bird in the text is from this article, 67.)

transcendental philosophy.[8] In fact, in one passage from the *Encyclopedia Logic*, Hegel explicitly discusses this complexity and ambiguity.[9] He notes that one construal of the subjective/objective opposition in Kant is the opposition between, on the one hand, the contingent, particular and subjective sequence of representations that are merely mine, and, on the other hand, the object over against these representations, which is universally shared among us and which determines my merely subjective representations. This is roughly equivalent to the subject/object distinction from the empirical standpoint. According to Hegel in this passage, what distinguishes Kant's idealism is that these 'universal and necessary determinations', which constitute the (empirically) objective, are determinations *of thought* — (he has in mind, obviously, the pure concepts of the understanding, the categories). 'Kant has called that which is in accord with thought (the universal and necessary) the *objective*, and rightly so' (EL, §41Z2). However, Kant's idealism is subjective idealism, according to Hegel, because the thought determinations (the categories) that constitute objectivity are 'again subjective'. Hegel does not mean, obviously, that the categories are subjective in the sense of being contingent, private, particular representations, since it is exactly *as* universal and necessary that they constitute the objectivity of representation. In what sense are the categories 'again subjective', then, if they are 'universal and necessary determinations', and, as such, constitutive of the objectivity of representation? Hegel writes:

Further, however, the Kantian objectivity of thinking is itself again subjective to the extent that the thoughts [i.e., the categories], although universal and necessary determinations, are *merely our* thoughts, and separated from the thing as it is *in itself* by an insurmountable gulf. (EL, §41Z2)

As I argue below, the suggestion here that the categories are subjective by virtue of being merely ours, as if the problem were that other thinkers might employ different categories, misrepresents both Kant's view and Hegel's own more considered interpretation of it. As we'll see, the insurmountable gulf to which Hegel refers here arises not because the categories by which *we think* may not hold for all thinkers, but because *we think at all*. The gulf is between *thought* and being and has its source in (Kant's conception of) the nature of ourselves as thinking beings. At this point I mean merely to have shown

---

[8] Sally Sedgwick, in rebutting this charge against Hegel's reading of Kant, points to several such passages in Hegel's works in her article, 'Hegel's Treatment of Transcendental Apperception in Kant'. See especially p. 153.

[9] Hegel, EL, §41Z2. (Please see 'Abbreviations' for my method of referring to the texts of Kant and Hegel.)

that Hegel sees that Kant redeems the objectivity of our knowledge from the empirical standpoint by means of transcendental reflection that finds *a priori* conditions for this object knowledge. Hegel's characterization of Kant's idealism as subjectivism does not betray, as some suppose, a failure to appreciate the transcendental dimension of Kant's idealism, but marks instead what might seem the undeniable fact that the transcendental conditions are, for Kant, 'again subjective' (in a sense yet to be determined).

However, it turns out not to be undeniable that the transcendental conditions are, as such, subjective. Kant scholars in fact dispute Hegel's claim that Kant's categories are subjective, arguing instead that only the forms of sensible intuition, space and time, are subjective.[10] My presentation of Hegel's interpretation begins by characterizing generally the epistemological problem to which Kant's critique of reason is addressed and the so-called Copernican revolution in epistemology as Kant's general solution to the problem. Against this background, we can formulate the controversy regarding the subjectivity of the categories more sharply.

[10] In this chapter, I will be considering in particular the work of two scholars, Karl Ameriks and Paul Guyer, who have both argued independently that Hegel is mistaken in interpreting Kant's categories as subjective. Karl Ameriks argues this in his article 'Hegel's Critique of Kant's Theoretical Philosophy'. Paul Guyer argues his case in 'Thought and Being: Hegel's Critique of Kant's Theoretical Philosophy'.

Those familiar with Ameriks's other important works will perhaps suspect me of attributing to Kant what Ameriks identifies as the so-called 'short argument' to idealism. Ameriks argues in his recent book, as well as in earlier papers, that Karl Leonhard Reinhold strongly influences the reading of Kant's project not only by other figures of the time (Hegel, inter alia) but by subsequent generations as well, chiefly through his recasting of Kant's argument to the idealist conclusion as an argument that proceeds summarily and simply from the mere concept of representation. (See Ameriks's *Kant and the Fate of Autonomy*, especially Chapter 3.) The influence of Reinhold's reading has been unfortunate, Ameriks contends, because '[f]or Kant himself ... there is no such short argument, for his transcendental idealism rests, first, on a series of complex considerations entailing the ideality of space and time, and, secondly, on an equally complex series of considerations requiring that all our theoretical knowledge is limited to spatiotemporal determinations (and hence is limited to their ideality)' (ibid., 164). The restriction of my focus to the role of our norm-governed intellectual activity in yielding knowledge and on Kant's interpretation of this role as having an idealist or subjectivist implication should not be taken to imply an endorsement of attributing to Kant the short argument. This restricted focus should not be taken to imply a denial that Kant's account of pure intuition in the Transcendental Aesthetic is essential to Kant's complete argument for transcendental idealism. My aim is not to reconstruct Kant's complete argument, but to make manifest the way in which Kant's identification of our essential reflective activity in knowledge is *a* source of the Kantian restriction of our knowledge or relativization of our knowledge to our human standpoint. Certainly Hegel (like many others) gives much more prominence to the articulation of the 'structure of the "I"' (chiefly in transcendental deduction of the categories), and much less prominence to the concerns about space and time, within the overall Kantian epistemological project than Kant himself does. But acknowledging this implies neither allegiance to the short argument, nor that what Hegel finds in Kant (namely the insightful and influential articulation of the structure of the judging subject and the subjectivist implications of that discovery) is not there to be found.

1.2 THE EPISTEMOLOGICAL PROBLEM

It will be helpful to review familiar, but important, general features of Kant's epistemology. Kant distinguishes fundamentally between two heterogeneous factors in all human knowledge: concepts on the one hand and intuitions on the other. These two factors correspond to two distinct faculties of human cognition: the faculty of thought or of the understanding on the one hand and the faculty of sensibility on the other. This distinction in faculties gives expression to the fact that we human beings are both active and passive in our knowledge: active insofar as we *think* objects, but passive insofar as objects impress themselves upon our sensibility. The faculty of thought (or of the understanding) is spontaneous, for Kant, in the sense that thought is a faculty for the synthesis of representations into higher, more general, representations. Thought, then, is a faculty of concepts, since concepts are those representations by means of which we collect many representations under one general representation. Kant distinguishes concepts from intuitions by their generality and by the fact that they relate to objects mediately, through other representations. Concepts, so understood as functions of unity among other given representations, are, independently of intuition, empty. Independently of intuition, concepts are insufficient for knowledge of an object.

Intuitions, in contrast, are singular representations that relate immediately to objects. But, like concepts, intuitions alone are not sufficient for knowledge of an object. This follows from the fact that our intuition is sensible and our understanding discursive. That our intuition is sensible implies that we are passive with respect to it. The content of intuition arises for us through the object's affection of our sensitive faculty. Our understanding is discursive in the sense that we can know an object only through thinking it, which implies that we must combine representations together as given to the faculty of sensibility; that is, we must bring given representations under concepts. So, neither concepts nor intuitions, neither thought nor sensibility alone, is sufficient for knowledge. Hence, perhaps the most quoted sentence in Kant's *Critique of Pure Reason*: 'Thoughts without content are empty, intuitions without concepts are blind.'[11]

---

[11] Kant, KrV, A51/B75. (Please see 'Abbreviations' for the manner in which I refer to the texts of Kant and Hegel.

Kant's general epistemological problem, to which the critique of pure reason is addressed, is the problem of the possibility of synthetic, *a priori* knowledge. What is this problem? In his *Prolegomena*, Kant describes the problem as arising for him from an encounter with Hume's reflections on the notion of causality (Prol., 4: 260). Hume's discussion of causality serves to put Kant on notice that universal and necessary knowledge of objects (which causal judgments presuppose) cannot be justified on the basis of experience. The possibility of *a priori* knowledge that is analytic poses no particular problem, because such knowledge expresses mere conceptual relations, not relations among real things or objects. The problem is to understand the possibility of *a priori* knowledge (that is, necessary and universal knowledge) that is not merely conceptual, but, at the same time, knowledge *of objects*. How is knowledge of the object possible prior to the object being given? How is synthetic, *a priori* knowledge possible? On this question depends the possibility, not only of metaphysics, according to Kant, but also of pure natural science and of mathematics.

In the preface to the second edition of the First *Critique*, Kant characterizes the so-called Copernican revolution in epistemology as the key to his solution to this epistemological problem (Bxvi). Knowledge of the object prior to the object being given is possible, Kant contends, only insofar as our knowledge presents necessary prior conditions on the possibility of the object of knowledge. On the hypothesis that objects must conform to our knowledge rather than our knowledge to objects, we can understand the possibility of synthetic, *a priori* knowledge; on this hypothesis alone, we can understand the possibility of universal and necessary knowledge that is, at the same time, knowledge of the object.

A sort of relativization of our knowledge to our standpoint—that is, a sort of subjectivism—seems to follow immediately from this strategy for solving the epistemological problem. Kant's view is that knowledge of the object prior to the object being given is possible just insofar as the object, as object of knowledge, is possible only through conditions that have their source in the knowing subject, that is, in us.[12] It follows from this move that we can know

---

[12] Though I am putting the point in terms of subjectivism rather than idealism, this accords with Allison's initial view, discussed above, that the very idea of these epistemic conditions brings with it a commitment to a sort of idealism.

Kant's procedure here—namely, finding the necessary conditions of objects of experience *in us*, as knowing subjects—implies that *we* (in the particular sense in which we refer to ourselves as the source of these conditions) do not belong as a proper part to the natural world we know or experience. (In *another* sense, we do so belong.) This is difficult to make sense of, and I cast no light on this dark doctrine. If one despairs of making sense of this doctrine, but still finds

objects only as they are for our knowledge, for us, not as they are in themselves. If we understand the basic doctrine of Kant's transcendental idealism as the claim that objects of our knowledge are objects only as they appear to us, not as they are in themselves, then his idealism is a consequence of his revolution in epistemology. Kant accounts for the possibility of *a priori* knowledge of objects by understanding the objects of knowledge to be merely subjective objects in the following sense: since the object of knowledge is possible only through conditions that have their source in the subject (through conditions which are, in some as yet unclarified sense, subjective), the object is merely an object for the subject. Kant purchases the possibility of synthetic, *a priori* knowledge at the price of the possibility of knowledge of things as they are in themselves.

Although this general story may seem uncontroversial as a general characterization of Kant's view, it is not. Our controversy arises out of the question: what is the nature of the 'subjective' conditions through which knowledge is relativized to us, to our cognitive faculties, on Kant's view? On a natural reading of some passages, anyway, the subjective (and subjectifying) conditions are twofold, corresponding to the duality in cognitive faculties that is a main feature of Kant's epistemology: first, the *a priori* forms of our human sensibility, space and time; and second, the *a priori* forms of our thought of objects, the pure concepts of the understanding or the categories.[13] Both sets of conditions are subjective in the sense that we impose them as conditions that are necessary for our knowledge of objects. Accordingly, in both cases the conditions have the consequence of relativizing our knowledge to objects *considered as* objects of knowledge for us, since, in neither case are the conditions understood as conditions of the things themselves. However, while some passages invite us to think of both sets of conditions as subjective, in this sense, other passages suggest that the sensible conditions on knowledge are

---

the general approach attractive or useful, one may attempt to purge the first-personal reference, at least with respect to the intellectual conditions in the Transcendental Analytic. That is, one may attempt to construe the referral to necessary intellectual conditions of experience in such a way that it is not first-personal (not to conditions that have their source in *us*, in any significant sense). (So, for example, Paul Guyer's incisive and exhaustive analysis of Kant's attempt to argue from transcendental apperception yields something like this despair, and, accordingly, Guyer holds up the arguments of the System of Principles, which are relatively free of the first-personal reference, as the more promising philosophically. See his *Kant and the Claims to Knowledge*). I believe that there is significant loss, with respect to what is philosophically interesting and promising in Kant's procedure, in purging the first-personal reference. I attempt in these first two chapters to highlight the structure of reflective subjectivity that Kant uncovers through his first-personal, reflective procedure.

13 See, for example, KrV, Bxvi–xvii, A89–94/B121–7, and especially B164.

alone subjective and ideal, while the intellectual conditions, the categories, are not.[14] According to the Hegelian interpretation, our cognition is relativized to our standpoint, not only or not primarily because of the ideality of the forms by which we passively intuit objects (though obviously that plays a role), but because thinking itself is subjective, on Kant's view, and we can know objects only through thinking them.

1.3 THE TRANSCENDENTAL DEDUCTION OF THE CATEGORIES AND SUBJECTIVISM

Because the Hegelian interpretation is essentially an interpretation of what transpires in Kant's transcendental deduction of the categories, I present here the deduction (in the second-edition version) so far as necessary to motivate Hegel's understanding of it. The deduction begins from the synthetic unity of apperception. With the synthetic unity of apperception Kant presents, according to Hegel, a conception of human subjectivity—a conception of what the 'I' formally consists in. The main claim of the deduction, as Hegel reads it, is that objectivity in our knowledge has its source ultimately in the synthetic unity of apperception, thus, in subjectivity. One can understand this claim as enacting the Copernican revolution in epistemology. As such, this claim contains, implicitly, both Kant's solution to the problem of the possibility of synthetic, *a priori* knowledge and the relativization of our knowledge to objects as they are for us.

The Principle of Apperception and Subjectivity

The transcendental deduction in the second edition begins with Kant finding pure apperception to be a necessary condition to which all representation (insofar as it is mine) must submit. In doing so, Kant declares the thinking subject to be a necessary condition to which all representations must submit. Kant presents the condition of apperception, famously, with the opening sentence of §16:

The *I think* must *be able* to accompany all my representations; for otherwise something would be represented in me which could not be thought at all, which is as much as to say that the representation would either be impossible or at least would be

---

[14] I will cite the passages, and discuss them at some length, in the last section of the chapter.

nothing for me. That representation that can be given prior to all thinking is called *intuition*. Thus all manifold of intuition has a necessary relation to the 'I think' in the same subject in which this manifold is to be encountered. But this representation is an act of *spontaneity*; i.e., it cannot be regarded as belonging to sensibility. (B131–2)

There are two main claims here. The first is that all representation (all representation that is 'for me' at least) bears a necessary relation to the 'I think' in the same subject in which the representation occurs.[15] This indicates a necessary unity among all my representations by virtue of which they are one and all mine. The second, implied in the last sentence, is that representation bears relation to the 'I think', not through mere *affection* or sensibility, but only through the subject's self-activity.

The move from the first of these claims to the second would seem to be crucial, since the second asserts the necessary role of my (thinking) activity, as knowing subject, in all representation. Presumably, this move reflects Kant's commitment to his conception of the human understanding as discursive. We can know objects only through thinking them, and for Kant, the act of thinking is, most basically, the act of combining representations according to a rule. Kant claims in the immediately preceding section (§15) that '*combination (conjunctio)* of a manifold [of representations in an intuition] in general can never come to us through the senses ... for it is an act of the spontaneity of the power of representation' (B129–30). He calls the act of spontaneity 'synthesis'. He writes further: 'We can represent nothing as combined in the object without having previously combined it ourselves, and [] among all representations *combination* is the only one that is not given through objects but can be executed only by the subject itself, since it is an act of its self-activity' (B130). Insofar, then, as we have turned up a combination in turning up the 'necessary relation' of all representations to the 'I think', we have, given this claim of §15, turned up an act of the subject's self-activity.

Kant is driven to speak, somewhat obscurely, of the subject's *self*-activity by the same consideration, I think, that impels him to refer to this combination

---

[15] Kant needn't be taken as denying the possibility of my having representations that cannot be made self-conscious—to which I cannot attach the 'I think'—as long as such representations would be 'nothing for me'. What particularly distinguishes a representation that is 'for me' from a representation that is merely in me (not for me) allows of various interpretations. Without pausing to defend the view, since the case I make here doesn't depend on it, I will mention that, as I read Kant, among those representations that are in me, only those are subject to the normative constraints he outlines here (only those are 'for me') which can figure in my knowledge claims, in my cognition of objects on their basis. (See Allison, *Kant's Transcendental Idealism* (1983) 137 and Allison, *Idealism and Freedom*, 47).

that he has uncovered as *original* combination. The act is original, it is self-activity, because it is identified with the responsible agency of the knowing subject, the locus or source of the cognitive claims. Kant explains, in a passage immediately following the opening of §16 quoted above: 'I call it [the act of spontaneity] ... the *original apperception*, since it is that self-consciousness which, because it produces the representation *I think*, which must be able to accompany all others and which in all consciousness is one and the same, cannot be accompanied by any further representation' (B132). What can Kant mean in claiming that the 'I think', while it must be able to accompany all other representations, 'cannot be accompanied by any further representation'? All my representations must allow of being made self-conscious in the sense that each must allow of being a substitution instance of x in the thought 'I think x'. But in the sense in which we say this of all other representations, we cannot say it of the representation 'I think' itself, exactly because this representation expresses our subjectivity. Kant claims that all representations bear a necessary relation to the 'I think' in the same subject in which they occur. But insofar as apperception, the 'I think', itself expresses *the necessary relating* of all cognitive representations to the identical subject, to me as the self-identical thinker of them, the 'I think' cannot itself be present to me as a particular content of representation. No particular representational content could express the 'mine-ness' (the necessary relation to me) of that content, in this sense, since *any* particular cognitive content (even if it were to represent me in some sense) must be again related to me, as the identical subject responsible for determining the cognitive relations in which the content stands. In short, no representational content could express the 'I' *as subject*. It follows that the 'I think' that must be able to accompany all my representations is necessarily empty of representational content of its own. This follows from its expressing my subject-hood, as it were. My presence to myself throughout my constantly changing representations, which is necessary, is, at the same time, necessarily not by way of any particular accompanying representation.[16] That Kant refers to the 'I think' that he here uncovers as the necessary condition of

---

[16] Hume argues that, since the self is supposed to be identical throughout the various representations it has, indeed throughout the course of its life, the impression from which the idea of the self is derived must, as he writes, likewise 'continue invariably the same, thro' the whole course of our lives'. He remarks further: 'But there is no impression constant and invariable' (*A Treatise on Human Nature*, 251). Whereas for Hume this fact poses an epistemological problem (whence, then, our idea of the self?), Kant shows it to be necessary, and draws important epistemological implications from it.

all my representations both as self-activity, incapable of being referred to any higher source, and as original combination, necessarily empty of any particular representational content of its own, indicates that it expresses the condition on knowledge imposed by my epistemic agency or subjectivity.

Kant draws important conclusions from the emptiness of this apperception. He writes later in §16 that the necessary 'relation of representations [to the self-identical subject] does not yet come about by my accompanying each representation with consciousness, but rather by my *adding* one representation to the other and by being conscious of their synthesis' (B133). This follows from the emptiness of apperception, taken independently of its relation to externally given representations. Kant continues: 'For the empirical consciousness that accompanies different representations is by itself dispersed and without relation to the identity of the subject.' Given that this necessary relating of representations to the identical 'I think' cannot proceed by way of relating them to the 'I think' over against them, since the 'I think' itself can have no content on its own, it must proceed by way of *my relating* the particular contents of representation *to each other* through an *a priori* synthesis of the manifold of given representations. Kant writes: 'synthetic unity of the manifold of intuition, as given *a priori* is thus the ground of the identity of apperception itself' (B134). My necessary presence to myself, as the identical subject throughout my representations, necessarily presupposes the relating of these representations together *a priori*, as my activity. Thus, the necessary identity of apperception presupposes an original synthesis of a manifold of given representations *a priori*.

Given the reading of Kant's claim in §16 that I am advancing here, it is important to stress another important consequence of the necessary emptiness of apperception. We cannot have knowledge of the 'I' or of the knowing subject through this representation. Through this representation 'I think' alone, nothing at all is thought. Considered independently of its relation to intuition, pure apperception is nothing epistemologically. Its whole meaning consists in its relation to the content that it necessarily conditions, but, in itself, necessarily lacks. On the reading advocated here, the condition of apperception expresses the necessary role of the subject in knowledge, and the structure of apperception is the bare structure of epistemic subjectivity. But this reading does not imply reading a 'metaphysics of the subject' into the deduction. The reading is compatible with Kant's claim in the Paralogisms that we cannot know what, metaphysically, the 'I' consists in.

The Main Claim of the Deduction

Kant claims abruptly in §17 of the second-edition deduction that this original act through which representations are related systematically to each other, thereby making possible their 'necessary relation' to me as the identical subject throughout these representations, is the self-same act through which representations gain their relation to an object. Kant writes, famously: 'the unity of consciousness is that which alone constitutes the relation of representations to an object, thus their objective validity' (B137). This claim, following immediately on the claims of §16, can seem—and has seemed to many commentators—quite unmotivated. The most Kant has argued in §16, it may seem, is that original apperception necessarily conditions representation of an object. It is, accordingly, a bit surprising to read Kant claiming here that original apperception constitutes the relation of representations to objects, hence their objective validity.

I think we can better understand both this claim and Kant's assumption of the right to make it if we attend to how Kant understands the objective validity of representation, or, as I will refer to it, the objectivity of representation. The objectivity of representation implies, for Kant, a constraint on how we must combine representations. It implies a rule for the combination of representations, a rule that holds universally and necessarily. In the following passage from the first-edition deduction, Kant presents what he means by the objective validity of representation:

We find [ ] that our thought of the relation of all cognition to its object carries something of necessity with it, since namely the latter is regarded as that which is opposed to our cognitions being determined at pleasure or arbitrarily rather than being determined *a priori*, since insofar as they are to relate to an object our cognitions must also necessarily agree with each other in relation to it, i.e., they must have that unity that constitutes the concept of an object. (A104–105)

What constitutes the concept of an object, for Kant, then, is that unity or order among representations by virtue of which they 'necessarily agree with each another'. This unity or necessary agreement of representations with one another by virtue of which they relate to an object is a function of their being subject to a rule in their combination. But, since combination is our act, the objectivity of representation is a function of *our* being subject to a universal and necessary (*a priori*) rule in the act of combination.

An illustration drawn from the *Critique* may help to clarify this point. If you and I are both looking over an object—a house, say—the particular sequence of representations that constitutes your representation of it and the particular sequence that constitutes mine are different. Suppose you see the roof before the door before the foundation, whereas the order of my representations is the reverse. Each of these sequences is merely 'subjective', reflecting the particular perspective of an individual subjectivity on the object. But neither sequence is, of course, determined 'at pleasure or arbitrarily'; in fact there is 'something of necessity' in both, insofar as each represents an object, further, the same object, though from different perspectives. The object is, as such, shared between us, though our perspectives on it are not. The objectivity of our representation consists in our being bound to relate representations together in a particular way, in such a way, namely, that representations 'necessarily agree with each other'. It is only in virtue of this necessary agreement of representations that we share the object between us. The objectivity of our representations consists, then, in our being bound, you and I, by a universal and necessary rule, in our combination or interrelating of representations. The source of the objectivity of representation is the source of these constraints or rules. What is that source?

Kant's Copernican revolution in epistemology, insofar as it is enacted in the transcendental deduction of the categories, consists in the claim that this constraint on the combination of representations by virtue of which they relate to objects has its source, not in the object itself, independently existing, but in us, in the synthetic unity of apperception. Kant writes in the first-edition deduction: 'the unity which the object makes necessary can be nothing other than the formal unity of consciousness in the synthesis of the manifold of representation' (A105). Just this, essentially, is the content of the above quoted passage from §17: that required unity or ordering of representations, which constitutes their relation to an object, their being of objects independent of our particular 'subjective' sequence of representations, is the *a priori* unity of consciousness.

Why does Kant think he has the right to this dramatic claim immediately on the heels of §16? The general interpretation of the claims regarding apperception advanced above helps, I think, to make Kant's transition to this claim seem less abrupt and unmotivated. Kant has argued in §16 that the necessary identity of the 'I think' throughout all my representations is possible only on the condition of an *a priori* synthesis or interrelating of given representations, a synthesis that must be self-ascribed, that cannot be ascribed to any higher source. So Kant has already arrived at an *a priori* (hence universal and necessary) unity or interrelation of representations, as a condition of the identity of apperception. At the beginning of §17, Kant identifies this necessary unity with that necessary and universally valid unity or interrelation by virtue of which representations relate to objects. On what grounds does he make this identification?

I take it that the realistic option is already precluded by the articulation of the condition imposed by our epistemic subjectivity presented at the beginning of §16. Why cannot the really existing object itself legislate or determine the rule according to which we must combine representations, and thus constitute the unity of our representations in virtue of which they relate to objects? If the legislation had its source in the independently existing object, then we could not understand combination as our act, as having its source in ourselves; we couldn't understand ourselves as subjects of judgment, in that sense. If combination is our act, not something that can come to us externally, then the unity of the activity itself (of thought, of judgment), hence the unity of the thinking subject as such, cannot be externally posited, but must be ascribed to itself. The unity of ourselves, *qua* subjects, must be a function of what we do, not externally determined. Hence, the unity of the subject must be self-constituted. This, I've claimed, is the source of Kant's use of the strange term 'self-activity' and of his speaking of the 'I think' as an original combination. But the rules that govern this activity are simply functions of its unity. And so, that the rules of this activity are externally legislated is precluded by our being the source of the activity, by our being subjects. Hence the (universal and necessary) rules of combination that constitute the objectivity of representation have their source in—are indeed nothing but expressions of—the necessary self-relating activity of the knowing subject as such.

I find Kant to be relying in the deduction on a consideration that he makes explicit only in his practical writings: namely, that in order to understand oneself as the source or the seat of norm-governed judgment, one must understand one's activity as the source also of the legislation for that activity. In *The Groundwork of the Metaphysics of Morals*, written between the two editions of the First *Critique*, Kant is explicit on this point:

Now, one cannot possibly think of a reason that would consciously receive direction from any other quarter with respect to its judgments, since the subject would then attribute the determination of his judgment not to his reason but to an impulse. Reason must regard itself as the author of its principles independently of alien influences. (GMS, 4: 448)

Though Kant does not speak here of original apperception, of course, he does speak of the conditions under which we can regard ourselves as the source of judgment. We can regard judgment as our activity only if the principles according to which judgment is governed also have their source in our activity. The alternative is one we 'cannot possibly think'; if judgment were bound by an externally legislated principle, it wouldn't be judgment at all. Hence, if judgment is understood as something we do, something we are responsible for, then the constraint on our combination (which constitutes the objectivity of representation) can be nothing else than the subject's self-legislation.

Independently of the question of the justification of this claim in §17, the Copernican revolution in epistemology insofar as it is enacted in the transcendental deduction consists in this claim: the claim, namely, that the general constraint on our act of combination that constitutes the objectivity of given representation (their relation to an object) just is the necessary combination required by the identity of apperception. In calling this the main claim of the deduction I mean that this move contains both Kant's solution to the problem of the possibility of synthetic, *a priori* knowledge and the basic Kantian limitation to our knowledge, namely, that we can know things only as they are for us, not as they are in themselves. Now I turn to unpacking these implications.

Kant's Solution to the Epistemological Problem

First, then, how does the claim of the deduction provide for the possibility of synthetic, *a priori* knowledge? We posed this question at the beginning as the question of how knowledge of the object is possible prior to the object being given. The solution of the problem goes by way of the deduction of the objective validity of the pure concepts of the understanding, which is Kant's immediate aim in the deduction. How, then, do we get from the claim of §17 to the objective validity of the categories? Kant gets there by way of a discussion of judgment in §19, but, for our purposes, the following point is sufficient: the categories have objective validity because they are the rules for the *a priori* synthesis of apperception. A way Kant has of putting the claim of §17 is that intuition has its relation to an object through being brought to the necessary unity of apperception. The pure concepts of the understanding, the categories, are those concepts by means of which the manifold of given representations is brought to this unity of apperception. They are the functions according to which the synthetic unity of apperception is determined. The pure concepts of the understanding necessarily apply to objects of our knowledge, since it is only by submitting to the *a priori* synthesis by means of these concepts that representations are of an object at all. As such, the pure concepts are 'concepts of an object in general', since, roughly, it is synthesis by means of these concepts that constitutes objectivity in knowledge for us.

Importantly, the synthetic unity of apperception, and, hence, the pure concepts as well, would not be 'objective conditions' were they merely conditions *I required* in order to know the object. If the categories were subjective, or merely ours, in this sense, then, far from being the ground of the possibility of our knowledge of objects, they could be taken to preclude that possibility. However, the categories are 'objective conditions'—hence, genuinely apply to objects—because they are, as Kant says, 'not merely something I myself need in order to cognize an object but rather something under which every intuition must stand *in order to become an object for me*' (B138). Only because these concepts, as rules of the *a priori* synthesis of apperception, are constitutive of the objectivity of representation for me, that is, constitutive of the relation of representation to the object as that which stands over against my merely 'subjective' sequence of representations and determines it, do they genuinely apply to the objects of our knowledge. Hence, we can have through the categories *a priori* knowledge (knowledge prior to the object being given) that is, at the same time, knowledge *of the object*.

Subjectivism as the Cost of this Solution

The limits to our knowledge drawn by Kant's transcendental idealism are, as Hegel understands it, implicit in this solution to the problem of the possibility of synthetic, *a priori* knowledge, thus, implicit in the main claim of the deduction. To repeat, the main claim is that the relation of our representations to objects consists in the unity these representations receive through being brought under the synthetic unity of apperception. The self-constituting unity of subjectivity constitutes the objectivity of our representations. It follows from this that objects of our knowledge are subject to the restriction of being merely for us, since it is only through conceptualization, through the synthetic unity of apperception, hence through our subjectivity, that objects of knowledge are possible for us. Independently of synthetic unity, knowledge is not possible for us. Consequently, knowledge of things as they are in themselves, that is, of things independently of the conditions that our cognitive capacities necessarily impose, in particular here, independently of synthesis, is impossible for us. Thus, *a priori* knowledge of objects is possible for us for the same reason that knowledge of things as they are in themselves is not: namely, for the reason that the synthetic unity of apperception constitutes the relation of representations to objects.

An important piece of the motivation for this distinction between things as they are in themselves and things as they are for our knowledge would be lacking if we neglected here to recall and to emphasize the following point: for Kant, thought itself is empty of content. It merely provides synthesis of a content that must be given to it externally through intuition.[17] Were this not the case, then the fact that objectivity has its source in thought or in our understanding wouldn't imply a distinction between the object as we know it and the thing as it is in itself, independently of our thought. But that this is the case is a fundamental claim of Kantian epistemology. Kant emphasizes that pure apperception itself is empty; it is a representation through which nothing manifold is given (B138). The emptiness of the categories follows from the emptiness of pure apperception, which in turn merely expresses the emptiness of our understanding generally. Kant writes in the second-edition deduction:

[The categories] are only rules for an understanding whose entire capacity consists in thinking, consists, i.e., in the action of bringing the synthesis of the manifold that is given to it in intuition from elsewhere to the unity of apperception, which, therefore, *cognizes* nothing at all by itself, but only combines and orders the material for cognition, the intuition, which must be given to it through the object. (B145)

So, again, because this content, this intuition, is *of an object* for us only through synthesis provided by our understanding, the pure concepts of the understanding—the categories—are a source for *a priori* knowledge of objects. But because thought itself is empty of content, because the pure concepts are merely rules for the synthesis of an externally given content, the knowledge that they make possible is knowledge of objects as they are for us, not as they are in themselves. As Hegel says in his lectures on the history of philosophy: the realm of objectivity in Kant is itself subjective in the sense that it 'remains enclosed within the circle of the subject, within the pure I of my self-consciousness, within the sphere of the thinking understanding'.[18]

This, then, is how I understand Hegel's interpretation of Kant's (epistemological) idealism as subjectivism. Kant's view is idealism insofar as it holds that objectivity has its source in thought. The basic thesis of idealism,

---

[17] Ultimately, the content of our knowledge derives from *empirical* intuition. (See B147–8.)
[18] Hegel, VGP, *Werke*, vol. 20, 35. *Hegel's Lectures on the History of Philosophy*, trans. and ed. E. S. Haldane and Frances H. Simson, vol. 3, 442–3.

according to Hegel, is the thesis that the real is thought or reason. But then, on Hegel's conception, Kant's idealism fails to be genuine idealism since Kant conceives of thinking—hence of the objectivity which thinking makes possible, as well—as subjective. There is, in other words, the insurmountable gulf between thought (the subject) and the 'in-itself' (reality or being) that Hegel referred to in the previously quoted passage from the *Encyclopedia Logic*: 'the Kantian objectivity of thinking is [] again subjective to the extent that the thoughts … are *merely our* thoughts, and separated from the thing as it is *in itself* by an insurmountable gulf.' That, in transcendental idealism, thought is subjective in this sense marks one striking and fundamental difference between Kant's idealism and Hegel's own absolute idealism, at least on Hegel's understanding of each.

1.4 ARE KANT'S CATEGORIES SUBJECTIVE?

The claim that, for Kant, thought is subjective will be made clearer by examining the major objection to this Hegelian interpretation of Kantian idealism. The objection is well expressed by Karl Ameriks and Paul Guyer in their respective articles on Hegel's critique of Kant's theoretical philosophy. Essentially, the claim of Ameriks and Guyer against Hegel's interpretation is, using Ameriks's words, that ideality does not attach to the categories as such in Kant.[19] Another way of putting this claim is that the categories are not as such merely 'ours'; they are not as such subjective. Since the categories are derived from the logical functions of judgment, and since the logical functions of judgment are, Kant sometimes suggests, the necessary rules of thought as such, the pure categories are not merely ours—they are not restricted to human cognition in particular. Of course, thought through the pure categories is *merely thought*; it isn't yet knowledge of an object. In order for the pure concepts to yield knowledge of an object, they must be applied to intuition, and this implies, in our case, that they must be applied to our particular *a priori* forms of intuition, space and time. As Ameriks and Guyer interpret Kant, the categories become subjective or ideal only through the necessary application of them to the pure forms of intuition, space and time. Guyer writes: 'Transcendental idealism applies to the categories only because of the transcendental idealism of the forms of intuition to which they must

---

[19] Ameriks, 'Hegel's Critique of Kant's Theoretical Philosophy', 24.

be applied in order to yield actual knowledge as opposed to mere thought.'[20] Ameriks and Guyer both argue that what is restricted to us is not the categories, not the forms of thought, but only the forms of sensibility, space and time. Only insofar as the categories are interpreted, as it were, by means of these ideal, subjective, human forms of sensibility are they themselves restricted in the scope of their application. Only the schematized categories are subjective, not the pure categories. Both Ameriks and Guyer rest an important part of their case against the interpretation of the categories as subjective on the fact that, for Kant, we can *think* things in themselves through the pure categories.

The first point in defense of Hegel's view is that the subjectivity of the categories has nothing to do with the question of whether they hold necessarily for all thinking beings as such or not. If the claim that a given set of epistemic conditions are subjective presupposes that we must have in mind another sort of cognition not limited by these forms, then the question of whether the categories are subjective depends on whether Kant envisions a cognition free from these forms or not. Ameriks and Guyer both emphasize that, since the categories are derived from the forms of judgment, they hold for all thinkers as such.[21] They maintain that, while Kant entertains the possibility of a discursive understanding with different forms of sensible intuition from our own, he does not allow for the prospect of thinkers with a different set of categories. Consequently, they argue, the categories, unlike the forms of sensible intuition, are not subjective. But this is a red herring. The question is not whether the categories hold for all thinkers as such, since, on Hegel's reading, the subjectivism derives from the role of thinking itself (whatever its pure forms) in our knowledge of objects.

If the claim that the categories are subjective requires a contrast with our cognition, the relevant contrast is not with another discursive understanding that employs a different set of categories, but rather with an intuitive understanding, for which, as Kant tells us, 'the categories would have no significance at all' (B145). Indeed, when Kant speaks of 'the peculiarity of human cognition', he most often has in mind, not our particular forms of sensible intuition (which would distinguish our cognition among other supposed finite knowers), but rather our understanding *as discursive* (which

[20] Guyer, 'Thought and Being: Hegel's Critique of Kant's Theoretical Philosophy', 189.

[21] Ameriks: '[The conceptual order of the categories] is one that holds for all thinkers' ('Hegel's Critique of Kant's Theoretical Philosophy', 24). Guyer: 'All thought takes the form of judgment, and the possible logical forms of judgment admit of an exhaustive analysis precisely in terms of his [Kant's] quite compact list of categories' ('Thought and Being: Hegel's Critique of Kant's Theoretical Philosophy', 187).

distinguishes us *as finite* knowers, in contrast to a supposed infinite or unlimited cognition).[22] Kant emphasizes that we can form no very determinate idea of an intuitive understanding—he even notes that we cannot assert the real possibility of such a thing—but it is clear that the idea of this contrasting cognition, by which we mark our own peculiarity, is of a cognition that, by virtue of knowing objects through actively intuiting them, has use neither for concepts (for general representations) nor for sensible intuitions. Such an understanding would be creative, hence not dependent. Such an understanding, he writes, 'would not represent given objects', but rather 'the objects would themselves [] be given' through its representing (B145).

Accordingly, for Kant, to know an object through thinking it, in contrast to knowing it through intuiting it, 'is always proof of limitations' (B71). How or why is limitation or finitude bound up with the very idea of cognition of objects through thought or through concepts? The answer is contained in the transcendental deduction of the categories, so far as we've surveyed its argument. Since knowing an object through thinking it is to know it through general representations, through concepts, such knowledge is inherently mediated and dependent. Thinking requires a content given to it externally through the senses. Thus, the cognitive operations of thinking an object and of sensing it reciprocally imply each other (insofar, that is, as either contributes to knowledge of an object). To know objects through the activity of thinking them is to be *passive* with respect to the content of knowledge. This content given externally to the thinking subject can only be of an object for the subject through the subject's combination of it according to *a priori* rules, that is, rules that have their source in the activity of the thinking subject, not in an external source. Consequently, to know objects through thought is to know objects only according to intellectual conditions that have their source in the subject. Thus, to know objects through thought is to know them only as they are for us, not as they are in themselves, independently of these necessary conditions. The cognition of a discursive understanding is inherently limited or finite, not (merely) because we cannot know everything, or because we cannot know anything in its complete individuality, but because we can only know objects according to subjective conditions, conditions that have their source in us, among which are the categories. The categories are subjective, in the sense that they are, because, far from being conditions of the things themselves, they are, as we've already heard Kant say, 'only rules for an understanding

---

[22] See, for example, B145. Also, KU, §77.

whose entire capacity consists in thinking, i.e., in the action of bringing the synthesis of the manifold that is given to it in intuition from elsewhere to the unity of apperception' (B145). At the end of the deduction, Kant puts the view I am attributing to him here about as explicitly as can be hoped:

It is by no means stranger that the laws of appearances in nature must agree with the understanding and its *a priori* form, i.e., its faculty of *combining* the manifold in general, than that the appearances themselves must agree with the form of sensible intuition *a priori*. For laws exist just as little in the appearances, but rather exist only relative to the subject in which the appearances inhere, insofar as it has understanding, as appearances do not exist in themselves, but only relative to the same being, insofar as it has senses ... As mere representations ... [appearances] stand under no law of connection at all except that which the connecting faculty prescribes. (B164)

There remains the point that Kant holds that, although we can't know things in themselves, we can *think* things in themselves through the pure categories. Guyer and Ameriks both take this doctrine to imply that Kant does not regard the categories as subjective. Does this doctrine have this implication?

Guyer claims that 'the reason Kant could argue that the categories, unlike space and time, could be used at least to *conceive* of things in themselves, even if not to acquire actual *knowledge* of them' is that 'Kant sometimes suggested that the categorical structure of judgment, or discursive thought, is by no means a peculiarity of human cognition in particular'.[23] If the doctrine that we can think things in themselves through the pure categories depends on the suggestion that discursive thought is *not* a peculiarity of human cognition, then the interpretive claim that the categories are subjective cannot be much threatened by this doctrine. The contrary view that discursivity *is* a peculiarity of our understanding is much better supported by Kant's texts.[24] If there is a contradiction between holding that discursivity is a peculiarity of our understanding and holding that we can think things in themselves through the pure categories, then one must conclude, not that for Kant the categories are not subjective, but rather that Kant's view is contradictory. But is there a contradiction between these doctrines? This depends on the difficult question of how to interpret thought of things in themselves in Kant, which cannot be

---

[23] Guyer, 'Thought and Being: Hegel's Critique of Kant's Theoretical Philosophy', 187.

[24] Have I perhaps misunderstood Guyer's claim quoted at the beginning of the paragraph? Is he saying, not that Kant sometimes suggests that the discursivity of our understanding is 'by no means a peculiarity of human cognition', but that Kant sometimes suggests that the categorical structure of discursive understanding is by no means a peculiarity of human cognition (though the discursivity of our understanding surely is)? But, then, as I've already argued, Hegel's claim that the categories are subjective does not depend on whether they hold for all thinkers or not.

wholly separated from the vexed question of how to interpret Kant's doctrine of transcendental idealism more generally. But we can make a few points here.

Kant himself warns against what I will call an 'objective' interpretation of thought of things in themselves through the pure categories. Such an interpretation seems implicit in Karl Ameriks's invocation of the doctrine (that we can think things in themselves through the categories) against Hegel's claim that the Kantian categories are subjective. According to the objective interpretation, pure thought through the categories has (or, at least, can have) an object, namely, things as they really are. Accordingly, we can say, by virtue of the capacity to think things in themselves through the categories, that the categorical structure 'holds of', or 'applies to', reality itself, independently of our way of knowing it. Such an interpretation may seem immediately to conflict with the Kantian doctrine that the categories cannot be employed transcendentally to know things as they are in themselves, but only empirically to know appearances. However, such an interpretation can attempt to accommodate that doctrine by maintaining that, though the categories are valid for all knowledge of objects whatsoever, pure thought through the categories, independently of application to our form of intuition, still falls short of knowledge by virtue of its relative indeterminacy or formality. On this view, that we can *think* things in themselves through the pure categories implies that the categories are *necessary* conditions for knowledge generally. That we *cannot know* things in themselves through the categories is merely a consequence of the fact that the categories are, though necessary, not *sufficient* for knowledge. In order to yield knowledge, the categories must be applied to some intuition, and the only intuition available to us is the sensible, according to our subjective forms, space and time.

I ascribe the objective interpretation of thought of things as they are in themselves to Ameriks on the basis of his objecting that Hegel misses the point that the categories have a pure meaning.[25] Hegel sometimes expresses the subjectivity of the Kantian categories by claiming that thought through the pure categories is thought of nothing at all.[26] In opposing such statements, Ameriks asserts that Kantian categories are not 'absolutely empty' independently of their application to intuition, as shown by the fact that we can think things in themselves through them.[27] Ameriks's interpretation of such pure thought is revealed in the following passage:

---

[25] Ameriks, 'Hegel's Critique of Kant's Theoretical Philosophy', 23–5.
[26] See, for example, Hegel, EL, §48A.
[27] Ameriks, 'Hegel's Critique of Kant's Theoretical Philosophy', 25.

On the basis of the distinction [between the pure and the schematized meaning of the categories] the Kantian can say that (contra Jacobi) what goes beyond the sensible is not a wholly amorphous domain but rather something which can be allowed some sort of conceptual order. This order is one that holds for all thinkers, and it can even be made determinate by us as long as we have another type of data than the spatio-temporal to make use of, as in fact occurs with our moral faculty.[28]

Ameriks infers from the fact that we can think things in themselves through the categories that the categorical structure actually applies beyond the sensible domain to reality itself, independently of our way of knowing it. The categories do not suffice for knowledge of things as they are in themselves only because the categorical structure is relatively indeterminate.

Kant himself warns against such an interpretation of thought of things in themselves through the pure categories. Though Kant's scattered remarks on pure thought through the categories and on thought of things in themselves are difficult to reconcile with each other, he consistently insists in such discussions that this thought is of no cognitive use for us. The most common way he has of saying this is to insist that the pure categories or pure thought is wholly devoid of meaning and significance (*Sinn und Bedeutung*).[29] As Ameriks reads Kant, Kant cannot really mean what he says in such passages. And, indeed, Kant does occasionally contradict the denial of all significance to the pure categories by ascribing to them a merely logical or transcendental significance.[30]

I offer the following hypothesis for reconciling Kant's apparently conflicting statements on this issue. What is correct (and important) in Ameriks's insistence that the categories have a pure meaning is just that the categories, as the pure forms of thought, do not derive from sensibility. They have an independent source in thought. Otherwise, pure thought, thought independently of all relation to sensible intuition, would not be possible for us at all. It is an important part of Kant's view that such thought is possible for us. As Kant writes in the following passage from the second-edition deduction, we have the capacity to think beyond the limits of our sensibility:

Space and time are valid, as conditions of the possibility of how objects can be given to us, no further than for objects of the senses, hence only for experience. Beyond these boundaries they do not represent anything at all, for they are only in the senses and outside of them have no reality. The pure concepts of the understanding are free from this limitation, and extend to objects of intuition in general, whether the latter be similar to our own or not, as long as it is sensible and not intellectual. (B148)

---

[28] *Ibid.*, 24.   [29] B149; A155/B194; A240/B299; B307–8, etc.
[30] See B186; B305.

However, the question is: of what cognitive use or significance to us is this independence from the limitations of sensibility on the part of the forms of thought? In particular, does this independence imply that reality itself, independently of the way that we must know it, is structured according to the conceptual structure of the categories? After pointing out this independence in the Phenomena/Noumena chapter, Kant explicitly warns against granting it *any* cognitive significance, while acknowledging the temptation to do so:

As far as their origin is concerned, the categories are not grounded on sensibility; ... they therefore seem to allow an application extended beyond all objects of the senses. But for their part they are in turn nothing other than *forms of thought*, which contain merely the logical capacity for unifying the manifold given in intuition in a consciousness *a priori*; thus, if one takes away from them the only sensible intuition possible for us, they have even less significance than those pure sensible forms, through which at least an object is given, whereas the kind of combination of the manifold that is proper to our understanding signifies nothing at all if that intuition in which alone the manifold can be given is not added to it. (B305–6)[31]

Contrary to Ameriks's objective interpretation then, far from its being the case that, in purifying our thought, we are able to gain a cognitive extension by virtue of freeing ourselves from the restriction imposed by our subjective forms of sensibility, Kant insists here that the pure forms of thought 'have even less significance' than the pure sensible forms. Moreover, he explains why they have even less significance: independently of their application to intuition, the pure forms of thought are purely thought, and, as such, lack all relation to an object.

Kant's repeated claim that the pure categories lack significance is not, as Ameriks holds, an exaggerated way of saying that they are relatively without significance, but rather a way of saying that they are completely empty, where this means that they lack any relation to an object. Independently of application to intuition, the categories are purely ideal. The pure categories 'are only functions of the understanding for concepts, but do not represent any object' (A147/B187). Or, again, they 'are merely the pure form of the employment of the understanding in regard to objects in general and of thinking, yet without any sort of object being able to be thought or determined through them alone' (A248/B305).[32]

---

[31] See also A146–7/B186–7, where Kant makes a similar point.

[32] Yet again, independently of application to intuition, the categories 'have no objective validity at all, but are rather a mere play, whether it be with representations of the imagination or of the understanding' (A239/B298).

Is Kant's repeated insistence that thought through the pure categories is thought without an object compatible with the doctrine that such thought is 'of an object in general', or, again, of things in themselves? To take thought 'of an object in general' first, Kant himself clearly detects no incompatibility, since he essentially asserts both claims in the single sentence quoted at the end of the previous paragraph. If we abstract in our thought from all application to intuition, then what remains is merely the formal unity of thinking (in its specific functions) for a possible intuition. Thought through the pure categories expresses merely the unity of thinking for any possible given (that is, sensible) intuition. Why is thought that expresses merely the unity of my thinking for any possible sensible intuition thought of an object in general? Kant's main claim of the transcendental deduction is that the necessary unity of thinking in a given manifold of representations constitutes the relation of those given representations to objects. The pure concepts of the understanding, the categories, are the functions of this necessary unity of thinking. Independently of being applied to given representation, they are mere functions of thought, without relation to an object. But they are the functions of thought through which alone intuition ('whether [it] be similar to our own or not, as long as it is sensible and not intellectual') is related to objects for us. As such, the categories are 'concepts of an object in general'.

It is more difficult to see how pure thought can be both empty and thought of things as they are in themselves. It's worth noting that Kant himself had advanced an objective conception of pure thought of things in themselves in his Inaugural Dissertation, as the following passage from that text shows.

[W]hatever in cognition is sensitive is dependent upon the special character of the subject to the extent that the subject is capable of this or that modification by the presence of objects and these modifications can differ in different cases according to variations in the subjects. But whatever cognition is exempt from such subjective conditions has regard only to the object. Consequently it is clear that things which are thought sensitively are representations of things *as they appear*, but things which are intellectual are representations of things *as they are*.[33]

Here the subjective element in cognition is explicitly identified as the sensible (or sensitive) element, whereas the objective element is explicitly said to be the intellectual. Sensible representations are said to be subjective, presumably, both because they are 'modifications *of the subject*' and because 'these modifications can differ ... according to variations in the subjects'. The objective

---

[33] Kant, InDiss, 2: 392.

representation, in contrast, is 'whatever cognition is exempt from such subjective conditions'. According to this conception, thought through the pure
intellectual concepts is *as such* objective, since it is cognitive representation
that is purified of the sensible/subjective; hence, thought through the pure
intellectual concepts is thought of things as they are.

Clearly, though, Kant's conception of thought through the pure concepts
of things as they really are must be significantly revised in the face of his
development of his critical question regarding these pure intellectual concepts
(namely, how can they have a relation to an object at all?) and of his critical
philosophy as an answer to that question. According to Kant's critical conception, thought through the pure intellectual concepts is empty in the sense that
such thought *lacks* relation to an object. Yet he continues to maintain that such
thought is (or can be) thought of things as they are in themselves. Why? How?

It might seem that, once Kant has dispensed with the assumption that the
pure intellect's representation, purified of all sensibility, is as such objective,
Kant should likewise dispense with the notion of noumena or of things in
themselves, as thought through the pure concepts. However, Kant emphasizes
in the Phenomena/Noumena chapter of the First *Critique* that the restriction
of our knowledge to mere phenomena implies conceptually the thought of
things in themselves/noumena. '[T]he understanding, when it calls an object
in a relation mere phenomenon, simultaneously makes for itself, beyond this
relation, another representation of an *object in itself* and hence also represents
itself as being able to make *concepts* of such an object ... ' (B306–7).[34] We
cannot assert the claim that we know only phenomena without thereby
ascribing to ourselves the *concept* of the object in itself, the noumenon.
However, though we cannot dispense with thought of things as they are in
themselves through the pure categories, we must reinterpret it.

I take it that the definition of the concept of the noumenon in the negative
sense in the Phenomena/Noumena chapter articulates the newly defined
conception of things in themselves/noumena, newly defined in accordance
with the critical philosophy. Kant defines the noumenon in the negative
sense as 'a thing *insofar as it is not an object of our sensible* intuition, because
we abstract from our manner of intuiting it'. The noumenon in the positive
sense is the thing considered as an object of a non-sensible intuition (B307).
We think through the pure concepts merely the noumenon in the negative
sense. The concept of the thing in itself/noumenon (in the negative sense) is

---

[34] See also A254–255/B310.

nothing but 'a concept setting limits to our sensibility' (A256/B311); it is, again, merely a 'boundary concept' (B310). Presumably Kant insists on this for the sake of the compatibility of the claim that we are required to think things in themselves through the pure categories with the claim that such thought is empty, in the sense of lacking all relation to objects.

However, Kant retains the conception of the Inaugural Dissertation to this extent: he continues to maintain that the concept of the noumenon/thing in itself is 'connected with the limitation of sensibility' (B311), not of our knowledge more generally, or of the limitations bound up with thinking. Though Kant sometimes characterizes the notion of the thing as it is in itself as the concept of the thing independently of both the sensible and the intellectual conditions on knowledge of objects,[35] much more often he presents it as the notion of the thing independently only of sensible conditions, as thought through the pure understanding.[36] The claim that we know the object only as it appears is the claim, for Kant, that we know it only as it affects our sensibility.[37]

However, this must not obscure the fact that intellectual conditions, namely the categories, are also relativizing or subjectifying conditions, and hence, that the notion of the thing in itself to which Kant is actually committed is the notion of the thing independently also of the rules of our understanding, according to which we must think it. As I've argued, Kant is committed to this by his conception of the discursive (as opposed to intuitive) understanding as inherently limited, along with his conception of the categories as 'merely rules' for such an understanding, rules or concepts that have no significance apart from this parochial way of knowing objects, and by his conception of thought through these pure concepts as empty thought. Kant's language in the Phenomena/Noumena chapter sometimes suggests that, if only we had a non-sensible intuition to which we could apply the categories, we could know the things that we, in the absence of this intuitive content, merely think. However, in other passages he implies what I think must be his more considered view, namely, that our cognition is limited not only by the fact that we can know objects through sensibility, but also by the condition—not unrelated, of course—that we can know objects only through thinking them.

---

[35] See, for example, Prol, 4:322.

[36] See Allison, *Idealism and Freedom*, 185, n. 13, for a list of passages.

[37] This is, arguably, a conceptual point for Kant, since he conceives of appearances/phenomena as 'beings of sense' (*Sinnenwesen*), and noumena, in contrast, as 'beings of the understanding' (*Verstandeswesen*). See B306.

He writes that the concept of a noumenon 'is not a special *intelligible object* for our understanding; rather an understanding to which it would belong is itself a problem, that, namely, of cognizing its object not discursively through categories but intuitively in a non-sensible intuition, the possibility of which we cannot in the least represent' (A256/B311–12). Hence, the concept of a noumenon/thing in itself is the concept of an object not only of a different intuition than our own, but of an entirely different sort of understanding as well. Despite what Kant sometimes explicitly says, thought of the things as they are in themselves must be, as it is in this passage, thought of things as they are independently of the necessary conditions by which *we* can know them, among which conditions are included the pure concepts of the understanding, even though we can only formulate the thought of such things through these very concepts (since, after all, they condition, and make possible, thought of objects as such, for us). If this is incoherent, then Kant's doctrine of thought of things as they are in themselves is incoherent. However, it is not incoherent, it seems to me, if one interprets thought of things as they are in themselves in the negative sense advocated by Kant. Despite the ambiguity in Kant's text, the main thrust of the doctrine of the noumenon in negative sense is that pure thought through the categories merely expresses the limits of our knowledge; it does not transcend that limit, even if only in thought alone.

The perspective on the status of pure thought for Kant that I advocate here seems to stand the perspective of Ameriks and Guyer on its head. For Ameriks, (and for Guyer too, judging from some of his statements),[38] we transcend through pure thought our particularity or our finitude or our subjectivity, as represented by the confines of the senses. They take the pure thought of things in themselves through the categories to testify to this transcendence. Against this, I contend that, when one attends to the full implications of the fact that pure thought, thought through the pure categories, is empty, then one sees that nothing so expresses our subjectivity or our finitude as pure thought. Pure thought is purely subjective. Accordingly, it is a misunderstanding of

---

[38] Whereas Ameriks seems consistently to maintain the view that the categories are not subjective, Guyer's position is less clear. He begins the cited article faulting Hegel for failing to acknowledge the significant reasons that Kant has for asserting the 'impassable gulf' between thought and reality (see p. 172), and then, later in the article faults Hegel for attributing this view to Kant at all. (More specifically, he faults Hegel for attributing to Kant the view that the categories are subjective, but, as I have tried to show, this view just amounts to the assertion of a gulf between thought and reality.) Also, in his earlier book, Guyer explicitly calls attention to the very parallelism between intellectual and sensible conditions, in terms of their subjectivity, that he denies in his attack on Hegel's reading in the article. See *Kant and the Claims of Knowledge*, 79–80.

Kant, I believe, to represent the Kantian limitations on cognition as arising from the drag which our limited sensibility puts on our (unlimited) thought, as if the problem were just that we cannot know as far as we can think. The limitation is more fundamental than this implies. The limitation is that we think at all, that we know through thinking, through general concepts.

We can encapsulate Hegel's understanding of Kant's epistemology as subjectivism in the claim that thought is for Kant subjective. This is what Ameriks and Guyer deny, in objecting to Hegel's interpretation. The categories are the necessary rules of the synthesizing activity (thought) through which alone *we* can have knowledge of objects. I think it is important that these concepts are, in comparison to the forms of our sensibility, subjective in a different, more fundamental, sense. Our pure forms of sensibility are simply brute facts about us, which bear no special relation to our conception of ourselves *as* knowing subjects. As I've tried to show in my discussion of the argument strategy of the deduction, the categories, in contrast, must be understood as internally legislated, as having their source in our activity (as opposed to having their source in the things themselves, independently of us) on pain of our not being able to understand ourselves as epistemic agents (as sources of judgment) at all. That Kant's categories are subjective, in the sense that they are, is bound up, then, with Kant's articulation of a structure of subjectivity, one of the central features of which is that a subject cannot, as such, understand itself to be bound by laws of which it is not the author. One of Hegel's deepest philosophical debts to the Kantian philosophy consists in Kant's articulation of the 'structure of the I' (as Hegel calls it). This debt imposes upon Hegel the burden of redeeming the Kantian claims made on behalf of the subject without the subjectivism that follows in Kant's system. We will see that the project of the *Phenomenology of Spirit* is to a significant extent determined by this task.

2

Hegel's Suspicion: Kantian Critique and Subjectivism

Our age is, in especial degree, the age of criticism, and to criticism everything must submit. Religion through its sanctity, and law-giving through its majesty, may seek to exempt themselves from it. But then they awaken just suspicion, and cannot claim the sincere respect which reason accords only to that which has been able to sustain the test of free and open examination.

Kant, *Critique of Pure Reason* (Preface, first edition)

Meanwhile, if the worry about falling into error sets up a suspicion of science … it is hard to see why we should not turn round and suspect this very suspicion. Should we not worry whether this fear of erring is not the error itself? Indeed, this fear presupposes something—a great deal in fact—as truth, basing its reservations and inferences on what is in itself in need of prior examination to see if it is true.

Hegel, *Phenomenology of Spirit* (Introduction)

Hegel begins his Introduction to the *Phenomenology of Spirit* by articulating a suspicion directed against Kant's methodology of critique, a methodology that in turn expresses an attitude of suspicion directed against the claims of traditional metaphysics.[1] Hegel's suspicion, very basically, is that the procedure of justification of Kantian critique already implicitly presupposes subjectivism. Kantian critique implicitly predetermines Kant's relativization of our knowledge to objects as they are for our cognitive faculties, not as they are in themselves. If, as the Kantian philosophy claims, we are confined in our knowing 'within the circle of the subject, within the pure I of my [our]

---

[1] Hegel does not mention Kant explicitly, and he might mean to target in his remarks at the beginning of the Introduction a broader field of epistemological inquiry, but surely Kantian critique is exemplary for Hegel of the sort of project that he has in his sights there.

self-consciousness',[2] this is not a result established and justified through the critical procedure so much as a presupposition hidden in that procedure from the beginning. As is typical of Hegel's treatments of Kant's philosophy, he leaves his objection here unspecified and contents himself with what amounts to little more than innuendo. In this chapter I flesh out Hegel's suspicion; I provide for it content and grounding.

In so doing, I build on the work of the previous chapter. There I portrayed Kant's subjectivism as arising (in part) out of Kant's articulation of the structure of epistemic agency in his transcendental deduction of the categories. The transcendental unity of apperception, which Kant presents as the highest condition of our knowledge, expresses that judgment, understood as a norm-governed activity of combining representations, is our own act, an activity the correctness of which is our own task or responsibility. This condition turns out to imply that the highest order norms of this activity must be self-legislated, in contrast to being constraints that have their source independently of our activity. In the deduction, Kant analyses the objectivity of given (sensible) representations—their relation to an object—in terms of a universal and necessary constraint on—a sort of legislation for—*our* activity of combining these representations. Since, in order to see the act of judgment as our own responsibility, we must understand the highest order norms of this activity to be self-legislated, the constraint which is the relation of the representations to objects is ultimately a constraint of our epistemic agency or subjectivity itself, not a constraint imposed on us from the outside, by the way the world is anyway, as it were. The highest order constraint imposed by our epistemic agency is the unity of that agency, the unity of the 'I think' itself. Thus, as Kant says, 'the unity which the objects make necessary is nothing other than the formal unity of consciousness in the synthesis of the manifold of the representations'(KrV, A105). As discussed in the previous chapter, the discovery of this formal constraint imposed by our epistemic agency enables the solution of Kant's epistemological problem of understanding how synthetic, *a priori* judgments are possible, though at the cost of subjectivism. Because the objects of our knowledge are partially constituted through the *a priori* constraints of our epistemic subjectivity or agency, we can know something of the objects of given representations *a priori*, prior to the objects being given through the senses. However, the

[2] Hegel, VGP, *Werke*, vol. 20, 35. *Hegel's Lectures on the History of Philosophy*, vol. 3, 442–3. (Please consult 'Abbreviations' for my method of citing the texts of Kant and Hegel.)

objects of our knowledge now must be understood as objects-*for-us*, whereas the things as they are in themselves transcend the limits of our knowledge.

Hegel suspects that Kant's methodology of critique already exemplifies this normative structure; since this normative structure is subjectivism, critique itself already is subjectivism.[3] The epistemological demand expressed in Kant's project of critique already implies that the norms of judgment are self-legislated, in contrast to being determined by the object(s) of pure reason's inquiry, what Hegel calls the 'absolute' and Kant the 'unconditioned'. The call for a critique of pure reason is the call to 'step back' from the metaphysical inquiry itself, from the attempt to know the unconditioned through pure reason, and determine in advance through reflection on our cognitive capacities whether or how such knowledge is possible for us. The suspicion is that this prior, self-reflective inquiry already effectively establishes, in its very stance of inquiry, the formal self-reflection as the highest condition on our knowledge of objects, thus precluding the possibility of metaphysical knowledge, understood as knowledge of the unconditioned. That the object of knowledge must conform to our knowledge rather than our knowledge to the object is a normative structure already implied in the epistemological project of critique, not a conclusion of that procedure. Hence, the critical procedure, which is to be a 'free and open examination' into the possibility of metaphysics,[4] in fact begs the question against that possibility from the beginning and has as a hidden presupposition our confinement in our knowing 'within the circle of the subject'.

I do not undertake in this chapter to prove this case against Kant's critical system. Whatever exactly such a demonstration would involve, it would clearly require more extensive discussion than I can give the issue here. I undertake here merely to make the best case for the *suspicion* within the scope of a chapter. This task requires reading Kant somewhat against—or, anyway, across—the grain of his writing. Hegel's suspicion arises through relating aspects of Kant's critical system that Kant himself does not discuss—or discusses only rarely—in relation to each other: namely, (1) the methodological revolution of critique and the allegedly new epistemological demand expressed in this new methodology; (2) the structure of agency or subjectivity (both epistemic and practical), particularly as regards the relation of the self-conscious agent

---

[3] In the early text *Faith and Knowledge*, Hegel writes: 'The Kantian philosophy plainly confesses that its principle is subjectivism and formal thinking through the fact that its essence consists in being critical idealism' (Hegel, GW, 301/67).

[4] Kant, KrV, Axi, *n*.

standing under norms (again, both practical and epistemic) to those norms; and (3) the conclusion of subjectivism, that is, the relativization of claims to the standpoint of the self-conscious, judging subject. The reading of Kant from which Hegel's suspicion is motivated is from a standpoint external to Kant's own, in the sense that the suspicion arises from holding Kant's system at arm's length, as it were, and noting structural similarities between aspects of Kant's system that Kant himself does not call attention to. Though we will see as we proceed that Hegel's suspicion of Kantian critique suggests an incipient hermeneutics of suspicion, our main aim here is to develop these structural similarities sufficiently to motivate Hegel's suspicion. In order to appreciate Hegel's attempts to come to terms with the epistemological project of critique, culminating in the *Phenomenology of Spirit*, we must first appreciate Hegel's suspicion.

2.1 WHAT IS KANTIAN PHILOSOPHICAL CRITICISM?

Again, I begin with a disclaimer. To answer the headline question of this section, one must collect and sift the scattered—usually brief and unspecific—passages in which Kant characterizes and motivates his critical enterprise. If there is a single, determinate answer to this question—an answer which holds of the entire critical project, from the first edition of the First *Critique* through the *Metaphysics of Morals*—I do not undertake here to provide it. Instead, I undertake to develop the outline of Hegel's reading of Kant's project of criticism. This undertaking imposes upon me the burden of showing that Hegel's reading is well supported by Kant's texts, but not that it is the all-things-considered best interpretation among salient alternatives.

If Kant's project of criticism, on the reading I give of it here, seems unfamiliar to us, even un-Kantian, this perception is owing not to a lack of support for this reading in Kant's texts, but rather to a significant shift in perspective on Kant's epistemology between the post-Kantians and us. The post-Kantian philosophers see Kant's critical enterprise primarily as the prior, reflective, epistemological inquiry through which metaphysics is to be set upon what Kant repeatedly calls 'the sure path of science' for the first time.[5] Prominent post-Kantian philosophers see Kant's project primarily in these terms partly because they themselves, inspired and energized by the philosophical promise

---

[5] See the first several paragraphs of the Preface to the second edition of the *Critique of Pure Reason*, where Kant characterizes the task in this way.

of Kant's critical turn, mean to finish Kant's work of founding the science of metaphysics, work they see Kant as having left unfinished. But, as concerns finally establishing metaphysics as a science, once and for all, we live in a more jaded age than that of Kant and his immediate successors. Our investment (or the investment of analytic philosophy, at least) in Kant's epistemology is quite different. The tendency in analytic philosophy has been to see the promise of Kant's epistemology in the task of articulating the *a priori* conditions of the possibility of ordinary empirical knowledge or of natural science (which are both presupposed as given, as *already* established), hence as an inquiry that significantly qualifies empiricism, by granting an essential role for *a priori* philosophizing, but as an inquiry that is securely hinged, unlike traditional metaphysics, to the constraints of experience.[6] Putting the contrast a bit too starkly for the sake of illustration: according to the post-Kantian orientation, Kant's critical turn finally enables the founding of the *a priori* science of the absolute, the science that has so far eluded metaphysicians in the tradition; according to the contemporary orientation, in contrast, Kant's critical turn finally destroys the pretensions to such a science once and for all, while at the same time showing the way toward the modest, but still philosophical task of articulating the *a priori* conditions of emphatically empirical science or knowledge. Both of these dimensions, despite the tension between them, are knit together in Kant's various presentations of his distinctive epistemological project. Hegel's reading of Kant's project of criticism is, if not *more*, then also not *less* supported than the significantly different reading of Kant's epistemological project common in the context of contemporary epistemology. The clash of interpretive orientations turns not so much on faithfulness to the relevant Kantian texts on methodology—which are, in any case, relatively vague, scattered, more or less metaphorical and rhetorical, leaving much playroom for interpretation—as on the interpreters' divergent perceptions of the promise of Kant's epistemological project. Consequently, my task is to develop Hegel's interpretation in such a way that we can see the richness of it, a richness obscured from us by common assumptions regarding what is philosophically interesting and promising in Kant's critical epistemology.[7]

---

[6] Important works by contemporary analytic philosophers or scholars on (dimensions of) Kant's thought that exemplify this tendency are the following: P. F. Strawson, *The Bounds of Sense* (trendsetting, in many ways); Paul Guyer, *Kant and the Claims of Knowledge*; Michael Friedman, *Kant and the Exact Sciences*; Karl Ameriks, *Kant and the Fate of Autonomy*.

[7] Hegel's interpretation of Kant's criticism is thoroughly mediated by the readings of thinkers who are also responding to Kant's criticism in this period: thinkers such as Reinhold, Fichte,

To begin with the generic concept, 'critique' means the activity of distinguishing true from false, or justified from unjustified, claims in one or another field of inquiry. To submit some claim or body of claims to critique is to submit it to testing or examination with respect to its validity or justification. As Dieter Henrich points out, the fact that the word 'critique' often carries a negative connotation both in and outside of Kant's writings, one associated with limitation and restriction, even though one could in principle come as well to a positive as a negative verdict in critical examination, follows from the fact that we are in general far more apt to assert beyond the bounds of what our grounds will support than to remain within those limits. It so often falls to the critic to deny and limit and discipline inquiry that critique becomes identified with those negative tasks.[8]

Critique is a negative inquiry in a technical sense as well. As noted, the critical inquiry takes as its object some set of positive assertions and examines them with respect to their validity or justification. It does not aim itself at positive knowledge, or, as Kant writes, 'it does not aim at the amplification of cognitions themselves, but only at their correction' (A12/B26). Thus, critique is distinguished from positive theory building or 'doctrine'. Whereas the practitioner of the object inquiry engages in building and extending the edifice of the theory in question, the critic tests the parts or whole of the theory with respect to their justificatory grounding. Criticism, then, partakes both of the particular dignities and the particular limitations of this merely negative task. On the one hand, critique reserves to itself the right of standing judgment over all domains of inquiry. As Kant likes to emphasize, in this 'age of criticism', no domain (neither religion, for example, nor political legislation) is so sanctified or high that it can rightfully exempt itself from critical examination.[9] On the other hand, critique is impotent on its own when it comes to generating (positive) knowledge. Because criticism can only discipline, not amplify, knowledge, its work awaits the presentation of some object inquiry for examination.

The major step in moving from the generic account of criticism to the specific concept of Kantian critique consists in specifying the object of Kantian criticism. As noted above, critique can in principle have any object. Any

Maimon, etc. Though I point occasionally, by the way, to the particular influence of particular thinkers, the story of this mediation does not belong to the story I tell here.

[8] See Dieter Henrich, 'Die Deduktion des Sittengesetzes: Über die Gründe der Dunkelheit des letzten Abschnittes von Kants *Grundlegung zur Metaphysik der Sitten*', 61. See also Kant, KrV, A709–11/B737–9.

[9] See, for example, the passage quoted as an epigraph to this chapter, Axi, *n*. See also A738/B766.

domain of inquiry consisting of claims that make demands upon the agreement of rational beings can be an object of critical investigation. However,
the *subject* of criticism, in the sense of that which criticizes, is always reason.
Kant likes to use the political or legal image of a tribunal to represent the
activity of criticism.[10] According to the analogy, in criticism reason sits in
judgment over some set of allegedly universal claims. The general question in
criticism is always whether the claims in the object inquiry measure up to the
standards of reason or not, and it is reason itself, or reason in us, that must
decide this question. But the question becomes considerably more complex
and interesting—it becomes, in fact, a somewhat different question—when,
as in Kantian critique, the specific *object* of critique is *also pure reason*.

It is clear from many passages in the *Critique of Pure Reason*—beginning,
perhaps, with the title—that Kant conceives of the object of his critical
inquiry, not as another object inquiry in the set of possible object inquiries,
but as the criticizing subject itself, namely pure reason.[11] Kant is most
explicit in the Introduction. There he characterizes reason as 'the faculty that
provides the principles of cognition *a priori*' (A11/B24). A system of pure
reason (which is equivalent, presumably, to a science of metaphysics) would
consist of reason's pure principles and the set of cognitions derived *a priori*
from them. In the Architectonic chapter of the Doctrine of Method at the
end of the book, Kant divides our cognitive power into two stems, one of
which is reason, by which he means the entire higher faculty of cognition,
and to which he contrasts the empirical faculty. Accordingly, he recognizes a
distinction there between two kinds of cognition: *cognitio ex datis*, cognition
based on what is given (empirical knowledge), and *cognitio ex principiis*,
cognition from principles (rational knowledge) (A835–6/B864–5). The task
of the critique of pure reason is not the attainment of rational knowledge,
that is, not the construction of a system of pure reason (a doctrine), but
what Kant regards as the prior task of investigating how and whether such
knowledge, or such a system, is possible for us. He writes in the Introduction:

But since [the creation of a system of pure reason] requires a lot, and it is an open
question whether such an amplification of our cognition is possible at all and in
what cases it would be possible, we can regard a science of the mere estimation

---

[10] See KrV, Axi–xii; A751/B779.
[11] I discuss in 2.4 below passages from the Preface and Introduction to the *Critique of Practical Reason* that suggest that the title of the First *Critique* should not be interpreted as I interpret it here.

[*Beurteilung*] of pure reason, of its sources and boundaries, as the propaedeutic to the system of pure reason. Such a thing would not be a doctrine, but must be called a critique of pure reason ... (A11/B25)

If critique is generically the process in which some object inquiry is brought before and judged by the tribunal of pure reason, the critique *of pure reason* is the process in which pure reason stands judgment over itself, judging the possibility of its own object inquiry or doctrine, called by the name 'metaphysics'.

That Kant understands the critique of pure reason as the self-reflection of pure reason—pure reason's critical gaze turned back against itself—is confirmed by the many passages in which Kant characterizes the critical project as reason's *self*-knowledge or self-examination.[12] Hegel's suspicion relies heavily on the conception of Kant's critical inquiry as pure reason's self-reflective inquiry, standing over against metaphysics proper, conceived in contrast as pure reason's object-directed inquiry.[13] If metaphysics is understood, in contrast to the prior critique of pure reason, as pure reason's object-directed inquiry, what are the distinctive objects of pure reason's inquiry in metaphysics? The short answer is what Kant calls 'the unconditioned'. According to Kant, human reason is led inexorably in its search for reasons, that is, in its task of giving the condition for that which is given to our cognitive faculties as conditioned, to seek ultimate satisfaction in the unconditioned, in that about which we cannot intelligibly ask the further question why it is as it is. This inquiry leads human reason into the realm of the supersensible. Kant argues in the Transcendental Dialectic of the First *Critique* that there are three forms of the unconditioned, hence, three 'objects' of pure reason in metaphysics, to which correspond the three 'doctrines' of traditional, special metaphysics. The unavoidable problems of pure reason concern specifically the supersensible objects of God (rational theology), the soul (rational psychology), and the world as a whole (rational cosmology). In the second-edition Preface to the First *Critique*, Kant contrasts the task of his criticism to the 'dogmatic procedure of pure reason', which consists in pure reason's attempt to cognize straightway these supersensible objects, '*without an antecedent critique of its own capacity*' (Kant's emphases), thus

---

[12] KrV, Axi; Axiv; Axx; Bxxiii; A12–13/B26; A763/B791; Prol, 4: 329.

[13] Though there are plenty of passages that suggest that Kant conceives of the relation of critique to metaphysics in this way, (as documented in the references in the previous footnote), there are some passages that suggest that Kant thinks of metaphysics itself as pure reason's self-knowledge, thus not as distinguished from critique in this respect. See Prol, 4: 327; KrV, B23.

clearly indicating that he thinks of the critical inquiry as pure reason's prior, *self-reflective* examination (Bxxxv–xxxvi).[14]

As I noted above and need now to explain, this turning back of pure reason's critical attention towards itself transforms the task of critique. The task of the critique *of pure reason* is not, as in critique generically, to determine whether the claims of the object inquiry measure up to the standards of pure reason (which are taken for granted as already established), but rather to determine or to establish the justified standards of pure reason themselves. In the critique of pure reason, it is the standards or criteria of pure reason's judgment itself that are in question or under examination. So, to employ the tribunal or legal metaphor of which Kant is fond, the task of critique here, when the object is pure reason itself, is not (or not *only*) that of applying established standards in a legal process, but of *instituting* or *establishing* or *founding* the legal order through constructing consensus on the fundamental principles or standards of pure reason. The critique of pure reason consists in the attempt to establish recognized, authoritative standards of justification through the process of reason's self-knowledge.

The case for reading Kant's project of critique as having this function of founding begins by noticing how he tends to characterize the task of critique as a response to a normative *crisis* which he takes reason currently to face, a crisis regarding the content and the *authority* of its fundamental norms or principles. What makes the critique of pure reason necessary, in particular, according to Kant's characterizations in the Preface to the second edition of the First *Critique* as well as in the *Prolegomena*, is that metaphysics, the science of pure reason, does not yet exist. Instead, metaphysics is a 'battlefield of endless controversies' in which the disputants (namely, the proponents of the opposing metaphysical systems) 'revolve ever around the same spot without advancing a single step'.[15] The situation of pure reason such that it calls for a critique is marked primarily by persistent and fundamental conflict or controversy within the domain of metaphysical inquiry.[16] The basic cause of this endless controversy, according to Kant's diagnosis, is that there is no

---

[14] See also Prol, 4: 329, where Kant contrasts a 'dogmatic inquiry into things', with the critical inquiry, which he characterizes as 'a subjective investigation of reason itself as a source of ideas'.

[15] KrV, Axiii; Prol, 4: 256.

[16] Kant's distinctively critical enterprise has its original impetus, not only in what he calls in the *Prolegomena* 'Hume's problem' regarding the concept of causality (Prol, 4: 260–1), but also in his discovery of the Antinomy of Pure Reason, which is pure reason's conflict with itself, in the absence of criticism, which conflict is expressed in the opposition between metaphysical systems, none of which can secure consensus for its claims.

agreement on the criteria (or on the norms or principles) of reason's judgment in metaphysics. Reason still lacks in its metaphysical researches what Kant calls 'a standard weight and measure [*ein sicheres Maaß und Gewicht*] [by which] to distinguish soundness from shallow talk' (Prol, 4: 256). Though metaphysics *as a natural predisposition* has always existed in the human spirit and always will, according to Kant, metaphysics *as a science* can only exist through supplying pure reason's 'want of a recognized standard'.[17] It is the specific task of the critique of pure reason to supply that want, which is why the critique of pure reason is, on Kant's conception of it, the necessary propaedeutic to the science of metaphysics, the prior investigation through which alone metaphysics *as a science* can come to be.

In the Introduction to the *Critique of Pure Reason*, Kant specifies the problem of that text as the famous problem: how are synthetic, *a priori* judgments possible?[18] This characterization of the task of criticism does not conflict with that according to which critique supplies 'the want of a recognized standard' for pure reason's object knowledge (metaphysics), but is rather a specification of that characterization. Kant understands the fundamental root of the crisis to consist in the failure of previous philosophy to notice that reason lays claim in metaphysics to a special sort of knowledge, namely synthetic, *a priori* knowledge. Previous philosophers have failed to notice that the possibility of this sort of knowledge poses a particular problem: namely, how can such knowledge possibly be legitimated or grounded? 'That metaphysics has until now remained in such a vacillating state of uncertainty and contradictions is to be ascribed solely to the cause that no one has previously thought of this problem' (B19).

As noted above, human reason 'driven by its own need' (B21), is led inexorably to pose problems regarding, specifically, the supersensible objects of God (whether He exists and what His nature is), the world as a whole (whether there is place for human freedom within it) and the soul (whether it is immortal). 'The science whose final aim in all its preparations is directed properly only to the solution of these problems is called *metaphysics*...' (A3/B7). Clearly, in posing such problems, pure reason transcends the realm in which experience can serve it as an arbiter of its claims. But, since pure reason aspires in metaphysics to more than merely analytical knowledge—that is, since reason in metaphysics claims substantive knowledge or knowledge *of objects*—logic is also not a sufficient ground. Thus, the previously unnoticed

---

17 See second-edition Preface, B19–24; Prol, 4: 367.
18 See Section VI of the Introduction to the second edition, B19–24.

problem posed by the possibility of synthetic, *a priori* knowledge is exactly the problem concerning its normative or justificatory basis: how can pure reason justify its claims to object knowledge in metaphysics if not by appeal either to experience or to the principle of general logic? Hence, the characterization of the critical task of reason as addressing the problem of the possibility of synthetic, *a priori* knowledge is but a specification of the previous characterization according to which critique supplies 'the want of a recognized standard', (or, 'the touchstone of the worth or worthlessness of all cognitions *a priori*').[19]

Kant presents the critique of pure reason *both* as a sort of tribunal or court before which claims are brought to be tried—that is, assessed or examined with respect to their validity—*and* as a sort of self-examination of pure reason through which the terms or criteria of pure reason's judgment would be established or instituted for the first time. This implies a significant mix of metaphors, or anyway a tension, in Kant's characterizations of the task of criticism, which is remarked by post-Kantian philosophers, but never addressed by Kant himself. The following passage from First *Critique's* Doctrine of Method exemplifies the tension between the two sorts of characterization.

> One can regard the critique of pure reason as the true court of justice for all controversies of pure reason; for the critique is not involved in these disputes, which pertain immediately to objects, but is rather set the task of determining and judging what is lawful in reason in general in accordance with the principles of its primary institution. Without this, reason is as it were in a state of nature, and it cannot make its assertions and claims valid or secure them except through *war*. The critique, on the contrary, which derives all decisions from the ground-rules of its own constitution, whose authority no one can doubt, grants us the peace of a state of law, in which we should not conduct our controversy except by *due process*. (A751/B779)

On the one hand, this passage, in accord with the others discussed above, represents the task of critique exactly as effecting the transition from metaphysics' condition as a battlefield of endless controversies (analogized here to a political state of nature, in which there is no recognized authority), to a condition in which claims can be assessed according to laws the authority of which is publicly recognized (that is, to the establishment of metaphysics *as a science*), exactly through establishing for the first time the publicly recognized first principles on which the authority of subsequent judgment depends. On

---

[19] KrV, A12/B26. However, the problem of the possibility of synthetic, *a priori* knowledge is broader than the problem of the possibility of metaphysics, since mathematics and natural science—which, unlike metaphysics, already exist as sciences—also consist of this sort of knowledge, according to Kant.

the other hand, Kant seems to present critique here as itself an established tribunal, in which the already-established norms or principles of pure reason 'whose authority no one can doubt' are merely to be applied, not established for the first time.[20]

Though there is an apparent tension between them, neither of these tasks of Kantian critique can be immediately dispensed with, neither the task of evaluation or examination, nor the task of foundation. The major problem for Hegel in the Introduction to his *Phenomenology of Spirit*, in determining the method of that work, is the problem of how both of these tasks can simultaneously be performed. As Hegel writes in setting up the problem, 'an examination consists in applying an accepted standard' (Hegel, PhG, 75/¶81). But the situation that calls for critical inquiry is exactly one in which we find ourselves lacking recognized standards or criteria. The critical inquiry, the self-examination of reason, is envisioned to meet this need. How can reason criticize when its object is itself and its aim to determine its own justified standards of examination? This is the problem of the possibility of the critical inquiry itself, which Kant, owing presumably to his focus on the problem of the possibility *of metaphysics*, notoriously overlooks.[21] I postpone to the last chapter an account of how Hegel deals with this problem. My aim in this chapter is to show how the unremarked combination of these two tasks in the project of Kantian critique leads to Hegel's suspicion that Kant's project of critique, the very stance of its inquiry, already is subjectivism.

2.2 HEGEL'S SUSPICION: INITIAL FORMULATION

On the one hand, the critique of pure reason, per the generic concept of critique, is a tribunal before which the claims of pure reason in metaphysics

---

[20] See also the passage in the Preface to the first edition, Kant's note to which contains the passage I quote as an epigraph to this chapter (Axi-Axii). It exemplifies the same tension.

[21] Hegel was hardly the innovator of the meta-critical gesture, the gesture of turning the critical gaze, directed by Kant against the possibility of metaphysics, back against the critical inquiry itself. So-called 'meta-critique' is one of the dominant themes of post-Kantian philosophy, a theme opened with the very first responses to Kant's critical project. In his book *The Fate of Reason: German Philosophy from Kant to Fichte*, Frederick Beiser discusses various of the early meta-critical responses to Kant's project, beginning with Hamann's early review of Kant's First *Critique*, (entitled *Metakritik über den Purismus der reinen Vernunft*), through Platner, Schulze, and Maimon. Meta-critique is not a monolithic movement. I will be restricted in my discussion in this work to *Hegel's* response to Kant's critique. In particular, I attempt to draw out Hegel's meta-critical objection that Kantian critique implicitly presupposes subjectivism, in order to set up discussion of Hegel's development of his methodology in the *Phenomenology* as a response to Kantian criticism.

are tried (assessed, examined) with respect to their validity (apparently by comparison with established standards or criteria of pure reason's judgment). On the other hand, the critical enterprise is a response to a sort of crisis regarding the content and authority of the fundamental standards or norms of pure reason itself; critique is to institute the recognized standards for the first time. But, putting these two characterizations together, we are bound to wonder about the content and, in particular, *the authority* of the norms or standards of pure reason employed in critical assessment itself. Whence do they derive? How are they validated? Add to this that the critique of pure reason is, in contrast to its object-directed inquiry in metaphysics proper, pure reason's *self*-examination, the reflection of reason back on itself. It would seem, then, that the critical enterprise itself already imposes a necessary condition on the possibility of metaphysics (as a science): namely, pure reason's antecedent self-examination in critique. It would seem that the new epistemological demand expressed in Kant's critical enterprise itself imposes a prior condition on metaphysical knowledge; and, given the preliminary notion of metaphysics as *a priori* knowledge *of the unconditioned*, there appears to be a tension on the face of it between the epistemological demand and the possibility of metaphysics.

Moreover, the epistemological demand embodied in the critical enterprise would seem itself to imply a sort of highest principle or norm for the judgment of pure reason, though one that is merely formal. As I will clarify below, the demand embodied in the call for a critique of pure reason that nothing—no principle or claim of pure reason—count for us as valid except insofar as it is validated through critical reflection (the reflection of reason on itself) is already a criterion or principle of pure reason. The prior self-reflection of pure reason itself serves us, then, as the ultimately authoritative standard (that is, as the 'touchstone') for the validity of all claims of pure reason, though this criterion is not itself validated through prior critique, but rather simply expressed in the demand for prior critique. The authority of such a principle implies Kantian subjectivism.

Otherwise put, Hegel's suspicion is that Kant's so-called 'Copernican revolution' in epistemology is enacted, not in response to the critical demand for justification—as a way to meet that demand, as it were—but *in the critical demand itself*, thus begging the challenge of its own justification. Kant explicitly presents the critical inquiry as entailing a complete reorientation in our perspective on knowledge. Criticism presents 'a transformation in our way of thinking [*eine Umänderung der Denkart*]' (Bxvi; Bxxii, *n.*). Kant famously compares this transformation to the Copernican revolution in astronomy, but

Kant's presentation also suggests revolution in the political sense of under-mining one assumed source of authority in order to establish another in its place. The political metaphor accords well with the passages that characterize the work of critique as establishing the legitimate, authoritative norms or principles of reason's judgment for the first time. The outcome of the critical inquiry, given these characterizations of its task, should be the general recog-nition of a legitimate authority for reason's judgment. According to Kant's description in a famous passage, the revolution enacted in the critical inquiry is the following: whereas it was assumed hitherto that our representations must conform to the objects in knowing (hence the independently existing objects were regarded as legislative for our activity of knowledge), through the revolution, it is supposed on the contrary that the objects must conform themselves to our knowledge (Bxv–xvi).

The Copernican revolution in epistemology is manifested primarily in two distinct ways and places within the body of the *Critique*.[22] In the Tran-scendental Aesthetic, Kant argues that all intuition that arises in us through the affection by objects of our faculty of sensibility must conform to the 'subjective' forms of intuition, space and time, which lie ready in the mind. This is the first respect in which the object must conform to our knowing, rather than our knowing to objects. Second, and much more importantly for our purposes, Kant argues in the Transcendental Analytic that the *laws for* appearances are legislated by the human understanding. That is, just as the forms according to which sensible intuition must be arranged lie ready in the subjective constitution of human sensibility, the most fundamental rules according to which we (or the understanding) *must combine* given sensible representations in order to generate knowledge of objects have their source in the understanding, not in any external source. The authority of these rules (which just are the pure concepts of the understanding) consists in the fact that, independently of their application, *we* could have no experience at all.[23]

As discussed in the previous chapter, that the constraint on epistemic judg-ment which the object makes necessary (simply *qua object*) is to be understood

---

[22] See KrV, Bxvi–xviii; also B164.

[23] Though each of these claims—that of the Aesthetic and that of the Analytic—enacts the Copernican revolution in its own way, the claim in the Analytic is more fundamentally related to critical inquiry, since it directly concerns a revolution in the legislating authority for our activity of judgment. That the position of the Transcendental Aesthetic and the basic arguments for it are already present in Kant's 1770 Inaugural Dissertation, prior to Kant's conceiving the critical project, supports the point that the Copernican revolution as enacted in the Transcendental Analytic is more fundamentally critical.

ultimately as self-legislated, as a constraint the knowing subject makes upon itself, implies immediately Kantian subjectivism; it implies the view according to which we can know objects only as they are *for us*, whereas the things as they are in themselves and the unconditioned transcend the limits of our knowledge. But the critique of pure reason, according to the view of it taken here, already implies that the self-reflecting rational subject is the ultimate validator or legislator of the authority of the claims of reason; thus critique already institutes, methodologically, in the very stance of the epistemological investigation, 'conformity to the subject' as the normative ground of our knowledge, and with it, of course, Kantian subjectivism. Hence, the promise of the critique of pure reason to determine the fundamental authoritative norms of pure reason in an unprejudicial 'free and open examination' is disappointed.

2.3 A SHALLOW SUSPICION?

To someone who appreciates Kant's critical project—who has felt the excitement of a powerful new beginning in epistemology aroused by appreciation of it—Hegel's suspicion is bound to seem relatively shallow, even if not totally unmotivated. Hegel himself subscribes to the dictum that criticism of a philosophical system has little weight unless it engages seriously with that in the system that seems compelling to its proponents. It may seem that Hegel's objection against Kant's project of critique, as construed above, does not engage very seriously or directly with what strikes students of Kant's epistemology as its substantial core. And so Hegel's apparently dismissive criticism of Kant's critical project is dismissed in turn by Kantians. Consequently, the Hegel–Kant engagement often strikes us, I think, as philosophically sterile.

However, contrary to initial appearances, Hegel's suspicion engages with what I'm vaguely calling the substantial core of Kant's critical epistemology, though on a *particular interpretation* of that core, an interpretation that differs from prominent current interpretations. Hence, in order to appreciate Hegel's suspicion, we need to take up the perspective from which Hegel's suspicion is summarily dismissed and point out how one misses from this perspective the force of Hegel's reading.

Hegel's suspicion, as articulated above, depends on seeing Kant's epistemological project both as a prior and founding epistemological inquiry relative to the science of metaphysics and as, in a sense, a subjective or self-reflective inquiry. It can seem, then, that Hegel's suspicion depends on inscribing Kant's critical project into the Cartesian foundationalist paradigm in epistemology. But is the interpretation of Kant's critical *Ansatz* according to which it is an exercise in foundational self-knowledge remotely charitable? After all, Kant is often credited with being the first to criticize effectively the broadly Cartesian epistemological presupposition according to which self-knowledge enjoys a justificatory privilege or priority in relation to other knowledge. Kant argues explicitly in his Refutation of Idealism that knowledge of one's own mind is not itself possible independently of knowledge of external objects (B274–9). According to Peter Strawson, one of the primary contributions of Kant's epistemology is to show the bankruptcy of *any* epistemological procedure that would have us 'work outwards' from some position of self-certainty, in which we allegedly possess certain, indubitable knowledge of our own minds, to knowledge of what is external or objective.[24] Would Hegel have us believe that Kant's critical procedure, despite this teaching within the body of the *Critique*, is itself to be understood as the foundational self-knowledge of reason relative to the object knowledge contained in metaphysics itself? Even if Kant's programmatic remarks occasionally suggest such a picture, why should we not follow Strawson's lead in rejecting what seems retrograde in Kant's project (including the subjectivism) and concentrate on that considerable portion of Kant's project that significantly advances the discipline of epistemology?

Relatedly, Kant is frequently made out to be an anti-foundationalist generally in epistemology.[25] According to some proponents of Kant's epistemology,

[24] Strawson, *The Bounds of Sense*, 19. See the whole of part one for a statement of a powerful and influential interpretation of the contribution of Kant's epistemology, of what are its 'very novel and great gains in epistemology' (29). To one who wholly accepts Strawson's interpretation of where the action is in Kant's epistemology, so to speak, Hegel's suspicion will seem lame. Though I do not find credible the outright rejection of Srawson's interpretation—how could an interpretation that is so evidently powerful philosophically be simply false?—I do believe that it is one-sided in various respects.

[25] Onora O'Neill discusses Kant's methodology of critique, focusing, as I do here, on the political and revolutionary terms in which he presents it, in her *Constructions of Reason: Explorations of Kant's Practical Philosophy*. However, contrary to my assertions here, O'Neill presents Kant's philosophical enterprise as being radically un-Cartesian, in the sense that it is neither first-personal nor foundational. (See especially pp. 4–9.) I maintain that there is a significant *respect* in which Kant's project is both foundational and self-reflective, though this respect is distinctive to Kant's project and not generically Cartesian. Karl Ameriks is another important contemporary interpreter of Kant's thought who construes it as contrary to the foundationalist impulse. (See in particular his recent *Kant and the Fate of Autonomy: Problems in the Appropriation of the Critical Philosophy*, part I.) As Ameriks makes clear, whether or to what extent Kant's epistemology is foundationalist bears on an old dispute about how to understand Kant's argument strategy in the transcendental deduction of the categories. What is the starting point of the argument, and what does it aim to establish? On one common reading, Kant's starting point is some sort of self-consciousness that, *as such*, is indisputable, and as such serves as a sort of foundation for the following argument. The argument

among the main contributions of Kant's 'revolution in method' is its showing us a way to do epistemology that is not foundationalist in orientation.
Transcendental philosophy consists in demonstrating that knowledge that is
presupposed as given (usually empirical knowledge) has *a priori* conditions.
Kantian epistemology, on this interpretation, is the articulation of the *a
priori,* conceptual framework that alone makes possible empirical knowledge
or natural science. This approach to epistemology is touted as something
new relative to the foundationalist tradition in modern epistemology, which
has both empiricist and rationalist strains. Kant's demonstration that sense
experience has *a priori* conditions frustrates the empiricist attempt to build
the edifice of knowledge upon the foundation of immediate sense experience.
Kant's demonstration that *a priori* concepts are validated *only as* necessary
conditions of the possibility of experience frustrates the rationalist attempt
to found the system of knowledge on supposedly self-evident principles or
intuitions of pure reason, independently of relation to experience.

If one sees Kant's revolution in methodology in these terms, then Hegel's
characterizations of Kant's method, on which he bases his objection to it, seem
to misrepresent Kant's project rather grossly. Hegel repeatedly characterizes
Kant's critical project as 'wanting to know before knowing, or of not wanting
to enter the water before one has learned to swim'.[26] Such a characterization,
however exactly it is to be interpreted, attributes to Kant's critical enterprise
a foundationalist ambition. Thus, commentators who read Kant's revolution
in epistemology along the lines sketched in the previous paragraph dismiss
Hegel's objections.[27] If Kant's transcendental procedure is to specify the
necessary (*a priori*) conditions of the possibility of knowledge—knowledge
that is either 'apparently indisputable' or simply 'assumed'—then Kant's
account in the critical enterprise is not, as Hegel sees it, knowing *before* one

---

proceeds to show the categories as necessary conditions of this indisputable self-consciousness.
(See for a prominent example, Dieter Henrich's 'The Proof Structure of Kant's Transcendental
Deduction', and 'Identity and Objectivity: An Inquiry into Kant's Transcendental Deduction'.) On
another reading, the whole argument takes for granted as given 'common knowledge' or 'experience',
understood as ordinary empirical knowledge, and consists in showing that the categories are the
necessary conditions of the possibility of that presupposed knowledge. (Ameriks argues the case for
the second reading. Besides the book cited above, see his article, 'Kant's Transcendental Deduction
as a Regressive Argument'.) The former reading is of course more easily inscribed into a Cartesian
foundationalist paradigm than the latter.

[26] Hegel, EL, §41Z1; *ibid.*, §10. See also Hegel, VGP, *Werke*, vol. 20, 333–4; Haldane and
Simpson, vol. 3, 428–9.

[27] See in particular the treatment of Hegel's criticism of Kant's project in Ameriks's 'Hegel's
Critique of Kant's Theoretical Philosophy' and Guyer's, 'Thought and Being: Hegel's Critique of
Kant's Theoretical Philosophy'.

knows, as if one had to know the *a priori* conditions first, as a condition of being able to claim possession of the knowledge.[28] In short, Hegel mistakes Kant's epistemological inquiry, which is an investigation into the *a priori* conditions of the possibility of knowledge, for a prior inquiry that aims to found or establish knowledge for the first time.

Such objections to Hegel's suspicion are based in part on a misunderstanding. While it is importantly true that Kant does not think that his inquiry is prior to, or founding with respect to, knowledge in general or empirical knowledge, he explicitly does conceive of the critical inquiry as founding with respect to *pure reason's* knowledge *in the science of metaphysics*. Granted that Kant does not hold that knowing how knowledge in general is possible is itself a prior condition of the possibility of knowledge, he does explicitly claim that knowing how metaphysics is possible (in the critique of pure reason) is a prior condition of the possibility of metaphysics as a science.[29] In *this* sense, Kant's critique represents the attempt to know (whether and how reason's object knowledge is possible) before knowing (the objects of metaphysics: God, the soul, the world as a whole). Further, though it is importantly true that Kant does not conceive the empirical subject's self-knowledge as prior or privileged with respect to its (empirical) knowledge of objects, nevertheless Kant conceives of critique as pure reason's foundational self-knowledge in relation to its science, the science of metaphysics.[30] Indeed, Kant in at least one place suggests that reason *cannot fail* to solve the problem addressed in the critical inquiry (namely, how and whether metaphysics as a science is possible), in contrast to its problems in metaphysics itself (having to do with its object, the unconditioned), exactly because reason is concerned with knowing *itself* in the critical inquiry. (See KrV, B22–3.)

---

[28] Ameriks deploys the claim that Kant's argument proceeds from knowledge that is simply 'assumed' or from 'common-sense presuppositions' against Hegel's understanding (*ibid.*). Guyer claims that Kant's argument begins from 'apparently indisputable' knowledge claims and argues to the 'cognitive capacities necessary to explain such claims', and he deploys this claim against Hegel's objection to Kant's method (*ibid.*, 186).

[29] If another passage is needed, in addition to those cited above, the following passage is nicely explicit: 'for [] critique must exist as a science ... before we can think of letting metaphysics appear on the scene, or even have the most distant hope of doing so' (Prol, 4: 261).

[30] See the quotations cited in 2.1. Kant does not clearly specify what he means by *reason's* self-knowledge, since he says little to characterize it beyond what he says to characterize the critique of reason itself, but it is clear that reason's self-knowledge is to be distinguished both from empirical self-knowledge, as knowledge of the contents of one's own, individual mind, and from rational self-knowledge, in the sense of knowledge of the soul as substance in the science of rational psychology. See Houston Smit, 'The Role of Reflection in Kant's *Critique of Pure Reason*', for a reading of Kant's account of transcendental reflection as an account of reason's self-knowledge in critique.

However, granted that Hegel (or, a defender of Hegel's position) can cite chapter and verse in defense of the reading of Kant's critical project that gives rise to the suspicion, such a defense is apt to leave us cold. Hegel's suspicion still seems to be based merely on Kant's programmatic remarks on method scattered in the margins of his project, to the neglect of the significant, detailed arguments on specific epistemological questions within the body of the critical system itself. The most that Hegel's case can show is a tension in Kant's writing—perhaps interesting, perhaps not so much—between the programmatic remarks on method and the teaching contained in the most important substantial arguments. But surely, in orienting ourselves to that in Kant's epistemology that represents a significant contribution and advance relative to the tradition, we ought to adhere, not to Kant's relatively unspecific, scattered, marginal remarks on method, but to the detailed, contentful arguments on specific issues.

Because of the force of this response to Hegel's suspicion, I need to motivate the suspicion further. Contrary to initial appearances, perhaps, Hegel's suspicion is not predicated on a lazy reading of Kant's critical project, according to which it essentially belongs to the old, familiar Cartesian paradigm. The Hegelian interpretation sees Kant's critical project as importantly innovative relative to the tradition, but its take on its innovation and contribution differs significantly from that indicated above. Because the interpretive and philosophical issues are many and complex, I cannot aim to do more here in support of Hegel's suspicion than sketch a sort of landscape that indicates how Kant's arguments within the body of his critical system as a whole relate, on Hegel's view of it, to the characterization of the critical inquiry discussed in 2.1. The picture should show exactly how what is innovative in Kant's project (on *this* view of it) is bound up with the presupposition of subjectivism.

2.4 DEEPENING THE SUSPICION: CRITICISM, AUTONOMY, AND SUBJECTIVISM

Hegel follows Fichte in taking the new, revolutionary element in Kant's critical philosophy to reside primarily in Kant's articulation of the structure of the subject or of the 'I'. Fichte models his own philosophical system, the *Wissenschaftslehre*, on Kant's critical system, as he interprets it. On his interpretation Kant proceeds by displaying as a necessary presupposition of all experience the structure of the self-relating activity of the (knowing and acting) subject and by deriving the fundamental constraints on (or norms for) the subject's judgment and action as *internal requirements* of the subject's self-relating activity. Kant's critical philosophy is above all a 'system of free-dom', according to Fichte's reading, since it consists in showing constraints that seem unreflectively to have their source outside of us to be self-legislated. Hegel's reading of Kant's critical system is deeply influenced by Fichte's. Indeed, when Hegel arrives in the development of his own *Science of Logic* at its highest concept, what he calls simply '*the* concept', (*der Begriff*, translated by Miller as 'the Notion'), he remarks that its basic structure is none other than that of Kant's self-relating subject, thus implying that his system as well (like Fichte's) is to a significant extent an adaptation of Kant's (on this reading of it).[31] Hegel's objection against Kant's philosophical criticism (namely, that it is in its very nature subjectivism) is closely bound up with what he takes to be revolutionary about Kant's system (namely, its discovery and articulation of the structure of the autonomous subject). In showing this relation here, I deepen Hegel's suspicion against Kant's criticism while dispelling the notion that his reading thoughtlessly conflates Kant's project with Cartesian found-ationalism. I undertake to specify the suspicion further, according to which Kant's critical project implicitly presupposes subjectivism in its very proced-ure, both by showing how the epistemological demand of critique expresses already a principle or criterion of reason, and by showing how that criterion consists in conformity to the formal self-relating activity of the subject.

In the Introduction to the *Phenomenology*, Hegel distinguishes the skeptical attitude of his protagonist in that text from another skeptical attitude, which he describes as follows: 'the *resolve* in Science not to give oneself over to the thoughts of others upon mere authority, but to examine everything for oneself and follow only one's own conviction, or better still, to produce everything oneself, and accept only one's own deed as what is true' (PhG, 72/¶78). Such a skeptical attitude might be said to presuppose, despite its overt suspicion and skepticism, the unexamined formal norm of 'conformity to the inquiring subject', in the sense that, insofar as the skeptical inquirer's own prejudices and convictions are not themselves examined or criticized, the

---

[31] Hegel writes in his *Science of Logic*: 'The Notion [*Der Begriff*], when it has developed into a *concrete existence* that is itself free, is none other than the *I* or pure self-consciousness ... ' (WL, Werke, vol. 6, 253/583). Hegel notes in this context that it is to Kant that we owe the original articulation of the structure of the 'I': 'It is one of the profoundest and truest insights to be found in the *Critique of Pure Reason* that the *unity* which constitutes the nature of the *Notion* is recognized as the *original synthetic* unity of *apperception*, as the unity of the *I think*, or of self-consciousness' (WL, Werke, vol. 6, 254/584).

criteria employed in the examination will inevitably (if only implicitly) be the inquiring subject's prejudices and convictions; and thus the skeptical resolve predetermines that only that will be acknowledged as valid which conforms to the unexamined, implicit prejudices and convictions of the inquiring subject.

Though for Hegel such a skeptical resolve shares with Kant's critical procedure the flaw that it precludes the inquirer's transformational education (*Bildung*) through the skeptical inquiry itself, the skeptical attitude exemplified in Kant's criticism pushes such a resolve to its limit: *nothing* counts as authoritative for us except insofar as it can be validated in critical reflection. Hence, whatever prejudices or convictions I might bring with me to the epistemological enterprise must not be allowed to have authority for me independently of validation in critical inquiry. The effect of pressing this demand is to empty all content from the standpoint of critical reflection, since any determinate content to be employed in criticism must itself be validated through critical reflection in order to have legitimate authority for the criticizing subject. Though it seems that this procedure deprives criticism of any standards at all to be employed in the testing of critical reflection, in fact it determines a formal criterion, namely conformity of content (necessarily given from elsewhere) to the self-relating activity of the subject, an activity which is necessarily empty of content on its own. Thus, Hegel frequently accompanies his objection that Kant's critical project is 'subjectivism' with the corresponding claim that it is 'formalism': the necessary self-relating activity of the subject is a mere form for content which must be given externally.[32]

In Kant's explication of the highest principle of *practical reason*, the categorical imperative, this normative structure is nearly explicit. In order to deepen Hegel's suspicion and in order to make the sense more clear of the claim that Kant's criticism presupposes the criterion of conformity to the formal self-relating activity of the subject, I display this normative structure in Kant's discussion of practical reason. I then make the case that the normative structure displayed there is the same normative structure that we have displayed in the transcendental deduction of the categories, which isomorphism anchors the case for Hegel's suspicion that Kant's criticism presupposes subjectivism.[33]

---

[32] This implies in turn the third epithet in Hegel's triumvirate of terms of criticism, namely 'dualism': the ultimate source of content must be absolutely opposed to the self-relating subject and its norms. (See Hegel, GW, 314/78.)

[33] I remind that, in relating together Kant's critical method, his conception of theoretical agency, and his conception of practical agency in this way—that is, by virtue of sharing a single normative structure—Hegel reads Kant against—or, anyway, across—the grain of his own writing. Kant

This serves several purposes: it makes more determinate Hegel's claim that Kant's criticism presupposes the criterion of conformity to the formal self-relating activity of the subject; it relates Hegel's suspicion regarding Kant's epistemology directly to Kant's philosophically rich articulation of the rational subject as a structure of autonomy; and it shows how Hegel's suspicion regarding Kant's philosophical criticism is a response to Kant's critical system as a whole, not merely to his doctrine regarding our cognitive faculties.

Critique and the Supreme Principle of Practical Reason

Though Kant himself does not draw attention to the parallel, Kant's claim that rational agency (a rational being with a will) acts 'in accordance with the representation of laws' (GMS, 4: 412) implies what we could call a 'necessary moment of self-consciousness' with respect to all practical content of the will parallel to the necessary moment of self-consciousness with respect to all cognitive content announced at the beginning of the transcendental deduction of the categories. To regard a person's behavior as the result of the person's will or as an expression of the person's agency—as opposed to regarding it simply as a product of natural causes—is to regard it as following from the person's (the rational being's) 'representation of laws'. As one would be apt to put the point today, responsible agency is action on the basis of the recognition of (or, anyway, responsive to) reasons. In regarding behavior as expressing agency, we regard the agent as acting on considerations (desires, inclinations, values, etc.) that she implicitly counts as sufficient reasons for acting as she does. This moment of 'taking the consideration(s) as counting as sufficient reason', which in the normal course of things may be deeply implicit, is what I mean by the necessarily presupposed 'moment of self-consciousness'.

Kant's famous skepticism regarding a person's capacity to know (or be certain of, anyway) her own practical reasons, the deeper principles on which she in fact acts, poses an immediate obstacle to my claim of a parallel between the moment of apperception in cognitive agency and a moment of apperception in practical agency.[34] The reasons a particular person recognizes are reflected

---

himself does not present matters in this way. I remind also that this way of reading Kant is strongly influenced by Fichte's reading. Frederick Neuhouser interprets Fichte's project as continuous with Kant's critical project, by virtue of Fichte's articulation of a fundamental structure of subjectivity (originally articulated by Kant in his account of apperception), a structure that is manifest in different ways in both theoretical and practical reason. See Frederick Neuhouser, *Fichte's Theory of Subjectivity*.

[34] For Kant's statements of this skepticism, see GMS, 4: 407–8; Rel, 6: 51; MS, 6: 392.

in what Kant calls her 'maxims' or her 'subjective principles of action' (see GMS, 4: 421, n.). A person's maxims are ordered in a hierarchical structure, reflecting the dependence of immediate practical reasons on more general, remote reasons. So, for example, I may have a maxim of exercising daily, which is dependent on a more fundamental maxim to preserve my health and mental well-being, which is in turn perhaps overridden frequently by my maxim of performing to the best of my ability in my job. Kant holds that, at the most fundamental level, there are only two sources of our practical reasons: our concern for our happiness, deriving from our sensible nature, and our interest in morality, deriving from reason. But no person can be certain, at the end of the day, how it stands with respect to her most fundamental maxim: whether the pursuit of self-love and happiness is conditioned by moral considerations fundamentally, or whether it is the other way around.[35] This skepticism seems to pose an obstacle to taking Kant's claim that we act on the basis of our representation of laws to imply a necessary moment of self-consciousness, to imply, that is, that one at least *can* become conscious, with respect to one's actions, of one's reasons for so acting.

However, this obstacle to the suggested parallel is merely apparent. We need to make a distinction in the context of practical agency akin to Kant's distinction in the theoretical context between empirical and transcendental self-consciousness (B139). When a person is challenged to give her reasons for performing a certain action—which challenge is always an open possibility, given the presupposition that human action is as such on the basis of the recognition of (or, anyway, responsive to) reasons—there is an ambiguity in the challenge (though one that rarely confuses us in practice). Suppose the challenge is put as the question: Why did you do that? One might take the challenge to mean: what were the ultimate considerations on which you in fact acted as you did? So interpreted, the question asks after your *subjective principle*, that is, your maxim. It takes empirical self-knowledge in order to answer such a question. Kant's above-mentioned skepticism concerns this empirical self-knowledge. One never knows, at least with complete certainty, what one's ultimate motivations are, and so we take 'I don't know' as an honest answer to the question, interpreted in this way. But more often the question is meant as a demand for *justification*: not as an inquiry into what you, as a matter of fact, took to be your reasons, but as a demand for your *justifying*

---

[35] I am influenced in the interpretation of Kant's view that I present here by Christine Korsgaard's 'Morality as Freedom', which is ch. 6 of her *Creating the Kingdom of Ends*.

reasons. That is, the challenge asks after *objective* principles. To plead lack of self-knowledge in response to this demand is to miss the point. One cannot claim ignorance of the justifying reasons of one's actions any more than one can claim ignorance of the justifying reasons of one's assertions. The necessary conceit is that actions (and assertions or judgments), as expressions of agency (practical or epistemic, respectively), express the agent's *recognition* of reasons. While this does not imply that the agent enjoys self-knowledge regarding why in fact she has done or said what she has done or said, it does imply that the task of justification is her own task; hence the justifying reasons must in principle be *available* to the agent in reflection (though not necessarily immediately available). If the justifying reasons were in principle unavailable to the agent in reflection, then we could not see her as a locus of responsible agency at all.

Although we are normally relatively uncritical regarding the practical reasons we recognize, that human action is as such responsive to reasons implies that we may assume the critical stance with respect to those reasons. What I mean by 'assuming the critical stance' is backing up from whatever reasons one takes to be authoritative for oneself and demanding insight into their authority (that is, justification in reflection) as a condition of recognizing their authority with respect to one's choice and action. The prerogative to make such a demand inheres simply in one's status as a responsible agent, as a rational being with a will. The demand for justification expressed in Kant's project of philosophical critique is just this demand expressed in the epistemological context of questioning the possibility of the science of pure reason, metaphysics.

Accordingly we confront an equivalent meta-critical problem regarding the standards to be employed in critical examination: if we suspend recognition of the authority for us of practical reasons conditional on their validation in critical reflection, what standards or principles can we possibly employ in critical reflection itself? All putative practical reasons, whatever their content, can have authority for us only on the condition of being validated through a test of reflection. But then it seems that there is nothing for the test of reflection to be; there's nothing to mediate our recognition of the authority of any practical principle, since we must be able to step back from each in turn, whatever its content, and ask why we ought to, or whether we can, recognize its authority.

As noted above, this critical reflection is meant to determine the *objective* principle of reason, the supreme principle of practical reason (as opposed to our subjective principles or maxims, the principles we in fact adopt for ourselves as authoritative); we are engaged here in the task of justification, not of acquisition of empirical self-knowledge. Kant teaches us to see *in the critical demand itself* the supremely authoritative, though merely formal, objective principle of practical reason. Whereas the demand that no candidate practical reasons have authority for us except insofar as they submit to and pass a test of critical scrutiny seems to deprive us of any criterion to apply in the test, the demand itself constitutes a formal criterion. How does the critical demand for justification in reflection itself constitute the ultimate (though merely formal) criterion of rational justification? 'The matter of a practical principle', according to Kant, 'is the object of the will' (KpV, 5: 27), that is, some end or purpose the will sets for itself. Clearly we derive much of what we *in fact* recognize as practical reasons from the various ends we set for ourselves; we represent our actions as necessary as means to such ends. But no such material principles can have authority for us simply as such (unconditionally); we can always step back from any such principle, or from the end from which it is derived, and question its authority in reflection. Kant finds a formal, objective principle in this deprivation of all matter from the will: 'Now all that remains of a law if one separates from it everything material, that is, every object of the will (as its determining ground) is the mere form of giving universal law' (KpV, 5: 27; cf. also, GMS, 4: 401, 421). Nothing remains to serve as our criterion (reason's criterion) in reflection but the very demand expressed in criticism itself: namely, the demand that nothing count for us as a reason except insofar as it be *recognizable as a reason* in reflection. How can one tell whether a candidate practical reason is recognizable as a reason in reflection? Since no contentful (material) considerations can be brought to bear without begging the question of their authority for us in turn, all that remains is to ask whether the candidate practical considerations have the *form* of practical reasons, which is universality.[36] This is determined by asking whether it is possible to will it (whatever its content) as a universal law without contradiction. *The universalizability test is the principle of reason implicit in the critical stance itself.*[37]

The critical reflection to determine the source and content of the objective principle of pure practical reason (the authoritative principle for our choice and action) has determined the process of critical reflection itself, or the

---

[36] For the claim that reasons or laws have the form of universality, see GMS, 4: 431, 436.

[37] See Onora O'Neill, *Constructions of Reason: Explorations of Kant's Practical Philosophy*, Part I: Reason and Critique. There O'Neill argues, as I have done here, that the categorical imperative, as the principle of autonomy, is articulated as the implicit principle of reason's critique. Among the ways that the Hegelian interpretation I elaborate departs from O'Neill's is in finding Kant's principle of apperception, as a principle articulating the self-determining activity of the knowing subject, to be likewise an articulation of the implicit principle of reason's critical activity.

self-relating activity of the acting subject, as the objective principle. Kant's characterization of this supreme principle as a principle of the autonomy of the will (GMS, 4: 433–4 and KpV, 5: 33–4) makes explicit the identity of the autonomy of the subject and the objective principle. We began with what seemed a relatively weak demand, a demand that reflects our status as practical reasoners who act on the basis of our reasoning: namely, nothing (no practical consideration or law) can have authority for us except insofar as we can have insight into its authority for us in reflection. Though this demand does not show on its face the implication that we are the authors of the principles that govern our wills, the reasoning above draws out this implication. When we generalize the demand, we see that the demand is itself the highest principle of the will: the only principles that have legitimate authority for our wills are principles that we authorize. Kant writes: 'The will is not merely subject to the law but subject to it in such a way that it must be viewed as also giving the law to itself and just because of this as first subject to the law (of which it can regard itself as the author)' (GMS, 4: 431).

Critique and the Distinction between Theoretical and Practical Principles

Though Kant explicitly relates the principle of pure reason to the self-activity of the acting subject as such in characterizing it as a principle of autonomy, he does not explicitly identify the principle with the activity of the *critique* of pure reason. Obstacles stand in the way of this identification. Kant draws a relatively sharp boundary between the role of reason in the task of cognition and its role in practical tasks. Kant conceives of the task of critique in the context of cognition as the task of drawing boundaries and limiting. As Kant famously puts the work of the critique of pure reason in the Preface to the second edition: the critical task is 'to negate [*aufheben*] knowledge in order to make room for faith' (Bxxx). As we might also put it, the realm in which *knowledge* is possible for us must be limited in order to make room for the prerogatives of *practical* reason. Thus Kant conceives the activity of critique differently in relation to the activity and principles of human cognition than in relation to the activity and principles of human rational agency.

Kant marks this difference in his titles for the First and Second *Critiques*. Kant explains in the Preface to the Second:

Why this *Critique* is not entitled a *Critique of Pure Practical Reason* but simply a *Critique of Practical Reason* generally, although its parallelism with the speculative seems to require the first, is sufficiently explained in this treatise. It has merely to show *that there is pure practical reason*, and for this purpose it criticizes reason's entire *practical faculty*. If it succeeds in this it has no need to criticize the *pure faculty itself* in order to see whether reason is merely making a claim in which it presumptuously *oversteps* itself (as does happen with speculative reason). (KpV, 5: 3)

In the context of theoretical knowledge, we tend to apply the principle of pure reason beyond the domain in which it has legitimate, though merely regulative, employment (namely, within the domain of possible experience) in order to acquire knowledge of supersensible objects. The critique of pure reason in the First *Critique* curbs pure reason's pretensions and shows the proper boundaries of its employment. However, in the context of practice, it is not *pure* reason that pretends to a use for which it is not fit; rather, it is *empirically conditioned* practical reason (that is, reason in the service of making us happy) that pretends to be absolute. Consequently, the work of critique in the context of practice is to curb the pretensions of empirically conditioned practical reason—or, what comes to the same, to show that there *is pure* practical reason. Hence, critique is of the faculty of practical reason generally, not merely of *pure* practical reason.

The activity of critique is understood here narrowly as the activity of setting boundaries of proper application or of curbing pretensions, in opposition to the interpretation I develop in this chapter, according to which the critique of pure reason inquires fundamentally into the basic norms of pure reason. The narrow meaning Kant attaches here to 'critique' is even more explicit in a striking passage appearing slightly later in the text: 'For, pure reason, once it is shown to exist, needs no critique. It is pure reason that itself contains the standard for the critical examination of every use of it' (KpV, 5: 15). This passage is striking for its implication that the First *Critique* is mistitled—or, anyway, that the 'of' in its title must be read, contra the custom, as solely genitive in case, not accusative: pure reason criticizes but is not criticized. Such a passage, when compared with those passages quoted in section 2.2 of the present work, which argues for interpreting 'critique' more broadly, casts doubt on the assumption that Kant has a definite, unitary, and stable conception of the project of critique throughout his development of the critical project. It is well known that, when Kant first published the First *Critique*, he had no plan to write two others, and that his conception of the principle of practical reason as a principle of autonomy was not yet worked out. The natural hypothesis, then, is that, as Kant elaborates his conception of the critical system throughout the 1780s, the First *Critique* is demoted from its initial position as constituting the critical endeavor as such to become but one part of the tripartite critical system. In the Preface to the Third *Critique*, the *Critique of Judgment* (the work in which Kant is self-consciously completing and unifying the critical system), Kant presents the First *Critique* as the critique of the faculty of the *understanding* in particular, since it is only the understanding that provides constitutive principles of *a priori cognition*; he presents the Second *Critique* as the critique in particular of the faculty of reason, since reason delivers constitutive principles only for the will or the faculty of desire; he presents the Third *Critique* as the critique in particular of the faculty of judgment, since it delivers *a priori* principles for the determination of the faculty of the feeling of pleasure and displeasure. (See KU, 5: 167–8.)

Though others no doubt see it otherwise, I believe that the reading of Kant's criticism according to which it is a fundamental inquiry, in the sense that it responds to a perceived crisis regarding the content and authority of the most fundamental norms under which we stand, renders Kant's project more philosophically interesting than a reading according to which it does not aspire to establish the content and authority of the most fundamental norms, but takes for granted certain norms of reason as already established or as not requiring validation. Such a reading may seem to render Kant vulnerable to the most obvious metacritical challenge: namely, what criteria could Kant possibly employ in critique itself if he means to establish through critique the most fundamental norms or criteria of reason? However, Kant does not avoid this metacritical challenge by virtue of not making an issue of, or by not questioning, the authority or content of such norms. Indeed, on the interpretation developed here, an interesting and initially promising *reply* can be mounted to the metacritical challenge. According to this reply, the ultimate criterion of the norm-governed activity of judgment, both moral and cognitive, is not simply presupposed without criticism in the context of Kantian critique, but manifested or displayed in the development of the critical project. The criterion (of conformity to the self-relating activity of the judging subject) receives its defense in the fact that we cannot coherently question it; to question it is to call into question our capacity to stand in judgment at all, to be the source of norm-governed judgment. But the presupposition that we are the source of norm-governed judgment, that we are responsible (epistemic and practical) agents, is presupposed in the very stance of critical examination. So, on this reading, Kant's critical project demonstrates how understanding ourselves as the source of norm-governed judgment (of epistemic and practical agency) implicitly presupposes that the ultimate norm for our judgment must be our (merely formal) self-relating activity.[38]

Such a reading finds in Kant's writings a project that is not only not fully explicit, but also not compatible with some of Kant's explicit doctrines. It belongs to Kant's official doctrine that pure practical reason is capable of a legislation that pure reason in its theoretical use is not. Whereas pure reason in its practical use is autonomous, and hence capable of generating a constitutive principle, pure reason in its theoretical use is restricted to a merely regulative use. Kant's official doctrine is that pure reason, while capable of determining the will alone (independently of any contribution by sensibility), is incapable of determining knowledge of any object alone. Thus, according to Kant's explicit doctrine, the normative configuration of human practical agency does not mirror the normative configuration of human cognition. Though Kant's highest principle in the sphere of practice may remind us in some salient respects of the principle of apperception, the highest principle of knowledge, Kant is happy to insist on the emptiness of the latter, independently of the contribution of sensibility, whereas pure practical reason is supposed to attain to complete self-sufficiency.

Among the ties that bind Kant to his doctrine regarding the asymmetry between theoretical and practical reason, I think, is his investment in presenting a merely *formal* idealism on the theoretical side.[39] Kant's idealism is merely formal in the sense that it is the mere *forms* of knowledge (both intellectual and sensible) that have their source in the knowing subject (in us), whereas the content for knowledge (the matter) must necessarily be given to us through our being affected by external objects. To this extent, dualism and formalism (according to particular interpretations of these terms, of course), far from constituting in themselves objections to Kant's system, belong explicitly to his teaching on the theoretical side. But it is supposed to be different on the side of practical agency. If the normative configuration on the practical side mirrored that on the side of theoretical knowledge, then either Kant would have to retract the claim that principles of theoretical cognition depend for their sense

---

[38] I don't pause to address the question of how such a strategy of defense relates to Kant's arguments in support of the validity of the supreme principle of practical reason in the Third Section of his *Groundwork of the Metaphysics of Morals* and in Book One, Chapter One of his *Critique of Practical Reason* (especially 5: 42–50). (For thorough discussion of the complexities of each of Kant's practical 'deductions' and of the issue of their relation to each other, see Henry Allison, *Kant's Theory of Freedom* and Dieter Henrich, 'Die Deduktion des Sittengesetzes').

[39] See his Prol, §13, remarks II and III (4: 288–93), and appendix, 4: 374–5.

and meaning on the contribution of sensibility (thus rendering his idealism material, according to his conception) or he would have to acknowledge the dependence of human practical reason on sensible conditions, which would threaten the doctrine of the autonomy of the will. Thus Hegel's charges of subjectivism, formalism, and dualism, which he applies to Kant's critical system of philosophy in general, seem to have different force depending on whether they are directed at the standpoint of theoretical or of practical reason.

The (brief) Case for Isomorphism

Hegel is well aware that the normative configuration of pure reason in its practical use is *supposed to be* different than the normative configuration in its theoretical use—that the highest principle of the former is supposed to be independent and self-sufficient, whereas the highest principle of the latter depends on sensible conditions for sense and meaning. But, according to Hegel's reading of Kant's criticism, reason does not attain in its practical employment to the self-sufficiency that is explicitly renounced for reason in its theoretical employment. The emptiness and insufficiency of the principle of practical reason expresses itself in the further development of Kant's system. In fact, according to Hegel's reading, Kant's principle of practical reason can be nothing else than the same empty self-relating activity which is the highest principle of knowledge, what Hegel calls in the following quotation 'the law of the abstract understanding': 'Kant had nothing else for the determination of *obligation* (for the abstract question is, what is obligation for the free will) than the form of identity, of non-contradiction, which is the law of the abstract understanding.'[40] Contrary to Kant's claim for it, the law of pure practical reason, the moral law, does not succeed in filling the 'vacant place' provided for by the merely formal idealism on the side of theoretical critique (see Kant, KpV, 5: 48–9). Hegel writes: 'Nothing further is available for the law which practical thinking makes for itself, for the criterion of the determination of itself, then again this *abstract identity* of the understanding, that no contradiction occur in the determination—thereby *practical* reason does not transcend the formalism which is supposed to be the limit of *theoretical reason*' (Hegel, EL, §54).

In completion of the case for Hegel's suspicion, I undertake here to display the isomorphism Hegel indicates between the normative structure

---

[40] Hegel, VGP, *Werke*, vol. 20, 368; Haldane and Simpson, vol. 3, 460.

elaborated in Kant's account of the highest norm of human knowledge and the normative structure elaborated in his account of the highest norm of the human will. I analyse the accounts in four parallel steps.[41]

Step One: The moment of apperception and norm-governed agency
Kant does not present the understanding as autonomous, but he does present it as a faculty of spontaneity and as 'self-active' (B130). The understanding must be understood as the locus of the norm-governed activity of judgment. As interpreted in the previous chapter, the principle of apperception, which Kant identifies with the understanding itself, expresses what I called the 'epistemic agency' of the knowing subject, that the subject is herself the source of the norm-governed activity, in the sense of being responsible for the conformity of the activity to its norms. That the 'I think' must be able to accompany all my representations expresses my epistemic agency in the following sense. Insofar as the representations given to me through the senses are available for judgment, that is, for claims regarding how things are objectively, they cannot stand in relations in principle hidden from my self-conscious reflection. If the representations that potentially figure in my judgments were in principle unavailable to me in reflection, then judgment would be at best something that happened *in me*, not something for which I could be expected to take responsibility, say by giving my reasons. That the 'I think' must be able to accompany all my representations expresses the necessary presupposition that judgment is my act, something I do.

So interpreted, the initial claim of Kant's transcendental deduction of the categories, the so-called 'principle of apperception', corresponds to the initial claim in his account of the norms of *practical* reason, namely, the claim that we (rational beings with a will) *act for reasons*; that is, that we derive our actions from our representation of laws. If the principle of apperception expresses the faculty of discursive understanding (our epistemic agency), then the latter claim expresses the faculty of practical reasoning (our practical agency). Whatever is the content of my will (in the sense that it is a practical consideration on which I act) must have been 'taken up' by me into my will, in the sense that I must (implicitly) see it as a sufficient reason to act as I do. Acting on reasons presupposes an implicit self-consciousness in the sense that one implicitly takes responsibility for the justification of one's

---

[41] Though it would require another study altogether—or, at least, a significant expansion of this one—to come to terms with Hegel's critique of Kant's account of practical reason, this analysis should show how Hegel reads Kant's practical reason as formalist, dualist, and, above all, subjectivist.

actions; should one be brought up short with a demand for justification, one's reasons must in principle be available in reflection. This is a presupposition of norm-governed, responsible agency.

Step Two: The emptiness or formality of the moment of apperception
In both the epistemic and the practical contexts, whereas the necessary presupposition of a moment of self-consciousness seems a relatively weak consideration, it turns out to have a surprisingly strong implication. We arrive at the strong implication by way of noticing the necessary emptiness or formality of the apperception. In the epistemic case, the 'I think' that must be able to accompany all my (cognitive) representations must itself be empty of content of its own, lest it fail to express the necessary relating *to me* (as knowing subject) of all my cognitive content. If the 'I think' had determinate content of its own, if it were itself to be 'for me' in judgment, then a further self-consciousness would be presupposed, namely, the being for me of the 'I think'. Since that is absurd, the 'I think' must be empty of all content on its own account.

A similar consideration holds in the practical context. The presupposed moment of practical self-consciousness, my recognition of the practical content on which I act as a reason, is necessarily empty of determinate content, since it is presupposed by all practical content for me. Whatever contentful normative considerations mediate my recognition of some practical content as a sufficient practical reason, these normative considerations must *themselves* be recognized by me as reasons; thus, the recognition of content as a practical reason cannot itself be expressed in determinate normative content.

Step Three: A priori apperception as the highest principle
In both the epistemic and the practical spheres, Kant shows that the necessarily presupposed self-relating activity, which is itself empty of particular content on its own account, constitutes the highest principle in its sphere. Starting with the epistemic case, I will merely remind us briefly of the steps discussed at fuller length in the previous chapter. In §16 of the second edition, Kant infers from the fact that the 'I think' must be able to accompany all my representations and from the fact that the 'I think' cannot itself be represented through any content of its own that the necessary identity of 'I think' across cognitive content is possible only through an 'original combination' through which alone the cognitive content can be said to belong to one consciousness. That is, the necessary relation *to me*, as knowing subject, of the sensible content that can figure in judgment, 'comes about, not simply through my accompanying each

representation with consciousness, but only in so far as I *conjoin* one representation with another, and am conscious of the synthesis of them' (B133). Hence,
all sensible content given to me to think must submit to this original combination. Kant writes: 'Synthetic unity of the manifold of intuitions, as generated
a priori, is thus the ground of the identity of apperception itself, which pre-
cedes *a priori* all *my* determinate thought … The principle of apperception is
the highest principle in the whole sphere of human knowledge' (B134-5).

Kant then claims in §17 that the required submission of given sensible
content to this *a priori* synthesis—that is, conformity to this presupposed self-
relating activity—*constitutes* the relation of these representations to objects
(B137). That given sensible representations 'relate to' objects expresses in a
highly abstract way their function as cognitive content, that is, as content on
the basis of which we make judgments about and know the world. Kant's
dramatic claim in §17 is that this abstract epistemic norm, that sensible
representations 'relate to' objects—as opposed to being cognitively useless
subjective determinations of consciousness—*consists* in their necessary conformity to apperception, to the empty self-relating activity. More specifically,
representations have the *unity* and coherence with each other necessary in
order to be representations *of* objects through their necessary submission to
the original combination of apperception. As Kant puts it in the first-edition
version of the argument: 'the unity which the object makes necessary can be
nothing else than the formal unity of consciousness in the synthesis of the
manifold of representations' (A105).

The argument means to establish the objective validity of the categories by
showing judgment to be the act through which given sensible representations
are brought to the unity of consciousness. Kant claims in the so-called 'metaphysical deduction' that '[t]he same function which gives unity to the various
representations *in a judgment* also gives unity to the mere synthesis of various
representations *in an intuition*; and this unity, in its most general expression,
we entitle the pure concept of the understanding' (A79/B104-5). Thus, the
pure concepts of the understanding (the categories), derived from the logical
functions of judgment, necessarily apply to the manifold of intuition, the
given sensible representations, insofar as the latter are brought to the necessary
unity of apperception. Hegel complains against Kant's procedure here, again
following Fichte, that the categories ought not to be simply lifted from the
table of judgments (which amounts, according to Hegel, to borrowing them
empirically from the logic textbooks), but ought rather to be derived *a priori*
from the necessary unity of self-consciousness, of which they are the necessary

forms.[42] However, that controversy need not detain us. The main point for our purposes is that the connections expressed in the categories are shown to apply necessarily to all sensible contents of cognition, to all objects of empirical knowledge, on the ground that the unity they express is the necessarily presupposed unity of the thinking subject itself, whose *a priori* self-relating activity (what Kant calls 'the original combination') constitutes the relation of sensible representations to objects. Kant thus takes himself to have shown that the understanding legislates for nature, rather than the reverse (B159–60). The basic ground of this reversal is that, only on its basis can we accommodate epistemic agency as expressed in the principle of apperception.[43]

A parallel reversal occurs for similar reasons in Kant's derivation of the supreme principle of practical reason, the categorical imperative. *Prima facie*, the authority of the reasons that it is our task in practical deliberation to recognize and follow is independent of our deliberative activity itself. Though it is our task to recognize and conform our activity to practical reasons, it would seem (initially, unreflectively) that the authority of the reasons is independent of the process of our recognition of it. However, critical reflection on our reasons and the source of their authority shows this not to be so. When we critically question what is for us the ultimate criterion of what counts as a reason, we see that, whatever content might be taken to condition our recognition of given practical content as a reason must itself be recognized as a reason by us in reflection. This implies that all the ultimate criterion could be is the formal requirement of our practical agency itself: namely, that nothing have authority for our wills except insofar as we can recognize it as a reason in reflection. And again, 'recognizing as a reason' can only have the formal meaning of being able to will as a universal law without contradiction, since any determinate content would itself have to be recognized as a reason in order to have authority for our wills. Hence the highest norm of our norm-governed activity of practical reasoning turns out not to have an external source—indeed to be nothing but a formal expression of the activity itself.[44]

---

[42] Hegel, VGP, *Werke*, vol. 20, 345–6 (Haldane and Simpson, vol. 3, 439–41); EL, §42A.

[43] Of course, in this short summary, I omit the important role of pure intuition in Kant's argument. Such justification as I have here to offer for this omission is contained in Ch. 1. I attempt to show there that the basic normative reversal that occurs in Kant's transcendental deduction of the categories (the Copernican revolution as enacted there) does not depend on the account of the *a priori* principles of sensibility in the Transcendental Aesthetic. However, Kant's full argument in the transcendental deduction of the categories does depend on the results of the Transcendental Aesthetic.

[44] The evident difference between the way in which the principle of apperception and the way in which the categorical imperative function for us as norms in their respective domains is a

Step Four: Subjectivism as consequence

That the highest principle for theoretical and practical activity is the conformity of content to the (in itself empty) self-relating activity of the subject implies subjectivism in both spheres. The conclusion of subjectivism is explicit in the theoretical domain, since Kant's conclusion there is that we know things only as they appear to us, not as they are in themselves independently of our cognitive faculties. I argued in the previous chapter that this subjectivism follows from Kant's argument articulating the normative structure of the judging subject in his transcendental deduction, not just (as some readers of Kant claim) from his articulation of the sensible conditions of human knowledge in the Transcendental Aesthetic. The *a priori* laws of connection implied by the categories apply to appearances only as prescribed by the knowing subject or by the understanding; consequently they do not hold of things as they are in themselves. Nevertheless, these laws of connection apply *a priori* to all objects of knowledge for us, since it is only by reference to conformity to such laws that we can make a principled distinction between representations which are of objects and the mere play of representations in the subject. However, this account implies that the objects of our knowledge are merely objects *for us*, since they are partially constituted through relations and connections prescribed *by us* or by the knowing subject as such. This much is explicit in Kant's official doctrine (at least, if my case in the previous chapter is granted).

---

major impediment to being impressed by this parallel. Whereas, as practical agents we represent the categorical imperative to ourselves (however dimly) as a norm that it is our responsibility to conform our actions to (and so, when we fail, we are intelligibly held responsible for the failure), as epistemic agents we do not represent the unity of apperception to ourselves as a norm it is our responsibility to conform our judgments to. This difference is striking and important, and would need to be thoroughly discussed in a fuller treatment of the claimed isomorphism. However, I do not think this difference immediately defeats my case for Hegel's suspicion, since, on second look, the alleged difference is not as sharp as it initially appears. On the one side, if the supreme principle of practical reason has application to our wills by virtue of being constitutive of our free willing, then how it can be understood at the same time as a guiding norm for such a will, a will that chooses its own principles, is an apparent problem for Kant's view. This suggests that its role may be more intrinsic, hence less different from that of the principle of apperception, than initially appears. On the other side, it would seem that the necessary unity of apperception must itself be understood both as constitutive of our cognitive activity and at the same time as a norm for it; hence our activity, and our responsibility for our activity, must be understood to be at stake, however remotely, in our conformity of our ordinary judgments to their more local logical and material principles. Hence there are grounds for the claim that the unity of apperception is not so much something we can take for granted as always already accomplished, but is rather itself a task for us, which is immediately exemplified in the concrete epistemic tasks of conforming our judgments to more local norms. If so, then the role of the principle of apperception approaches within its sphere to that of the categorical imperative within the practical sphere.

In this chapter, I have attempted to elaborate Hegel's suspicion that this normative structure, and hence, this subjectivism, is implicit from the very beginning in Kant's critical procedure, a procedure which is supposed to be 'free and open', unprejudiced and undogmatic with respect to the highest norms of reason (Axi, *n.*).

Again, however, according to Kant's official doctrine, matters are different in the context of practical reason. Kant holds that the resources of our pure practical reason enable us to overcome the subjectivist limitations of the standpoint of theory (though only from the practical standpoint). However, Hegel suspects that Kantian practical reason cannot attain to this self-sufficiency because the subjectivism is implied in the very standpoint of Kant's critical project.[45] Kant's doctrine that 'morality leads inevitably to religion'—largely regretted by contemporary Kantians—may be read as in effect confessing that the principle of pure practical reason is not sufficient, that its determinate application also requires a supplement from an indeterminate beyond.[46] Hegel interprets Kant's claim that the object of pure practical reason, the highest good, merely *ought to be* as the expression in the context of practical philosophy of the subjectivism expressed in the context of theoretical knowledge with the claim that we can *know* things only as they are *for us*. The subjectivism of Kant's practical reason is further explicated in his doctrine of rational faith. Kant argues that the object determined through our pure practical reason, the highest good, the world in which virtue is rewarded by proportional happiness, depends on our *faith* in the existence of God as the author of nature and in the immortality of our souls. With respect to these moral ideas (God, the immortal soul), the resources for *knowledge* are lacking, and reason determines a relation of *faith*. In the Canon of Pure Reason in the First *Critique*, Kant distinguishes faith (*Glaube*) from knowledge on the basis of the strength of the grounds on which a proposition is held to be true: in the case of faith, the grounds are merely *subjectively*, not objectively, sufficient (A822/B850). Our relation to the object of pure practical reason as well as its content is determined only through *our* subjective limitations.

---

[45] Recall Hegel's comment from the *Encyclopaedia Logic*: 'Nothing further is available for the law which practical thinking makes for itself, for the criterion of the self-determining activity, then again this *abstract identity* of the understanding, that no contradiction occur in the determining activity—thereby *practical* reason does not transcend the formalism which is supposed to be the limit of *theoretical reason*' (EL, §54).

[46] Kant's claim that 'morality leads inevitably to religion' is in the Preface to his *Religion within the Boundaries of Mere Reason* (6: 8). See also KpV, 5: 129.

Hegel comments on Kant's account: 'But the *good* which is posited as the final end of the world [the moral world] is determined from the beginning only as *our* good, as the moral law of *our* practical reason.'[47]

The subjectivism of practical reason can be seen to be internal to the procedure by which we arrive at the highest practical principle. The principle at which we arrive expresses the demand that we act on no practical consideration except insofar as we can 'recognize it as a reason', that is, will it as a universal law. But this demand is evidently merely formal; it expresses a form for given content, just as the principle of apperception does. Hence the demand to be moral has no content for us except insofar as our sensible nature—in itself independent of our rational nature—supplies us with desires, inclinations, ends, plans, and projects. Only insofar as the given sensible content conforms to the form of practical reason (that is, is capable of being universal law) can it be regarded as good or as properly determining our will. Our practical task, as imperfectly rational beings, is determined as that of conforming our sensible natures to the rational form or of imposing rational form upon a recalcitrant and alien sensible nature. As such, the determination of our practical task depends on the very opposition that we are to overcome through the completion of the task. Our practical task consists of bringing the moral world to be, so far as this lies within our power. As briefly discussed above, the realization of the moral world in which virtue and happiness form a harmonious unity, though it is *our task* and the end of our striving, depends on our *belief* (faith) that sensible nature is *not* ultimately independent of reason. Hence we must believe in God as the author of nature. But, were we to actually realize the moral world, or were it to be realized by any means, the practical task of free (but finite) beings such as ourselves would lose its sense, since, again, the determination of that task depends on the difference between the way the world is and the way it ought to be. Hence, we must represent the final end of

---

[47] Hegel, EL, §60. Hegel quotes from Kant's *Critique of Judgment*, §88: 'And yet [the concept of a] final purpose [*Endzweck*] is merely a concept of our practical reason; we cannot infer it from any data of experience, so as to judge nature theoretically [in terms of it], nor can we apply it to the cognition of nature. There is no other possible use for this concept except for [our employment of] practical reason according to moral laws; and the final purpose of creation is [nothing other than] that constitution of the world which harmonizes with the only [thing that, by way of a final purpose,] we can indicate determinately according to laws: the final purpose that our pure practical reason has, namely, insofar as it is to be practical' (KU, 5: 455). Hegel focuses here in particular on the reference to *our* pure practical reason. According to the official doctrine, as *pure* practical reason, this reason is not supposed to be merely *ours* (that is, *pure* practical reason is not supposed to be restricted to a subjective standpoint). But the subjectivism that is internal to the procedure slips out.

our activities as necessarily receding from us, even as we advance towards it. Hegel comments: 'The absolute good remains [in Kant's critical system] something that merely ought to be, without objectivity; and so it ought to remain [*Das absolute Gut bleibt Sollen ohne Objektivität; und dabei soll es bleiben*].'[48]

I briefly summarize this long section. Hegel suspects that the attempt to determine the fundamental norms or criteria of reason in a *prior* reflection on our capacities (in particular, in a prior *self-reflection*, a reflection of reason on itself) implicitly predetermines the subjectivism at which the critical inquiry arrives. He suspects that the epistemological demand expressed in the critical project, namely that the norms be vindicated or legitimated in a prior self-reflective inquiry, already establishes conformity to the self-relating activity of the subject as the highest principle of our judgment. To those who appreciate Kant's critical philosophy, who see it as marking a new beginning in epistemology and in philosophy in general, Hegel's suspicion is apt to seem relatively facile and unresponsive to the most philosophically innovative aspects of Kant's thought. Defenders of Kant are apt to respond to this suspicion with several objections: the suspicion rests on a false interpretation of Kant's idealism as subjectivism; the suspicion rests on a false interpretation of Kant's criticism as continuous with Cartesian foundationalism and privileging of self-knowledge; the suspicion rests on a reading that fails to observe Kant's distinctions between understanding and reason, on the one hand, and between theoretical and practical reason on the other.

I have attempted to show in this section that Hegel's suspicion responds directly to the most innovative and fundamental arguments and claims of Kant's philosophy, on a plausible interpretation of those. According to Hegel's interpretation, Kant's subjectivism is intimately bound up with his revolutionary articulation of the structure of the (knowing and acting) subject, according to which the highest norms or principles governing the (epistemic and practical) activity of the subject (of the 'I') must be understood to be self-legislated, to be indeed formal expressions of that self-activity itself. Hegel writes: 'It is a great advance when the principle is established that freedom is the ultimate hinge on which the human being turns, the ultimate pinnacle which allows nothing further to be imposed upon it, so that humanity recognizes nothing, no authority, insofar as it contravenes its freedom.'[49] This is the great advance of Kant's critical philosophy, according to Hegel's reading. The supreme

---

[48] Hegel, VGP, vol. 20, 372; Haldane and Simpson, vol. 3, 464.
[49] Hegel, VGP, vol. 20, 388.

principle is freedom, the self-determination of the rational being. One can of course disagree with Hegel's interpretation of Kant on any number of points, but I think one cannot charitably accuse him of reading Kant lazily or superficially. To the contrary, Hegel's suspicion depends on a subterranean probing, as it were, that finds an *implicit* normative structure in the critical project itself. Self-determination of the subject is the principle implicit in the critical project from the beginning; this principle is made explicit in the course of the critical inquiry itself, first in the articulation of the highest principle of knowledge for us, the principle of apperception, and then in the articulation of the supreme principle of practical reason, the categorical imperative. I have attempted in this section to detail Hegel's suspicion that the normative structure implied in the critical method and articulated in the transcendental deduction and in the derivation of the supreme principle of practical reason presupposes subjectivism—or rather: this normative structure just *is* subjectivism. According to Hegel's interpretation, Kant's elaboration of the structure of subjectivity, according to which the norm-governed activity of the subject must be understood as a structure of autonomy, is expressed as subjectivism.

I will argue in Part II of this study that Hegel's defining struggle in his articulation of the method and project of the *Phenomenology* is to do justice to the articulation of the principle of the rational subject as self-determination or autonomy (which is owed above all to Kant's critical system) while freeing it of the implication in Kant's system of subjectivism. I will argue that this requires a transformation of the project of philosophical critique (by Hegel), a transformed process of criticism that requires in its turn the transformation of the critical inquirer (the criticizing subject) through the process of criticism. Hegel's philosophical criticism does justice to Kant's articulation of the structure of the subject as autonomy while overcoming subjectivism by articulating a self-transformational criticism.

2.5 DIRECTIONS OF RESPONSE

My defense of Hegel's reading and suspicion from attack on one flank has perhaps only exposed his case on another. The lack of detailed development of Hegel's interpretation of Kant's critical system opens his reading to the charges that I have been responding to in the previous section: superficiality and unresponsiveness to the innovations, relative to the tradition, of Kantian criticism. I have developed Hegel's interpretation in the direction indicated by his undeveloped points regarding Kant's critical project. Hegel's critical interpretation of Kant's criticism finds at its core a normative structure. According to this normative structure, the highest principle for our norm-governed activity expresses our self-relating activity itself; but the self-relating activity is itself a merely formal norm, which, as such, makes reference to a necessarily independent source of content. Kant's procedure solves the problem of discovering and articulating the highest principle by finding it in the subject's self-relating activity, but at the cost of subjectivism (that is, of relativization to the standpoint of the subject). However, the more convincing this reading of Kant is, perhaps the more philosophically attractive the Kantian position seems, and so the less Hegel's reading seems to support an objection (or even suspicion) against it.

After all, as indicated above, this Hegelian reading, even though it does not correspond to Kant's explicit presentation, seems to set up a *defense* of the subjectivist principle of critical reason. Just by virtue of expressing the stance of critical questioning as such, the principle seems immune from critical challenge. In attempting to challenge critically the principle of apperception, we would implicitly be presupposing it, since we would perforce be occupying the standpoint of norm-governed, self-conscious judgment in demanding justification of the principle. Similarly, if we were to challenge the authority of the categorical imperative for us, we would be presupposing the principle, insofar as the principle expresses the activity of practical deliberation and of acting on reasons. There is a sense in which the principle is 'presupposed in' the procedure of critique, but not in the sense that the critical philosopher arbitrarily or dogmatically adopts it as a principle, but in the sense that the principle expresses formally the activity of critical reason as such. If Hegel finds the norm to be presupposed in Kantian criticism in this sense (as I am claiming), then where is the objection in that finding?

We must distinguish two different critical responses to Kantian criticism, on this interpretation of it. According to the argument I advance in Part II, Hegel's own position at Jena develops from the first of these responses to the second. According to the first, Kantian critique is to be rejected *tout court*, on the ground that it is as such subjectivism. Hegel displays this attitude to Kantian criticism in his early Jena writings. The problem with Kantian criticism, according to this response, is not that it fails to meet a demand for epistemological justification that it itself expresses, but simply that its principle is subjectivism; the objection is to subjectivism as such. Hegel—in this respect like many contemporary philosophers—is strongly averse to the strain of subjectivism and dualism that he finds dominant in modern Western philosophy. The task in opposition to this strain is to articulate a procedure of epistemology that is innocent of modern subjectivism and dualism. I will argue in Part II that Hegel responds to Kant's project of philosophical critique in the early Jena writings by rejecting the epistemological demand that it exhibits and thereby the critical project itself. Hegel's early challenge to Kantian critique depends on showing it to be *optional*, to show in contrast to it a different epistemological procedure that does not presuppose subjectivism and dualism. Though Hegel does not have a fully worked-out alternative in his early Jena writings, the writings strongly suggest a dialectical procedure modeled on that of the ancient skeptics. The strong virtue of ancient skeptical procedure, over against modern epistemological procedure, including Kantian critique, is that it is innocent of modern subjectivism and dualism.[50]

In the previous chapter, I defended Hegel against the claim that he misreads Kantian idealism as subjectivism. In this chapter I have argued that Kant's subjectivism is implicit in his methodology, in the very epistemological project of critique. Despite contemporary aversion to subjectivism, some contemporary commentators would defend Kant's position against Hegel's objection by arguing that Kant's subjectivism is well motivated. Paul Guyer expresses this stance directly: 'Hegel treats Kant's subjectivism, his insistence on an impassable gulf between thought and object, as mere dogma, indeed almost as a failure of nerve ... Hegel does not engage in internal criticism in his response to Kant's theoretical philosophy ... His arguments are external; he argues that Kant's conclusions fall short of his own philosophical expectations.'[51]

I undertake in Part II to convince that this is not so. That it appears so is at least partly owing to the fact that Hegel's explicit treatments of Kant's philosophy are often relatively summary and external. However, in Part II I present the case that Hegel's *Phenomenology* is (among other things, of course) a sustained *internal* critique of Kant's philosophical criticism—internal in the sense that Hegel's project proceeds in response to the epistemological demand expressed in Kant's criticism, but critical in the sense that it shows that demand to require a more radical procedure than Kant's own, a procedure that culminates in the end, not in subjectivism, but in absolute idealism.

---

[50] Michael Forster argues that Hegel's epistemology is derived from the method of the ancient skeptics (see his *Hegel and Skepticism*). I argue in Ch. 3 below that Hegel's judgment of ancient skepticism as superior to modern turns on his conception of it as free of the subjectivism and dualism that plagues modern epistemology in general.

[51] Paul Guyer, 'Thought and Being: Hegel's Critique of Kant's Theoretical Philosophy', 171.

Thus, Hegel moves from the response in the early Jena writings of rejecting the epistemological demand expressed in Kantian criticism as inherently subjectivist to the response of accepting that demand with his *Phenomenology*; with the *Phenomenology*, Hegel still rejects Kant's procedure, but now on the grounds that Kant's criticism itself fails to meet the epistemological demand expressed in the critical turn. Hegel comes to see that the problem with Kantian critique is not that it is subjectivism *per se*, but that the subjectivism *is presupposed* (dogmatically) in the method; the problem is that its end position (subjectivism) is dogmatically presupposed in its procedure. Hegel's problem with Kantian critique comes to be, not that as criticism it is subjectivism, but rather that it is not critical enough.

I argue in Part II that Hegel's epistemological project in the *Phenomenology* becomes necessary for him when he recognizes, against his own earlier view, that the epistemological demand expressed in Kantian critique is a valid demand.[52] His recognition of it as valid turns on his recognition of it as expressing, or as backed by, the individual subject's autonomy (or, rather, as Hegel calls it, his *Selbständigkeit*). Hegel remains an opponent of Kantian subjectivism; he continues to maintain that the subjectivism is presupposed in Kant's method of inquiry. But now he can no longer dismiss the justificatory project of Kantian critique as issuing from an illegitimate demand for justification. The challenge now is to develop a new procedure of criticism that can fulfill the demand without presupposing subjectivism and dualism. The transformational procedure of Hegelian critique is designed (at least in part) in order to redeem the individual autonomy insisted upon by the modern subject without the cost of subjectivism and dualism with which it is associated in Kantian criticism.

2.6 CRITIQUE AND SUSPICION: UNMASKING THE CRITICAL PHILOSOPHY

Lastly I develop further the relation of critique and suspicion, adumbrated in the pair of quotations chosen as epigraphs to this chapter, and the conception of Hegel's reading of Kant's criticism as an *unmasking* of it. Hegel's philosophical development runs roughly contemporaneously with a crucial

---

[52] I do not want to contend that this is the only thread in the story of the development of Hegel's multifaceted project. However, I will be tracing this thread and emphasizing its significance in Part II of this study.

period in the development of philosophical hermeneutics. The manner in
which Hegel takes up and develops philosophical criticism in this period
is no doubt influenced by developments in hermeneutics. As we will see
more clearly as we proceed, philosophical critique is more explicitly and
immediately intertwined with the discipline of *interpreting* philosophical
systems (or products of spirit, in general) on Hegel's conception of it than on
Kant's. Fichte's reading of Kant's critical philosophy importantly points the
way in this respect as well. Fichte finds and manifests the 'spirit' of Kant's
philosophy submerged within—and in some respects contradicting—the
letter of Kant's texts.[53] The sort of reading that Fichte's interpretation of
Kant's system exemplifies is inherently fueled by suspicion, in the sense that
the interpreter suspects to find an implicit meaning (what the text *really*
means) hidden behind or underneath its manifest meaning.

Of course, Fichte's critical interpretation of Kant's system amounts to a
defense of it; the critical interpretation is meant to redeem it from various
objections, objections that depend (according to the interpretation) on a
dogmatic, spiritless interpretation, an interpretation blinded by the dead
letter. Thus, Hegel's critical interpretation differs from Fichte's in being
driven by a more fundamental suspicion. Like the full-fledged 'philosophers
of suspicion' who emerge out of this tradition (Marx, Nietzsche, and Freud),
Hegel, in his interpretation of Kant's philosophical critique, wants to know
the source of the difference between the manifest and the latent meaning.
Hegel suspects that the Kantian critical philosopher is engaged in a process of
intentional (though unconscious) masking of the truth (from himself, above
all).[54] Hence part of the work of the critical (unmasking) interpretation is
to manifest the motives for self-deception. In this section, I present Hegel's
interpretation of the hidden motives of Kantian philosophy, the motives
hidden by and from the Kantian philosopher himself.

Hegel emphasizes in his reading of Kant's critical gesture the element of
suspicion. As Hegel reads it, the critical gesture is *prima facie* motivated
by suspicion. Critical suspicion is directed at the alleged *a priori* science of
reason, metaphysics. Kant presents the current condition of pure reason in
its pursuit of knowledge of its objects, such that it stands in need of critique,
as *disoriented*, as lacking trustworthy points of reference by which to orient

---

[53] Fichte, '*Introductions to the* Wissenschaftslehre', I, 4, 231–2/63–4.

[54] Fichte accuses dogmatist philosophers, among whom are those who interpret Kant according
to the letter rather than the spirit of his philosophy, of masking themselves (their freedom and
selfhood) from themselves.

itself in its inquiry. He characterizes the current condition of metaphysics as 'a mere random groping, and, what is worst of all, a groping among mere concepts' (Bxv). Reason is driven by needs it does not fully understand to pursue satisfaction in the realm beyond possible experience, but, in that realm, it loses its bearings and falls into self-conflict. Kant prescribes the activity of critique, as the self-examination of reason, for this condition of disorientation. Reason is to orient itself through self-knowledge.

Kant's conception of reason as in its nature systematic, as constructing systematic unities, (which is nicely captured with the metaphor of orienteering), feeds the suspicion directed against it. In orienteering, if one makes an error in a significant point of reference, then one is apt to construct a mental map of the terrain that is not only wrong in this or that point, but *systematically wrong*. Other available points of reference are interpreted in terms of the mistaken one. Of course, in literal orienteering one's mental map is apt to be corrected by encountering an unexpected stream, valley, or mountain peak. But in metaphysics, beyond the realm of possible experience, there is no independent check on reason's systematizing.

In the *Critique of Pure Reason*, Kant defines 'dialectic' as a 'logic of illusion' (A293/B349), and it is hard to overemphasize the importance of this conception of dialectic for the direction of post-Kantian philosophy. The negative teaching of Kant's Transcendental Dialectic, namely, that we cannot have metaphysical knowledge of the supersensible objects of the soul, the world as a whole or God, follows as a fairly immediate consequence of the main claims of the Aesthetic and the Analytic; Kant's negative arguments do not of themselves give a new direction to philosophical inquiry. However, Kant's articulation of the *logic* of reason's illusions in transcendent metaphysics does recast philosophical work. It follows that the work of the critical philosopher is not only to show whether and how metaphysics is possible or to draw limits to our knowledge, but also to uncover and display through reason's self-knowledge the logic of reason's illusions. Since these illusions result in reason's self-conflict beyond the sphere of possible experience, if reason can in self-examination comprehend the sources of the illusion—and comprehend the sources of reason's true need expressed in its transgressions—reason can be brought through such self-knowledge into unity with itself; reason can be brought only in this way to true and stable satisfaction of its deepest needs, which express themselves in frustrated self-conflict in the history of metaphysics. The task now for reason becomes that of achieving self-unity out of a condition of self-conflict through a process of self-knowledge.

The perception that pure reason's illusion has a logic or is systematic further heightens suspicion. If reason forms a system of its illusion, driven on by its own needs, then where can one stand, what can one rely on, to criticize the illusion or the false claims that result from it? If one suspects not only error, but systematic error, then one is apt to suspect the terms of criticism themselves; one is apt to suspect that they are themselves expressions of pure reason's illusory needs (or of the illusory interpretation of real needs). And where is the end of it?[55] Critique would seem to require a standpoint outside the systematic illusion from which to recognize and criticize it as such. Hegel reads the significance of the gesture of reason's critique as stepping back to a position *before* and *outside* metaphysics itself in these terms.

Contemporary philosophers tend to look askance at (to be suspicious of) the attempt to achieve a critical standpoint genuinely 'outside' the system of claims or norms that is the object of criticism. Contemporary philosophers tend to dismiss foundationalist ambitions in epistemology, not only as impossible to fulfill, but as expressing a false need of reason. A favorite contemporary image of an alternative (non-foundationalist) procedure of critique derives from Otto Neurath: the image of rebuilding one's ship while on the open sea. The point of the image is to express that criticism of our science or knowledge occurs only *within* that ongoing concern, not from a standpoint outside of it. A fixed, self-standing standpoint of criticism, outside the ongoing enterprise to be criticized, is neither possible nor necessary: not possible because there are no transcendent, self-certifying principles; not necessary because, even granted this lack, everything is nevertheless in principle subject to criticism and revision, though not all at once, but piecemeal, holding in place the larger whole while the part is criticized.

The terms of Hegel's objection against the enterprise of Kantian critique resonate with Neurath's image. As already noted, Hegel repeatedly criticizes

---

[55] Though the Meditator's motivation of radical doubt in Descartes's First Meditation is similar to this intensified suspicion in the context of philosophical criticism, the latter also differs in significant respects from the former. The basic point of the Meditator is that, since the inferences we draw from false premises will be corrupted, error is apt to run through our system of beliefs if we're wrong about even some of our more or less fundamental beliefs. So we do best to scrap all our beliefs and start again from the beginning (just as a person worried about the rot in her basket full of apples would tip out the whole lot and examine each in turn before placing it back in the basket) (see Descartes, *The Philosophical Writings of Descartes*, II, 324). But there are at least the following two respects in which critical suspicion goes beyond the Meditator's motivation of radical doubt: (1) Kant's articulation of a 'logic of illusion'; and (2) Kant's anthropomorphizing discourse, according to which reason has 'interests' and 'needs' and seeks 'satisfaction' or 'peace', which raises the suspicion that reason may be motivated to resist its own realization.

Kant's criticism with the analogy from Scholasticus: criticizing our cognitive faculties prior to employing those faculties in cognition is like wanting to learn to swim before one enters the water. Hegel's simile for Kantian critique shares with Neurath's image the implicit denial of the possibility of an independent, self-certifying critical stance outside (or before) the system of claims that is to be criticized; criticism must take place within the cognitive enterprise itself, despite the perils of such a procedure.

We come again to the question of whether, or in what respect, Kant's project of criticism counts as foundationalist. Though many contemporary epistemologists would sympathize with the anti-foundationalist thrust of Hegel's simile, many would regard it as uncharitable to impute to Kantian criticism a foundationalist ambition.[56] Again, though, the question depends on what we mean by epistemological foundationalism. As noted above, while there are respects in which Kant's criticism is clearly not foundationalist, there are other respects in which it clearly is. While Kant does not attempt to ground the norms of reason in something outside of reason itself (in a transcendent being) or in self-evident or indubitable truths, Kant's inquiry means to establish the fundamental standards of pure reason's inquiry for the first time, and thereby found metaphysics as a science.

Though the need to get back before the beginning of the cognitive enterprise in order to properly found it tends to be felt today as a false need of reason, Kant's inquiry responds to such a need in one significant respect. The sort of criticism illustrated by Neurath's image of rebuilding a boat on the open sea fails to allow for *revolutionary* critique, and Kant's criticism has revolutionary ambitions. Neurathian criticism seems on its face to be conservative; the procedure of criticism analogized to rebuilding a boat on the open sea, plank by plank, seems to preclude the possibility of revealing reason to be suffering under a *systematic* illusion, standing in need, not merely of piecemeal reformation, but of basic normative revolution or transformation. Hegel interprets the epistemological challenge expressed in Kant's critical project (again, following

---

[56] O'Neill's interpretation of Kantian criticism in her *Constructions of Reason* is representative. She interprets Kantian criticism as essentially anti-foundationalist; indeed as offering us 'a way between the cliffs of a transcendent vindication of reason and the whirlpools of relativism' (42). She claims that Kantian criticism provides a model of *recursive*, in contrast to foundational, justification (ix, 21, 38). By recursive justification she means that claims of reason are justified to the extent that they meet their own criticism, as opposed to being justified by, or with respect to, an alien or transcendent authority (see 15–16, 38). I have no quarrel with the characterization of Kant's project as anti-foundationalist, to the extent that foundationalism is supposed to require appeal to a transcendent authority relative to reason itself (or appeal to any 'givens' that are supposed to be exempt from criticism themselves).

Fichte) in terms consonant with the contemporary revolutionary challenges
to traditional political authorities. The epistemological demand that nothing
be recognized as authoritative for our reason except on condition that it be
validated in reason's self-reflection expresses a deep suspicion of traditional
authority and ways of justification in the realm of metaphysics. Accordingly,
Kant advertises his critical inquiry, not merely as a reform of previous procedure and authority, but as a revolution and 'transformation in our way of
thinking [*eine Umänderung der Denkart*]'.[57] Part of the point of his famous
analogy with Copernicus's revolution in astronomy is that the change in orientation or perspective is a total change, a change that leaves no reference point
fixed. That critique be *prior* to reason's object-directed inquiry reflects the
need to have a fixed point from which to question the whole normative framework at once. The need that the critical standpoint be *pure*, in the sense that its
norms not be determined by uncriticized content or presuppositions, reflects
the depth of critical suspicion. Accordingly, the highest norms or principles
that emerge in the course of Kantian criticism, the principle of apperception in
the sphere of human knowledge and the categorical imperative in the sphere
of human action, are themselves pure principles: they are *a priori*, timeless,
and formal with respect to the content derived from the 'ongoing' concerns of
developing culture and tradition. That Kant's supreme principle of practical
reason, the categorical imperative, is a fixed principle of criticism relative to
developing culture and tradition is of particular significance. As we will see in
the sequel, Hegel aims in his *Phenomenology of Spirit* to present a criticism that
fulfills the radical, revolutionary ambitions of Kantian critique without benefit of a transcendental standpoint of criticism. Indeed, as we will see, Hegel
holds that only a criticism that foregoes the fixed, transcendental standpoint
can fulfill the revolutionary ambitions inherent in the Kantian project.

It is indeed true that Kant frequently writes as if the ultimate standard
of success for his critical enterprise is the roughly coherentist standard of
reason's agreement with itself. From the famous first sentence of the first-
edition Preface of the First *Critique* through the final sentence of the entire

---

[57] KrV, Bxvi. See the whole context of the beginning of the Preface to the second edition,
where Kant models his Copernican revolution in epistemology on the revolutions enacted in Logic,
Mathematics, and Natural Science, whereby these were also set upon the sure path of science for
the first time. It is important not to be misled by the fact that Kant initially presents the revolution
in the hypothetical mode, that is, as a sort of hypothesis to be tested by determining whether it
succeeds in resolving reason's age-old self-conflict. Kant takes care to tell us later in the Preface that
the change in point of view is proved in the *Critique* itself apodeictically, not hypothetically (Bxxii,
n.).

work, Kant presents the trajectory of critical inquiry as that of bringing pure reason, which Kant finds *in conflict with itself* in its current condition (ceaselessly asking questions which it is powerless to answer) to a condition of satisfaction or peace (*Befriedigung*). However, this coherentist standard of reason's self-agreement or satisfaction is vague; indeed, it proves to be equivocal, in the context of the suspicion encouraged by Kant's criticism. If, as Kant suggests, reason fails to achieve unity with itself because it fails to understand its 'true' needs and interests, then it is a short step to the conception of reason as prone to *fake its own satisfaction* and to disguise from itself or bury its self-conflict, just as individual rational beings do. Encouraged by Kant's critical suspicion, Hegel takes this step.[58] The question becomes: what counts as reason's *genuine* satisfaction? How are we to tell?

The critique of pure reason, according to Kant, not only draws determinate limits to our knowledge, according to which we cannot have knowledge of the supersensible objects about which we cannot fail to inquire, but it teaches us further to rest satisfied with these limits through reinterpreting our interest in these objects. What human reason *really wants* with respect to the supersensible objects of metaphysics, though human reason has long been confused about this, is practical faith, not knowledge. When we come through reason's self-knowledge in critique to clear consciousness that reason's real interest in these objects is practical, not theoretical, we will no longer chafe against the boundaries to our cognition made determinate in that critique.

Hegel views it differently, of course. Whereas Kant presents his doctrine of transcendental idealism as the one system in which reason can stably satisfy its (genuine) interests and needs and avoid self-conflict, Hegel sees in Kantian

---

[58] Perhaps the more important encouragement derives from Fichte. In the First Introduction to his *Wissenschaftslehre*, Fichte presents the fundamental conflict between philosophical systems as that between what he calls the system of 'idealism' and what he calls the system of 'dogmatism'. Because they differ from each other in their conception of the first principle of the system of philosophy, neither the dogmatist nor the idealist can refute the other. Each system ultimately expresses the self-conception and the *interest* of its respective adherents; the idealist system expresses the conception of the self as free and self-determining and the interest of the self in its freedom and self-determination, while the dogmatic system expresses the conception of the self as a thing and as determined by causes outside of itself. 'The kind of philosophy one chooses', Fichte famously writes, 'depends on what kind of human being one is: for a philosophical system is not a dead instrument [*ein toter Hausrat*], which one can pick up or put down as one pleases, but rather it is animated by the soul of the human being whose system it is' (Fichte, *Introductions to the* Wissenschaftslehre, I, 4, 195/20). Essentially Fichte explains the dogmatic system of philosophy as an expression of the fear and avoidance of human freedom. As we will see, Hegel similarly explains critical philosophy, not as a fear of freedom, but as a fear of truth or of the absolute. In both cases, the fear reduces to fear of self-loss; the difference is accounted for by the differing interpretations of the self.

subjectivism and limits to cognition the institutionalization (as it were) of reason's self-*dis*satisfaction and self-conflict.[59] Again, Hegel views the major transitions within Kant's critical system back through the lens of Fichte's interpretation and re-presentation of it. Though Kant presents the step from the theoretical to practical standpoint as enabling us to inhabit the supersensible realm that must remain for us from the former standpoint a transcendent beyond, human reason's quest for transcendence is not satisfied through this transition. The old antagonism between our finite standpoint and the infinite, thoroughly self-determining standpoint re-emerges upon the new ground of practical reason, now as the opposition between what we are (a human will, affected by sensible impulses) and what we ought to be (a purely self-determining will) (or as the opposition between the existing world, in which virtue and happiness do not correspond and the moral world). Another transition, now from morality (or practical reason) to religion, is prescribed finally to effect the reconciliation of human reason with itself. However, the old opposition between our finitude and our infinitude is not so much overcome in religion as made manifest and confessed. The reconciliation of the self-opposition is not effected through philosophy; rather we are supposed to be *reconciled to the self-opposition* through coming to understand it as our human condition. This is especially clear in Fichte's *Wissenschaftslehre*, at the end of which we are delivered over to an endless practical striving to become the completely self-determined being that we both ought to be and can never become. Fichte's doctrine of infinite practical striving is but an interpretation and re-presentation of the Kantian doctrine according to which we are delivered over in the end to an endless practical striving to achieve virtue.[60] Thus, on Hegel's reading, the critical system that begins with the chafing of human reason against itself in metaphysical inquiry, in its vain attempts to achieve self-unity and satisfaction through knowledge of the absolute, ends with the same exasperated condition transposed into an endless *practical* task.[61]

[59] In this too, Hegel follows others who respond to Kant's critical system before him, perhaps particularly in this case Friedrich Jacobi. In the supplement to his book of dialogues, *David Hume über den Glauben, oder Idealismus und Realismus. Ein Gespräch*, Jacobi famously expresses the instability he finds in Kant's critical system with the oft-repeated statement that without the presupposition of things in themselves he cannot enter the critical philosophy, but with that presupposition, he cannot remain within it. (See 1983 reprint, 209–30; English translation: *The Main Philosophical Writings and the Novel 'Allwill'*, trans. and with an introductory study, note, and bibliography by George di Giovanni, (Montreal: McGill—Queen's University Press, 1994), 331–8). The conception of human reason as eternally frustrated and at odds with itself in the critical system surely owes its currency among post-Kantians partly to Jacobi's supplement.

[60] KrV, 5: 83, 128; Rel, 6: 51.

[61] This general reading is of course very tendentious and I don't mean to be defending it here.

Kant's interpretations of the dialectical inferences of pure reason as 'the sophistications not of men but of pure reason itself' sets the stage for later philosophers of suspicion (A339/B397). The sophistications and illusions that structure significant metaphysical systems arise not from the accidental faults and foibles of their authors but from the nature of reason's activity itself.[62] Not only does illusion have a logic, but it expresses a misunderstood interest of reason; the metaphysical system expresses a *genuine* need *in a distorted way*. Later philosophers of suspicion undertake to lay bare the logic of illusion as expressed in the object of criticism. This task includes not only identifying the *genuine* need (or desire) that drives the expression, but also the source of the distortion that it suffers in expression, which, according to the philosophers of suspicion, is also motivated. The philosopher of suspicion suspects a reason, generally unconscious, for the distortion itself. If, as I have been suggesting, Hegel's suspicion of the suspicion expressed in Kantian critique prefigures philosophies of suspicion, then what account does Hegel offer of the interest expressed in Kant's critique? Granted Hegel's interpretation, what is the (perceived) interest behind Kantian subjectivism and limits to knowledge, or behind the Kantian subject's projection of the unconditioned into an inaccessible beyond?

In the Introduction to the *Phenomenology*, Hegel expresses the suspicion that the 'mistrust of science' expressed in the critical inquiry 'reveals itself rather as fear of the truth' (PhG, 70/¶74). This suspicion is explained more thoroughly in Hegel's earlier Introduction to the short-lived *Critical Journal of Philosophy* that he and Schelling published at Jena (from 1802–3). That introduction is entitled 'On the Essence of Philosophical Criticism Generally, and its Relationship to the Present State of Philosophy in Particular'. I will discuss more thoroughly in Chapter 4 the conception of philosophical critique presented in this piece. I refer here to the conception to round out the picture of Hegel's suspicion of Kantian critical philosophy. What is the meaning of Hegel's claim that criticism's 'mistrust of science' 'reveals itself rather as fear of the truth'?

According to Hegel's presentation in this early introduction, philosophical systems, which are the objects of philosophical criticism, are the products of essentially two drives (or interests): one genuine and one illusory. The authentic drive is the drive to express 'the Idea' (what is also known as 'the

---

[62] It is perhaps not such a long step from here to the account of the *history* of metaphysics, not as a mere *random* groping among concepts, but instead as the logic of reason's illusions. And from there it is a short step to the *Phenomenology*.

absolute' and as *'das Objektive'* and which is the object of cognition in philosophy). Since philosophy just is the cognition of the Idea, if the Idea is not at all expressed in a (supposed) philosophical system, then the system does not count as a genuine philosophy at all, and the work of criticism is to reveal its inward nothingness.[63] When the Idea is expressed in a philosophical system, the work of the critic is 'to make clear the manner and degree in which it emerges free and clear and the extent to which it has developed itself into a scientific system' (WdpK, 172/275). Because philosophy is the self-knowledge of reason and reason is at all times and places one and the same, philosophy is also essentially one (*ibid.*). That there is nonetheless a diversity of philosophical expressions—various philosophical systems, all expressing the Idea of philosophy—is due to the other drive behind philosophical expression. Hegel claims that 'subjectivity or limitedness' mixes itself into the presentation of the Idea of philosophy in the particular system (*ibid.*). I take Hegel to mean that the particular subjectivity which aims on the one hand to express the absolute aims also on the other to express its own subjectivity—which, as Hegel claims, is 'incompatible with the true energy of the Idea'—as itself absolute. In cases such as this, philosophical criticism 'has to apply itself especially to the way that philosophy looks when masked by this subjectivity—it must tear the mask off' (*ibid.*). The task of unmasking is accomplished by adhering to the *genuine* need expressed in the philosophical system. Hegel explains:

> When it emerges here that the Idea of philosophy is truly present, then criticism can adhere to the demand and to the need that expresses itself, to the objective factor [*das Objektive*] in which the need seeks satisfaction and refutes the limitedness of the form out of its own authentic tendency toward complete objectivity. (*Ibid.*)

Hegel's passages strongly suggest that what distorts the expression of the philosophical Idea in a given philosophical system—which expression itself responds to a genuine need—is the *misguided* desire to express subjectivity or limitedness, as conceived in the particular case, as itself absolute.

Hegel specifically addresses the case of 'the critical philosophy', under which category he includes not only Kant's system, but those of his followers, Reinhold and Fichte as well (WdpK, 175–6/278). What distinguishes the critical philosophy, according to Hegel here, is that, though the Idea of philosophy is relatively clearly cognized within it, 'subjectivity has striven to ward off philosophy insofar as this is necessary for its own preservation'

---

[63] Hegel refers to these pretenders as 'Unphilosophy' and explains how the philosophical critic must approach them at WdpK, 173–4/276–7.

(*ibid.*). Because 'the true energy of the Idea is incompatible with subjectivity', subjectivity is negated in the face of the pure expression of the Idea in philo- sophy—negated, anyway, as something self-standing on its own account, outside of relation to the absolute. The critical philosophy is characterized by the attempt to preserve self-standing subjectivity. Hence, according to Hegel's critical suspicion directed against the critical philosophy, critical philosophy is most fundamentally an expression of defense against philosophy itself on behalf of self-standing finite subjectivity. This misguided self-defense is the ultimate source of the normative configuration of critical philosophy, of its principle of self-standing subjectivity and of its subjectivism, though the practitioners of critical philosophy are unaware of this latent meaning of their enterprise.

Hegel's suspicion is nicely illustrated in significant respects by Plato's fam- ous allegory of the cave in his *Republic*. Plato's allegory allegorizes philosophic- al education, what Plato calls 'the upward journey of the soul to the intelligible realm'.[64] Plato presumably means his allegory to shed light on (among other things) the puzzling circumstance that people *resist* philosophical education, despite the fact that philosophical knowledge benefits them incomparably. In Plato's allegory, when the enlightened one—he who has been dragged from captivity in the cave out into the upper realm and who has come to know the source of being and goodness directly—returns to the darkened cave and its captives in order to help others to the enlightenment he has experienced, he is regarded with great suspicion and fear. Plato is interested in the fact that people misprize philosophical education exactly because they lack it. The gulf between the philosopher and the cave-bound people whom he would liberate consists in their respective conceptions of the most fundamental criteria of truth and goodness. The people resist and refuse to consent to philosophical enlightenment because, by the standards constitutive of their unenlightened existence, they cannot but judge the way the philosopher would lead them as a path of harm and self-loss. What philosophical education requires, according to Plato's allegory, is not only change in one's opinions and beliefs—there is nothing deeply threatening about that—but change in the most fundamental standards on the basis of which one assesses the good and judges what is true. What is required is a complete reorientation of the soul, a turning of the whole soul around (as Plato's Socrates puts it at 518c). The upward journey of the soul to the intelligible realm requires self-transformation, and that is

---

[64] Plato, *Republic*, 517b.

the source of the resistance to it. From the perspective of its starting point, the upward journey of the soul necessarily appears as a path of self-loss.

The *Phenomenology of Spirit* is Hegel's rendering of the upward journey of the soul to the intelligible realm. The pathway of the *Phenomenology* is the path of philosophical education, beginning at the standpoint of natural or ordinary consciousness, characterized by its most basic criteria or standards of judgment, and ending at the standpoint of philosophy, characterized by revolutionized standards. As in Plato's allegory, Hegel's rendering of philosophical education requires a turning of the soul around. Hence, as Hegel writes in the Introduction, the path of the *Phenomenology* has for natural consciousness a 'negative significance, and what is in fact the realization of the concept counts for it as the loss of its own self; for it does lose its truth on this path. The path can therefore be regarded as the path of *doubt* [*der Weg des Zweifelns*] or more precisely as the path of despair [*der Weg der Verzweiflung*]' (PhG, 72/¶78).

In Part II, I offer an interpretation of Hegel's method in the *Phenomenology* as a radically critical method; what specifically makes it radical is that the most fundamental norms of judgment, through which the criticizing subject's activity is determined as it is, are put at stake in the critical inquiry itself, which implies that the criticizing subject must put herself at stake in the inquiry. In this chapter, I have articulated Hegel's suspicion that *Kantian* philosophical criticism presupposes subjectivism exactly through precluding the transformation of the criticizing subject. The epistemological demand of Kantian criticism implicitly presupposes, as the highest norm of reason to which all given content must conform, the formal self-relating activity of the criticizing subject itself. Kantian criticism implicitly confines us within the magic circle of our own self-consciousness, even as we unavoidably locate our final and true destination in the realm beyond the boundaries of this circle. We have seen how the epistemological demand of Kantian critique is bound up with the conception of the judging subject as autonomous and self-standing. We examine in Part II how Hegel struggles with the problem of redeeming the modern subject's claim to autonomy (to *Selbständigkeit*) without presupposing subjectivism. I argue that Hegel's methodological solution to this problem in his *Phenomenology* is his self-transformational criticism.

PART II

HEGEL'S TRANSFORMATION
OF CRITIQUE

Introduction

It is very unhappy, but too late to be helped, the discovery we have made,
that we exist. That discovery is called the Fall of Man. Ever afterwards,
we suspect our instruments ... Once we lived in what we saw; now, the
rapaciousness of this new power, which threatens to absorb all things,
engages us. Nature, art, persons, letters, religions—objects, successively
tumble in, and God is but one of its ideas.

R. W. Emerson, 'Experience'[1]

When Hegel arrives at the university at Jena in 1801, he takes up his position
in the shadow of his friend from their days together as theology students at
the Tübingen Stift, F. W. Schelling. Schelling is at the time the philosophical
luminary reigning and holding court at the university at Jena, the most recent
in the brief line of luminaries that also includes K. L. Reinhold and Fichte.
Schelling is also recognized at the time as the leading philosopher in the
resplendent circle of Romantics that had formed in Jena. In Hegel's first
philosophical publication in his new position at Jena, entitled 'The Difference
Between Fichte's and Schelling's Systems of Philosophy', published in 1801,
Hegel attracts to himself some of Schelling's reflected light. The intellectual
public gratefully receives the essay for performing the needed service of differ-
entiating Schelling's so-called 'identity philosophy', associated with Romanticism, from the Kantianism of Fichte's system, and of highlighting the former's
virtues in contrast to the latter's vices. Hegel also publishes in those early Jena
years (1802–3) a number of unsigned articles for the *Critical Journal of Philosophy*, which was a short-lived journal jointly edited by him and Schelling and
generally regarded as an organ of Schelling's philosophy. Though it would
be a significant misunderstanding to see Hegel in his early Jena publications

---

[1] *Ralph Waldo Emerson: Essays and Lectures*, ed. by Joel Porte (New York: Library of America, 1983) 487.

as simply a mouthpiece for Schelling's philosophical ideas, it is true that, when he authors the early Jena essays, the distinctive conceptions of his own mature thought have yet to take shape. However, when Hegel leaves Jena just a few short years later, in 1806, all in a rush, ahead of Napoleon's invading army, he carries with him the manuscript of his *Phenomenology of Spirit* (to be published in 1807), which both marks a clear break from Schelling's system and contains definite expression of the core ideas of his own.[2]

Those recent commentators on Hegel's thought whose work 'rehabilitates' him as an epistemologist focus in particular on his Jena writings, for the simple reason that Hegel's preoccupation with issues epistemological is most evident there.[3] However, the prejudice of the older commentators, criticized by the more recent, according to which Hegel is blithely indifferent to the justification of his metaphysical claims, is also founded to a great extent on comments Hegel makes in his early Jena writings. Hegel at several places in those writings seems to dismiss the demand to justify knowledge of the absolute from a standpoint that does not already presuppose it.[4] Some comments in those writings do indeed seem explicitly to affirm dogmatic procedure in metaphysics and thus to mark a relapse back into pre-critical metaphysics. However, with the discussion of Hegel's objection in Part I as background, we can read such passages differently; we can see them, not as the rejection of the demand to justify metaphysical claims as such, but as the rejection of the demand of Kantian *critique* in particular. The implicit presupposition of the demand of critique, according to Hegel's objection, is that we possess in ourselves, in our critical standpoint, over against the standpoint of metaphysics, a criterion by which to test the validity of the claims of reason in metaphysics. Hence the critical procedure dogmatically (and implicitly) presupposes subjectivism and the *impossibility* of the knowledge the possibility of which it is the main business of the procedure to question in free and open inquiry. In Chapter 3,

---

[2] A thorough treatment of Hegel's development while at Jena is provided by H. S. Harris in his book *Hegel's Development: Night Thoughts (Jena 1801–1806)*. A shorter treatment is provided by Terry Pinkard in his recent biography *Hegel: A Biography*.

[3] For example, Michael Forster's case in defense of Hegel's epistemology draws heavily on Hegel's *Critical Journal* article on the relation of skepticism to philosophy. (See Forster, *Hegel and Skepticism*.) To a significant, though lesser extent, Kenneth Westphal also relies on this early article by Hegel. (See Westphal, *Hegel's Epistemological Realism*.) Robert Pippin's case for reading Hegel as essentially completing Kant's critical project relies heavily on Hegel's remarks on Kant's system in the *Critical Journal* article *Faith and Knowledge*. (See Pippin, *Hegel's Idealism: The Satisfactions of Self-Consciousness*.) See Ameriks's survey of this and other recent work in his essay 'Recent Work on Hegel: The Rehabilitation of an Epistemologist?'

[4] The passages will be noted and discussed in Ch. 3 below.

I discuss an article Hegel publishes in the *Critical Journal of Philosophy* (in 1802) on the relation of philosophy to skepticism. Examination of this article, which is densely concerned with epistemological issues, is particularly helpful for demonstrating that Hegel's rejection of the epistemological demand of criticism is not a self-conscious embrace of dogmatic procedure in philosophy; rather, in this article Hegel advocates the employment of the epistemological procedure of the Pyrrhonist skeptics in preference to that of modern skeptics, exactly on the ground that the ancient skeptical procedure is 'infinitely more skeptical' than modern procedures. In bringing out such points, the reading I offer in Part II is in accord with (and much indebted to) that of recent commentators. However, I believe that recent commentators have, in their rehabilitation of Hegel as an epistemologist, underplayed the significance of the transformation of Hegel's views on epistemological procedure while at Jena, the transformation between the view presented in the early Jena writings and that exemplified in the very project of the *Phenomenology*. As I interpret this transformation in Part II, Hegel reverses himself while at Jena on the question of the legitimacy of the epistemological demand of Kantian critique. The main task of Part II is to show how Hegel's project and procedure in the *Phenomenology of Spirit* take shape through his coming to recognize that the project of Kantian critique cannot simply be rejected or dismissed, as he does in the early Jena period, but rather must be undertaken and completed. I show that the method of the *Phenomenology of Spirit* takes shape through Hegel's transformation of Kant's critical procedure, a transformation required by the objection to Kant's procedure interpreted in the previous chapter.

The story of Hegel's change from his rejection of the project of Kantian critique to his adoption and transformation of it while at Jena is intertwined with the story of Hegel's developing response to *skeptical* procedures and positions at this time, particularly his views regarding the difference between ancient and modern skepticisms. The above-mentioned *Critical Journal* article on the relation of philosophy to skepticism is a review article of the work of the post-Kantian skeptic, Gottlob Ernst Schulze. By means of a discussion of this article in Chapter 3, I show that Hegel's attack there on Schulze's skepticism—his strong rejection of Schulze's skeptical demands, taking the demands to be an expression, crude though they be, of distinctively modern epistemological demands—far from expressing Hegel's dismissal of epistemological scruples, *itself expresses* his strong epistemological scruples. Taking Hegel's case against Schulze's skepticism as a case against distinctively modern skepticism in general, Hegel's case calls to mind a strand of criticism of

'Cartesian' or modern skepticism familiar to us in contemporary philosophy. I quoted in the Introduction the following passage from John McDowell, who is a distinguished proponent of this strand of criticism: 'It is the source of the basic misconception of modern philosophy that the task of philosophy is to bridge an ontological and epistemological gulf across which the subjective and the objective are supposed to face each other.'[5] According to 'the basic misconception of modern philosophy', the fundamental epistemological project is to demonstrate that our representations, to which our epistemic access is immediate and of which we therefore have *certain* and indubitable knowledge, correspond to the *objects* outside the mind which they purport to represent. As Hume puts the skeptic's challenge, 'By what argument can it be proved that the perceptions of the mind must be caused by external objects, entirely different from them though resembling them?'[6] So formulated, the challenge looks insurmountable. However, as McDowell's passage indicates, the problem is with conceptions that underlie the skeptic's challenge, not with our knowledge. According to this strand of criticism of modern skepticism, we escape the skeptic's thrall, not by answering his demand for justification, but rather by seeing how that demand is founded on fundamental misconceptions of the *tasks* of human knowledge. The extent to which Hegel's case against Schulze's 'most recent' skepticism anticipates this contemporary criticism of modern skepticism is remarkable. Hegel too refuses to meet the skeptic's challenge, but instead argues that that challenge itself is based on a fundamentally distorted conception of the epistemological *task*. Further, Hegel understands the modern philosopher mistakenly to conceive the epistemological task as that of bridging a perceived gulf between our (supposedly inner) concepts and the (supposedly external) being or things that these concepts are supposed to represent. However, I attempt to show in my discussion of Hegel's article that it is not so much Descartes and Hume that lurk in the background of Hegel's case against Schulze's skepticism as Kant and his critical project.

The surprising circumstance that contemporary analytic philosophers increasingly engage with Hegel's 'epistemology' (and even with his metaphysics) is mostly explained by the fact that Hegel's thought lends itself to being enlisted as an ally in the ongoing contemporary struggle against Cartesian dualism in these fields. Yet I believe that there are very significant divergences

---

[5] McDowell, 'Knowledge and the Internal', 889.
[6] David Hume, *Enquiry Concerning Human Understanding*, in *Enquiries Concerning Human Understanding and Concerning the Principles of Morals*, 152–3.

between Hegel's orientation in epistemology and even that version of contemporary response to modern skeptical demands that may most remind us of Hegel's thought. Hegel is not the friendly ally in the contemporary case against modern, Cartesian epistemology that he may initially seem to be.[7] The relation of Hegel's developing epistemology to strands of contemporary criticism is not a major theme of this work, but I note in this introduction two major respects in which Hegel's orientation diverges from the strand of contemporary criticism mentioned above, because these differences help us to see, I think, why the *Phenomenology of Spirit* must take the form it has, bloated and baroque as it may seem to us; it takes the convoluted form it has in *response to*, not in rejection of, epistemological demands.

The first difference concerns the relation of Cartesian skeptical challenges to distinctively philosophical ambitions and presuppositions. Whereas contemporary philosophers in opposing Cartesian skepticism tend to fault distinctively *philosophical* presuppositions for the offending dualism, and to elevate the *ordinary* standpoint as innocent of the distorting preconceptions that make the skeptic's challenges seem pressing, for Hegel the reverse is true: the offending dualism is rooted in ordinary consciousness, and the standpoint from which the (modern) skeptical challenges are seen to be completely unmotivated is the opposing standpoint of *philosophical cognition*.[8] The relevant contemporary critic of modern skepticism conceives the task of his criticism, not, of course, as the task of refuting or answering the skeptic directly—granted the terms implicit in the skeptic's demand for justification, such a refutation is impossible—but rather as the task of showing the skeptic's standpoint, from which the demand for justification seems pressing, to be both *optional*, and, further, based on dubious assumptions. If these assumptions are 'the basic misconception of modern philosophy', as McDowell has it, then presumably they are deep-rooted and powerfully tempting. In the face of this, the task of the critic of modern skepticism is to return us to a condition of innocence, a condition innocent of the fateful moves that have saddled us with modern skepticism. The symbolism of the Fall of Man, as employed in the Emerson passage used as an epigraph, strongly suggests itself here: in our lost condition of epistemological innocence, the condition which

[7] For a discussion of the ways in which Hegel's critique of modern skepticism differs from that of John McDowell, despite surface similarities, see William Bristow, '*Bildung* and the Critique of Modern Skepticism in McDowell and Hegel'.

[8] Robert Stern emphasizes this difference in his article, 'Going Beyond the Kantian Philosophy: On McDowell's Hegelian Critique of Kant'.

it is the task of criticism to recover for us, we lived at home in the natural and social world; we recover from our contemporary alienated condition in epistemology by means of patient insight into the disastrous intellectual sins that cast us out of that world.[9] But, speaking generally, the contemporary critics figure the voice of temptation as the voice of the philosopher within us, and the original and unalienated condition as our ordinary condition, in which we rely in our knowledge claims on ordinary criteria.

In his early article on philosophy and skepticism, written in the sphere of influence of the Romantic Schelling, Hegel's criticism of Schulze's skepticism implies that the work of such criticism is to return us to a condition of innocence, back before the offending dualism and subjectivism characteristic of modern times. But, while acknowledging this affinity to contemporary criticism, we must also recognize the following difference: in rejecting distinctively modern epistemological demands as inherently subjectivist, Hegel means to affirm the possibility, not of empirical knowledge of middle-sized dry goods, but of rational or metaphysical knowledge. Hegel's conception of the 'object' of metaphysical knowledge in the early writings is distinctly Platonic, as indicated in the preferred label, 'the Idea'. According to his conception of it in this period, the Idea, the *Urbild* from which all difference and determination ontologically derive, excludes from itself all difference and opposition. Whatever difference there may be between Hegel's and Schelling's philosophical conceptions in this early Jena period, Hegel too, like Schelling, conceives of the object of philosophical knowledge as an *identity* above all. His rejection of the epistemological demand of the modern skeptic—represented most immediately by Schulze's skeptical demands, but as I hope to show, more importantly by the demands of Kantian critique—depends on his conception of the object and task *of metaphysics* in particular. As Hegel conceives it, the modern skeptic demands justification of cognition of 'the Idea' from a particular standpoint, a standpoint in which he conceives of himself as self-standing (*selbständig*), independently of his relation to that Idea, the alleged ground of all being, the possibility of knowledge of which he means to question in his skeptical/critical inquiry. According to Hegel's critique of it, this conception

---

[9] Playfully employing the symbolism, J. L. Austin objects to Wisdom's view according to which knowledge of 'sense-statements' is infallible in 'Other Minds' as follows: 'This seems to me mistaken, though it is a view that, in more or less subtle forms, has been the basis of a very great deal of philosophy. It is perhaps the original sin (Berkeley's apple, the tree in the quad) by which the philosopher casts himself out of the garden of the world we live in.' J. L. Austin, *Philosophical Papers*, 3rd edn., 90.

of the task of philosophical cognition presupposes the criteria of *ordinary consciousness*; it presupposes the dualism between representation and object represented that is characteristic of ordinary cognition, and thereby begs the question against *rational* or *philosophical* cognition, which can be nothing else, given its object, but the expression of the presupposed Idea. But, again, Hegel's rejection of this epistemological demand, as the discussion of Hegel's skepticism article will show, is a rejection of a particular epistemological demand in favor of what he regards as the more demanding epistemological procedure of the ancient (more specifically, Pyrrhonist) skeptics. As he conceives it, the procedure of the ancient skeptics, in attacking 'the dogmatism of ordinary consciousness', which is what is expressed in modern subjectivism, elevates us to the standpoint of philosophy and its cognition of the Idea.

A further task of the discussion of Hegel's Skepticism article in Chapter 3 is to show how Hegel's rejection of the project of philosophical critique is embedded within a broader conception of the relation of philosophy to its history and to the history of culture in general in this early Jena period. In conceiving the object of philosophical cognition in this period on a Platonic model, he conceives it as an ontological ground elevated above the processes of change and development. Moreover, in these writings he already conceives of the *knowledge* of the Idea in philosophy as one with the Idea itself; knowledge of the Idea is the self-knowledge of reason, and, as such, identical with it. Therefore he maintains that philosophy can no more develop, according to its nature, than the Idea itself can. *A fortiori*, if there is a distinctively 'modern' dispensation in philosophy—a modern skepticism or a modern idealism, for example—Hegel is committed to viewing it, so conceived, as alien to the true philosophy, which is one and the same in all times and places. Hegel conceives the work of philosophy in these writings as the work of recovery and expression, over against time and development, of the eternal, changeless *Urbild*. To the extent that the attempt at philosophy succeeds, it shows its identity with the earliest, and with all true, philosophy. Insofar as Hegel does trace historical developments in what passes itself as philosophy, as he does in the Skepticism article, where he recounts the story of the development of skepticism from its oldest 'and most noble' appearance through its succeeding manifestations in Plato's Academy to its 'most recent' manifestation in Schulze's Humeanism, he presents these stages of development as so many steps in the decline and corruption of philosophy, as reflecting the decline in the culture generally, from the extraordinary expression of culture in Socrates' Athens to the bourgeois philistinism of contemporary Europe. Though it is perhaps impossible to say what Hegel's considered view on such matters was in 1802 (and perhaps not so important to know), the Skepticism article (as well as other pieces of that period) manifest the spirit of Romanticism which envelops him in Jena at the time, at least to the extent that they express a yearning for the lost harmony and greatness of Greek culture, a yearning explicitly counter to the broader Enlightenment culture of contemporary Europe, which he sees as corrupted by modern dualism and subjectivism.

I go into these matters, to the limited extent that I do, because they form the context that allows us to understand the motivation of Hegel's 'return to the point of view of Kant and Fichte' while at Jena and the consequences of it, which include the project of the *Phenomenology of Spirit*.[10] Hegel returns to the standpoint of philosophical critique; he comes to recognize, against his own earlier rejections of it, the *validity* of the epistemological demand expressed in the project of Kantian critique. Again, the distinctive epistemological demand of Kant's critical project is the demand that the claims (or, in particular, the criteria or principles) of metaphysics be legitimated *to us*, in our standpoint of critical self-reflection, explicitly set over against that of metaphysics, as a prior condition of our recognition of their authority for us. The argument of Part I has shown this epistemological demand to be bound up with subjectivism. However, Hegel comes to recognize the distinctively modern epistemological demand to be based, not on mistakes or misconceptions or illusions, but rather upon a *discovery*, moreover, as Emerson has it in the passage used as an epigraph, upon a *self-discovery*. This self-discovery is (or, is supposed to be, anyway) distinctively modern—indeed, it is supposed to be a discovery that, as much as any single thing, defines our condition as modern. It is hard to overestimate the significance of Hegel's recognition of the validity of the epistemological demand of philosophical critique for the development of his own distinctive philosophical system.

What motivates Hegel's turn (or return)? The affinity between the epistemological demand of Kantian critique, as that challenges the traditional authority of the claims of pure reason in metaphysics, and the demands for justification of traditional authorities, both religious and political, made on behalf of ordinary citizens at the time, is widely recognized in the wake of the publication of Kant's First *Critique*. Fichte's re-presentation of Kant's critical system as a 'system of freedom' helps cement this conception. According

---

[10] The quoted phrase is taken from Hyppolite, *Genesis and Structure of Hegel's* Phenomenology of Spirit, 5–6.

to Fichte's re-presentation, nothing has validity for the reflecting self except insofar as it is shown to be, through the procedure of reflection, a necessary condition of the self's own self-positing activity, the principle of which is the highest principle of philosophy. As a theology student at the Tübingen Stift in the early 1790s, Hegel ardently admires Kant's critical system; and his admiration of it is not separable from his seeing Kant's demands for the justification of traditional authorities as enacting the same revolution in the realm of the intellect that was then being enacted in France in the realm of politics. Given Hegel's enthusiasm for the Enlightenment ideals of the freedom, equality, and dignity of each human being, *qua* rational being, and given the perceived fact that the epistemological demand of Kant's critique expresses these ideals, Hegel's rejection of this epistemological demand in the early Jena writings is not a stable position. He must make room in his developing philosophical system for the claims of the individual to freedom, equality, and dignity. This, I believe, is the pivot on which Hegel returns to the standpoint of Kantian critique while at Jena.

In the early Jena writings one sees Hegel implicitly reject the *right* of the individual subject to demand of philosophical claims that they be validated in a process of critical reflection from a standpoint explicitly set over against the standpoint of metaphysics, a standpoint in which the individual claims to be self-standing, independently of its relation to 'the Idea'. As Hegel sees it, to make this demand is to arrogate to oneself an authority that precludes the authority of reason's principle, thus foreclosing the possibility of metaphysical knowledge and predetermining confinement in one's knowing within the circle of self-consciousness. In Chapter 4, I document how Hegel explicitly reverses himself on just this point. I show how, in justifying the need for the *Phenomenology of Spirit* in both the Preface and Introduction to that work, Hegel appeals to the *right* of ordinary consciousness to make this epistemological demand. Further, he finds this right to be grounded in turn in the individual's immediate claim to *Selbständigkeit*, to being self-standing, of which status it is immediately certain independently of its relation to the absolute. What Hegel comes to recognize here is what he later calls, in the *Philosophy of Right*, 'the highest right of the subject', the right of the subject not to recognize anything that it does not have insight into as rational.[11] The discovery of this right constitutes the distinctively modern in philosophy and culture.

---

[11] Hegel, PhR, §133. (Please see 'Abbreviations' for the manner in which I refer to the texts of Kant and Hegel.)

I noted above that there are two main differences between Hegel's criticism of distinctively modern epistemological demands and that of contemporary critics, differences which make Hegel at best an ambiguous ally of these critics in their struggles against modern Cartesian dualism and subjectivism. The first is that Hegel, in direct opposition to contemporary critics, finds the Cartesian dualism and subjectivism to be rooted in the standpoint of *ordinary* cognition, as opposed to the standpoint of distinctively philosophical cognition. The second is that Hegel conceives the distinctively modern epistemological demands to be founded, not on mistakes or misconceptions, but on a self-discovery, and hence unavoidable for philosophy. If the distinctively modern gulf across which the subjective and the objective are supposed to face each other opens through a self-discovery rather than through a mistake or misconception, then we cannot reject the task of overcoming this gulf through a direct engagement with the skeptical standpoint. Once Hegel comes to the recognition that the epistemological demand of Kantian critique is backed by a self-discovery, Hegel can no longer complacently reject Kant's critical project and the epistemological crisis to which it responds in favor of an ancient epistemological procedure. I show in Chapter 4 that the *Phenomenology of Spirit* responds to approximately the same crisis for metaphysics that Kant makes vivid and responds to in his *Critique of Pure Reason*, the same crisis that Hegel dismisses in his early Jena writings.

Now that Hegel recognizes a distinctively modern philosophical discovery, the question arises: what is the nature of the truth philosophy would express such that a distinctively modern discovery is possible? The pressure generated by this recognition splits his traditional Platonic conception of 'the Idea' at the seams. Hegel responds to this problem with what is perhaps his most defining and bold philosophical claim: what philosophers have forever striven to know ('the Idea' or 'the absolute' or 'God') is not set over against development and change, but itself *becomes what it is* through an historical process of development and self-knowledge. As Hegel puts it in the famous sentence in the Preface of the *Phenomenology of Spirit*: 'everything turns on grasping and expressing the True, not only as *Substance*, but equally as *Subject*' (PhG, 22–3/¶ 17). Having come to recognize the right of the subject to make its epistemological demand, *vis-à-vis* the claims of the metaphysician, Hegel is brought to the claim that the truth the metaphysician would know itself has the form of subjectivity. This metaphysical claim is difficult to grasp, and I don't attempt in this study to expound it. I focus rather on the epistemological pressures that underlie it.

In Chapter 5, I argue that two main pressures determine Hegel's method of criticism in the *Phenomenology*. First, Hegel objects against the procedure of Kantian critique that it presupposes subjectivism and the impossibility of metaphysics. Hegel alludes to this objection throughout his corpus, including at the very beginning of the Introduction to the *Phenomenology of Spirit*. This objection implies that Hegel cannot simply 'return to the standpoint of Kant and Fichte' once he has recognized the legitimacy of the epistemological demand expressed in Kantian critique. However—and this is the second pressure—once he recognizes the right of ordinary consciousness to make its demand for justification over against the standpoint of metaphysics, Hegel must undertake the project of this demonstration, starting from this standpoint, a standpoint within which the absolute is not presupposed, but rather, on the contrary, regarded as a transcendent other. If Hegel prosecutes criticism in the style of Kant and Fichte, his method too will presuppose subjectivism and the impossibility of knowledge of the absolute; but if he simply rejects the demands for justification of the claims or criteria of metaphysics, from the self-certain standpoint of ordinary consciousness, set over against that of metaphysics (as Schelling does in this period), then, as he says in the Preface in the *Phenomenology*, he condemns metaphysics to being the private and inward possession of a few isolated souls; metaphysics does not exist, as it properly should, as a public property of all. It does not exist as a science. The existence of metaphysics (as a science) depends on the completion of the critical task.

I argue that the key to Hegel's transformation of Kant's procedure of criticism is his determination of a critical procedure according to which the standards or principles that the criticizing subject brings to bear in criticism are equally at stake in the critical inquiry with the knowledge under investigation. Insofar as the configuration of the criticizing subject is defined by the highest principles that it recognizes, this implies that Hegel's criticism is *self-transformational* criticism; the criticizing subject is transformed through the process of criticism. The presupposition of subjectivism in Kant's procedure of critique is implicit in the fixity of the standpoint of its criticizing subject, over against metaphysics. The key to Hegel's attempt fully to meet the epistemological demand of critique is his construction of a procedure that lets the epistemological crisis fully flower and become existential, that is, become a crisis in the existence of the criticizing subject. Hegel's famous claim in the Introduction to the *Phenomenology* that the procedure of justification there is not only a way of doubt (*ein Weg des Zweifels*), but much more a way *of despair* (*ein Weg der Verzweiflung*), by which he means minimally that it is a way of self-loss and self-realization for the person who undertakes it, cannot be ascribed to Romantic ornamentation of the text, but rather expresses the key to his attempt rigorously and fully to meet the epistemological demand of philosophical critique, in particular, to respond to that demand without implicitly presupposing subjectivism. This is what I shall argue in Part II.

3

The Rejection of Kantian Critique: Philosophy, Skepticism, and the Recovery of the Ancient Idea

3.1 HEGEL'S EPISTEMOLOGY IN THE SHADOW OF SCHELLING

According to Hegel's objection against Kant's project of philosophical critique, as interpreted in Chapter 2, that project, though it consists explicitly in questioning the possibility of metaphysics in a free and open inquiry, in effect implicitly precludes the possibility of knowledge of the absolute and, further, confines us in our knowing to a realm of mere appearances. This objection leads Hegel initially simply to *reject* the project of Kantian critique. Hegel's rejection of the critical project is indicated in several statements from his early Jena writings. The main task of this chapter is to elaborate Hegel's conception of epistemological procedure and philosophical knowledge in this period, insofar as these conceptions can be teased out of his early publications. I focus mostly in this chapter on Hegel's article entitled 'Relation of Skepticism to Philosophy: Presentation of its Various Modifications and Comparison of the Most Recent with the Ancient', published in the *Critical Journal of Philosophy*.[1] I focus on this article because, as the title indicates, the relation of philosophy to epistemological procedure is its main concern. A general comprehension of Hegel's conceptions of epistemology and metaphysics in his early Jena period is required in order to appreciate the account in the succeeding two chapters according to which Hegel's coming to recognize the validity of the epistemological demand of Kantian critique, as against his earlier rejection of it, makes the specific project and procedure of the *Phenomenology of Spirit* necessary for him.

[1] I indicate this work with the abbreviation 'VSP', and provide page references within the body of the text. Please see the 'Abbreviations' for information regarding how I cite the texts of Kant and Hegel.

Hegel's rejection of the epistemological project of Kantian critique in his early Jena years is indicated by those scattered passages in the writings of that period in which he claims that the procedure of philosophy must simply presuppose the absolute. In a passage in the Skepticism article, Hegel explicitly rejects the task of grounding the principle of philosophy; he claims that philosophy (or metaphysics) does nothing else than express and know the philosophical principle that is presupposed in everyday life.[2] Similarly, in a passage in his essay on the difference between Fichte's and Schelling's systems of philosophy, Hegel rejects the epistemological task of justifying the principles of philosophy in a prior inquiry relative to the system of metaphysics proper. He claims there that to undertake the task of justifying and grounding such principles outside of or before philosophy proper frustrates the very task that it attempts.[3] Further, Hegel begins his Introduction to the *Critical Journal*, 'On the Essence of Philosophical Critique in General and its Relation to the Present Condition of Philosophy in Particular', with the claim that the activity of critique must simply presuppose its criterion, that is, the absolute, as the condition of objective judgment. Such passages express Hegel's rejection of the demand that the principle of metaphysics be legitimated or justified in a prior inquiry, as a condition of the possibility of the system of metaphysics proper. Thus such passages express a rejection of the project of philosophical critique.[4]

---

[2] The passage reads as follows: 'In daily life, says Herr Schulze, we *presuppose* that identity [of thinking and being, of concept and thing]; that it is *presupposed* in daily life means that it is not present in consciousness. "*The recent metaphysics seeks to ground* [*ergründen*] *the possibility of this identity*"; but that the recent philosophy seeks to ground the possibility of the identity *presupposed* in ordinary life is no true saying, for this metaphysics does nothing but express and know that presupposed identity. Just because that identity is presupposed in daily life, the ordinary consciousness posits the object always as an other relative to the subject … ; metaphysics brings this identity, which is for ordinary consciousness merely presupposed and unconscious, to consciousness; this identity is its absolute and only principle' (VSP, 255/342).

[3] The relevant passage concerns the possibility that philosophy has as its presupposition some need to which it responds. 'It is, however, inapt to regard the need for philosophy as a presupposition thereof', Hegel writes. A presupposition (*Voraussetzung*) is a pre-positing, a proposition (*ein Satz*) *before* philosophy proper. But 'it can be demanded of propositions that they justify themselves. The justification of such propositions, as presuppositions, is supposed to be not yet philosophy itself, and so the activity of establishing by and giving grounds [*Ergründen und Begründen*] begins/comes undone [*losgehen*] before and outside philosophy' (Hegel, Diff, 25/94). Though the context of this passage is not one in which Hegel addresses the epistemological project of Kantian critique, the passage expresses in an exemplary way Hegel's rejection in this period of the attempt to establish the principle of philosophy in an epistemological procedure *in advance of philosophy or the system of metaphysics proper*. Michael Forster helpfully discusses this passage, though without relating it to the project of critique. (See his *Hegel and Skepticism*, 110.)

[4] Some will object that such passages are not restricted to the early Jena period, but are to be found throughout Hegel's corpus. For example, Hegel's famous characterization of the procedure

Against the persistent temptation to take such passages to show that Hegel's thought represents a relapse into pre-critical, dogmatic metaphysics, a few points must be made. Although there is *a sense* of dogmatism in which Hegel does explicitly embrace dogmatism here, this sense is *defined by Kant*, and opposed by Hegel himself. Recall how Kant defines 'dogmatism' in the Preface to the second edition of the *Critique of Pure Reason*:

[This critique] is opposed only to *dogmatism*, that is, to the presumption that it is possible to make progress with pure knowledge, according to principles, from concepts alone (those that are philosophical), as reason has long been in the habit of doing; and that it is possible to do this without having investigated in what way and by what right reason has come into possession of these concepts. Dogmatism is thus the dogmatic procedure of reason, *without previous criticism of its own powers*. (Bxxxv)

By this conception of dogmatism, Hegel is a confessed dogmatist in this early Jena period. If it is dogmatism to begin with the absolute straightway, without benefit of a prior inquiry in which the principle of rational cognition is validated and established, then Hegel embraces dogmatism in these writings. But even putting aside the main point of the subsequent chapter—namely, that Hegel's embrace of dogmatism in this sense is temporary and that he returns to the standpoint of Kant in his *Phenomenology*—one can see that Hegel's embrace of dogmatism in this sense is no mere relapse. It is not as if the rigorous epistemological spirit expressed in Kant somehow passes Hegel by. Hegel self-consciously *rejects* the epistemological demands and procedure of Kantian critique; he rejects them on the basis of the considerations adduced in Chapter 2 above. The critical procedure implicitly presupposes subjectivism and the impossibility of metaphysical knowledge; if rational cognition is possible for us, then only if its possibility does not wait for validation on a prior self-reflective inquiry.

---

of Kantian critique as wanting to know before one knows, or of wanting to learn to swim before entering the water, occurs in his discussions of Kant's philosophy in his *Encyclopedia Logic* and in his *Lectures on the History of Philosophy* (see EL, § 41Z1 and § 10; VGP, *Werke*, vol. 20, 333–4; Haldane and Simpson, vol. 3, 428–9). If such later passages express essentially the same rejection of the procedure of Kantian critique as those mentioned above from the early Jena period, then Hegel's rejection of Kantian critique is not restricted to that period, as I claim. As I understand them, such post-*Phenomenology* passages express Hegel's rejection, not of the project of philosophical critique *per se*, but of Kant's specific critical procedure, which, as untransformed, and not transformational, presupposes subjectivism. Hegel would not need to transform the project and method of Kant's critique in his *Phenomenology* if he didn't reject the *specific form* the critical project takes in Kant's writings. I must leave for the following chapter the argument for the claim that the project of the *Phenomenology* involves taking on the critical enterprise in a sense that Hegel rejects it in his early Jena writings.

However, granted Hegel's rejection of the specifically *critical* demand to justify the claims of reason in metaphysics (in Kant's sense of critique), what becomes of the general demand that metaphysical knowledge be demonstrated and justified, according to Hegel? What conception of the proper demands and procedures of epistemological justification does Hegel set over against the critical demand and procedures in this period characterized by his rejection of critique?

One of Hegel's main occupations in his early Jena writings is to characterize the philosophical positions of Kant and Fichte—also, but less significantly, of Reinhold and Jacobi—and to mark in contrast the difference and superiority of Schelling's system. He characterizes the systems of Kant and Fichte, in contrast to Schelling's, principally in terms of their subjectivism: knowledge in their systems is ultimately relativized to the standpoint of the transcendental 'I' and the absolute is rendered inaccessible relative to our knowledge. As I demonstrate in Part I above, the subjectivism of Kant's account expresses his intensification of the requirements of epistemology *vis-à-vis* metaphysics. The critical philosopher demands that the criteria of rational cognition be legitimated to us in a prior reflection on our cognitive capacities, as a condition of the possibility of metaphysics. I argue in Part I that the key claim of the Transcendental Analytic of Kant's *Critique of Pure Reason*, the claim that the principle expressing the self-activity of the knowing subject, the principle of apperception, is the highest principle of our knowledge, to which all content of our knowledge must conform, merely elaborates and makes explicit a principle implicit already in the original epistemological demand of the critical project. Hence the subjectivism that Kant explicitly derives from the principle of apperception is already implicit in the epistemological demand of critique. According to Hegel's reading, Fichte's system conforms generally to the Kantian pattern. The principle of the early *Wissenschaftslehre* expresses the pure self-activity and self-consciousness of the 'I'. While it expresses an identity of subject and object, Hegel characterizes the identity, as that expressed in Kant's principle, as a merely *subjective* identity, to which the absolute identity is absolutely opposed. Hence, as in Kant's system, so in Fichte's: one never attains to the cognition of the absolute after which one strives; instead the system implicitly asserts the absoluteness of finite subjectivity over against the absolute.

Schelling's system is superior, according to Hegel in his early Jena writings, because its principle, in contrast, is the *absolute* identity of subject and object, on which the self-consciousness of the particular, finite subject itself depends for its existence.[5] However, granted my account in Part I, if it is true that the principle of the subjective idealisms of Kant and Fichte, the principle that expresses the self-consciousness and self-activity of the finite, knowing subject, expresses in turn the intense epistemological demand with which Kant gives the original impetus to the movement of German idealism, then there is a tension between the demands of epistemology, as expressed in the critical project, and the demand to express or to know a fully objective or fully absolute principle in philosophy. Schelling's system of idealism is further evidence of this tension, insofar as he in effect sacrifices epistemological rigor in the effort to express the absolute identity. This exchange becomes more or less explicit in Schelling's explicit embrace of the esotericism of philosophy. Schelling is content to deny that there can be any *demonstration* of philosophy's principle, if what we mean by such a demonstration is that the principle be legitimated to ordinary rational beings who recognize the force only of common, ordinary reasons and for whom the claims of metaphysicians seem incomprehensible flights of fancy. Schelling's denial of the possibility of elevating an ordinary rational person to the standpoint from which she has insight into philosophy's principle through the provision of reasons the force of which she has the capacity to recognize expresses his sacrifice of epistemology to metaphysics. Schelling uses the conception according to which the highest principle, the unconditioned, is known through an *intuition*, an intellectual intuition, rather than discursively, to defy demands for its demonstration. Thus, *Schelling's* system really is dogmatic in the way that Hegel's is often assumed to be: that is, not only in the specific sense of 'dogmatism' defined by Kant, but also in the general sense of not undertaking the demonstration or justification of philosophy's principle to any rational person, assuming only that person's common, ordinary rationality.[6]

The tension between the demands of epistemological rigor, characteristic of what Kant calls the 'age of criticism', on the one hand, and the demand for genuine objectivity or absoluteness in philosophical cognition on the other is the productive tension at the core of Hegel's development at Jena, culminating

---

[5] Hegel, Diff, 94–115/155–74.

[6] For an expression of Schelling's disdain for the demand that the principle of philosophy be demonstrated towards common cognition, see his *Fernere Darstellungen aus dem System der Philosophie*, 414. For a discussion of Hegel's stance towards Schelling's dogmatism in his Jena writings, see Forster, *Hegel and Skepticism*, 100–1. For a defense of Schelling's early philosophical writings against the common conception of them as dogmatic, see Frederick Beiser's discussion in his *German Idealism: The Struggle Against Subjectivism, 1781–1801*, 475–6, 577–95.

in his *Phenomenology of Spirit*. If Schelling lets the need for expression of a genuinely objective principle cancel the opposing demand of the individual subject for justification and demonstration of this principle, we need not suppose that Hegel does likewise, even in this period of his close association with Schelling, when his publications are occupied with defining the difference of Schelling's system and showing it to advantage in contrast to the subjectivism of Kant and Fichte. Though Hegel does reject the specific epistemological demand expressed in the project of Kantian criticism in this period, Hegel is presumably already uncomfortable with the dogmatism of Schelling's absolute idealism. The difficulty posed by the objection to Kant's critique is to define a rigorous epistemological procedure that does not preclude from the beginning the possibility of cognition of the absolute. How can dogmatism (in the general sense) be avoided without presupposing subjectivism?

The *Critical Journal* article on the relation of philosophy to skepticism presents Hegel's view on this matter in the early Jena period. There Hegel defines 'dogmatism' in its original opposition to skepticism (as against the Kantian sense, in which it is opposed to criticism); there he criticizes distinctively modern epistemological demands and procedures as *dogmatic* in the genuine sense, by virtue of being structured by the fixed opposition between subject and object; there he praises in contrast an ancient skeptical procedure (that of the Pyrrhonist skeptics) on the grounds that it manages to be completely or radically skeptical; he argues, moreover, that this ancient skeptical procedure, or at least what he calls its most noble expression, far from implying the denial of the possibility of philosophical cognition, is but the negative side of the true philosophy, of the expression of the absolute. However, we'll see that Hegel is able there to unite epistemology and metaphysics by appeal to the procedures of the ancient skeptics only by conceiving the epistemological procedure as the recovery of an ancient (indeed Platonic) Idea, over against modernity and the Enlightenment. The instability of this position for Hegel, child of the Enlightenment that he is, sets the stage for his return to the project of Kantian critique.

3.2 SCHULZE'S SKEPTICISM CONTRA THE CRITICAL PHILOSOPHY

In the title of Hegel's *Critical Journal* article concerning the difference between ancient skepticism and modern, 'Relation of Skepticism to Philosophy:

Presentation of its Various Modifications and Comparison of the Most Recent with the Ancient', what Hegel means by 'the most recent' skepticism is the skepticism expounded by Gottlob Ernst Schulze. Hegel's essay (1802) is a review of Schulze's 1801 publication *Kritik der theoretischen Philosophie*. Schulze's skepticism is peculiar in several respects. Yet I will read Hegel's attack on Schulze's brand of skepticism as implying an attack on modern skepticism in general, and also, more particularly, as embodying Hegel's objection against Kant's epistemological procedure in his project of philosophical critique.[7] This will need defense. We must first set the intellectual scene of Hegel's article.

In the context of discussion of the critical philosophy in the immediate wake of its appearance, Schulze's critical attacks on the Kantian philosophy were, as Frederick Beiser reports, 'the first generally recognized threat to the apparently impregnable critical fortress'.[8] Schulze achieved his reputation primarily through his so-called *Aenesidemus*, an anonymously published skeptical attack on the critical philosophy that appeared in 1792.[9] Aenesidemus is a first-century skeptic, famous for, among other things, his metaskeptical attack on the skeptical school of the Academy. He attacked that school for teaching the 'dogma' that knowledge is impossible. Schulze figures himself as standing with respect to the Kantian critical philosophy as Aenesidemus stands with respect to Academic skepticism: that is, he presents himself as more radically or consistently skeptical than the critical philosophy, since, on his view, the latter condemns the dogmatism of metaphysics only upon the basis of dogmatic epistemological claims. Schulze maintains that the negative claim of the critical philosophy, the claim that we cannot know the unconditioned or anything of things as they are in themselves, is not skeptical enough, since, contra the critical philosophy, we cannot know anything of the origins or conditions or limits of our knowledge either. As Schulze portrays himself, he turns the skeptical spirit inherent in Kant's critical philosophy against itself, that is, against the positive epistemological claims underlying the limits to our knowledge posited by the critical philosopher. In his review of Schulze's later work

---

[7] In taking Hegel's attack on the 'most recent' skepticism of Schulze to imply an attack on modern skepticism in general, I follow Michael Forster. (See his *Hegel and Skepticism*, chapter 1.) However, I read Schulze's skepticism as a stand-in primarily for the skepticism of Kantian critique in relation to metaphysics, not, as Forster does, primarily as a stand-in for Cartesian and Humean skepticism. These differences will emerge more fully as we proceed.

[8] Beiser, *The Fate of Reason*, 267. Beiser's chapter devoted to explicating and assessing Schulze's skepticism begins with an account of its considerable influence.

[9] More fully: *Aenesidemus, oder Über die Fundamente der von dem Herrn Professor Reinhold in Jena gelieferten Elementarphilosophie: Nebst einer Vertheidigung des Skepticismus gegen die Anmaassungen der Vernunftkritik.*

Hegel accepts the implied standard here of achieving a position or procedure that is maximally undetermined by unjustified presuppositions; and Hegel argues that the position or procedure that most nearly meets that standard is not that of Schulze or of Kant—or of Hume, who is the real patron of Schulzean skepticism—but rather that of the Pyrrhonist skeptics of antiquity.

Schulze's skeptical attack in *Aenesidemus* immediately targets the supposedly new and improved version of the critical philosophy as presented in Karl Leonhard Reinhold's so-called *Elementarphilosophie*. Reinhold develops his philosophical system in several published works between 1789 and 1792.[10] Reinhold's system responds primarily to the felt need for a new *presentation* of the critical philosophy, a presentation that will give to it the systematic form of a science. It is felt that in Kant's presentation, the critical philosophy fails to show the unity of theoretical and practical reason; it is felt further that Kant's presentation fails clearly to show how space and time, as forms of sensibility, and the categories, are ultimately derived from a single source in the human mind. Reinhold exerts great influence in the development of post-Kantian philosophy through his attempt to construct a system in which all the basic elements of the critical philosophy (space, time, the categories, the supreme principle of practical reason) are derived *a priori* from a single, foundational principle.[11]

Though Reinhold takes Kant himself not to be clear or explicit on this point, the most fundamental concept in the critical philosophy, as he sees it, is the concept of *representation* (*Vorstellung*). In contrast to the dogmatic procedure of previous philosophy, the critical philosophy proceeds by deriving *a priori* propositions, or universal and necessary features of the realm of human experience, as requirements of our faculty of representation, that is, as demanded by our way of representing things. So interpreted, the critical procedure *begins* properly from the concept of representation. Accordingly, Reinhold proposes as the first principle of philosophy a principle that expresses the universal and necessary structure of our representational consciousness. This

[10] Beiser devotes an informative chapter to the development and demise of Reinhold's *Elementarphilosophie* in his book *The Fate of Reason*. See also the discussion by Ameriks in *Kant and the Fate of Autonomy*, part II. Part of Reinhold's work entitled *Über das Fundament des philosophischen Wissens* is translated under the title *The Foundation of Philosophical Knowledge* and published in di Giovanni and Harris (eds.), *Between Kant and Hegel: Texts in the Development of Post-Kantian Idealism* (abbreviated BKH), 54–103.

[11] Karl Ameriks argues in his book *Kant and the Fate of Autonomy* that Reinhold's recasting of the critical philosophy as a foundational project misconstrues the critical philosophy and gives an unfortunate turn to subsequent German philosophy. (See in particular the introduction and chs. 1–3.)

principle, called 'the principle of consciousness' (*der Satz des Bewußtseins*), reads as follows: 'In consciousness, the subject distinguishes the representation from the subject and the object and relates it to both.'[12] Granted this first principle, as expressing the universal and necessary form of our representational activity as such, the task is to derive from it *a priori* the complete set of principles of practical and theoretical cognition.

Though other principles in the system are to be validated as derived from the principle of consciousness, the latter, as first and most fundamental, can be derived from no higher. How then is this first principle to be itself known and justified? Reinhold addresses this question as follows:

So determined—independently of all philosophizing, for the latter depends on this original determinateness for its correctness—the concept of representation can only be drawn from the CONSCIOUSNESS of an *actual fact* [*Tatsache*]. This fact alone, *qua fact*, must *ground* the foundation of the *Elementarphilosophie*—for otherwise the foundation cannot rest, without circularity, on any philosophically demonstrable proposition. It is not through any inference of reason that we know *that in consciousness representation is distinguished through the subject from both object and subject and is referred to both*, but through simple *reflection* upon the actual fact of consciousness, that is, by ordering together what is present in it.[13]

The first principle is known by reflection on what is an immediate and certain actual fact of consciousness (*Tatsache des Bewußtseins*). Reinhold writes: 'My principle expresses, *qua principle of consciousness*, only the *actual fact* through which the concept of representation is determined ... Its ground is consciousness, and [more precisely], the fact in consciousness which it expresses' (BKH, 71).

In 'The Foundations of Philosophical Knowledge', Reinhold presents the critical philosophy as the single safe passage between the perils of dogmatism (represented chiefly by the philosophies of Locke and Leibniz) and skepticism (represented chiefly by the work of Hume) (BKH, 57–65). In *Aenesidemus*, Schulze presents himself as defending Humean skepticism against the defeat it has allegedly been dealt at the hands of the critical philosophy. On Schulze's interpretation of the critical philosophy, it means to conquer Hume's doubts 'by deriving a certain part of human cognition from the faculty of representation' (BKH, 106). That the critical philosophy derives the relevant

---

[12] Karl Leonhard Reinhold, *Beiträge zur Berichtigung bisheriger Mißverständnisse der Philosophien*, vol. 1, 167.

[13] Reinhold, *The Foundations of Philosophical Knowledge*, in *Between Kant and Hegel* (BKH), 70. Please see 'Abbreviations' for the full bibliographical information on this text.

part of human cognition from the faculty of representation within us rather than from objects outside us constitutes the claimed advance over previous dogmatic metaphysics and the alleged immunity from Humean skeptical attack (BKH, 118).

However, Schulze, as Aenesidemus, finds that Hume's skeptical arguments are just as valid against the procedure of the critical philosophy as against the earlier dogmatisms. The two most important skeptical weapons Schulze draws from Hume and employs in his counter-attack against the critical philosophy are Hume's skeptical attack on the concept of cause and Hume's challenge to the justification of the step from knowledge of one's representations in consciousness (which Schulze admits is, as such, indubitable and certain) to knowledge of the objective features of things represented. Accordingly, we can summarize two core points of Schulze's Humean skeptical counter-attack against the critical philosophy as follows. First, since the critical philosophy (on his interpretation of it) reasons on the basis of the causal principle from a certain segment of human knowledge to its causal ground in our faculty of representation, the basic procedure of the critical philosophy presupposes the validity of the causal principle, which Hume had already attacked skeptically. Schulze writes: 'Hume would [] require [the author of the *Critique of Pure Reason*] to explain to him what right he had to apply the principle of causality in the groundwork of critical philosophy, and how he could presume, at the very outset of its construction into a system, that a circumstance such as the presence of synthetic necessary propositions in us is the effect of a cause different from them (be this cause what you will)' (BKH, 115). Second, Schulze attacks Reinhold's inference from actual representation to the objective existence of a faculty of representation (BKH, 107–108). All that can be confidently inferred from the undeniable fact of representation is the *representation* of a faculty of representation, not the actual existence of such a faculty external to our representation of it. Schulze describes the characteristic inference of the critical philosophy as follows: 'It [] infers the objective and real constitution of what is to be found outside our representations from the constitution of the representations and thoughts present in us; or, again, it proves that something must be constituted *realiter* in such and such a way because it cannot be thought otherwise.' Schulze continues:

But it is precisely the validity of this kind of inference that Hume questioned. And he declared it to be a sophism because we know of no principle by which we can determine to what extent our representations and their characteristics agree with what is objective and its characteristics, or to what extent something present in our thoughts refers to anything outside them. This inference is the foundation on which every dogmatism is grounded. (BKH, 116)

Schulze's sweeping claim about dogmatism here is noteworthy: every dogmatism is grounded on the inference to the characteristics of what is objective from the characteristics of what is present immediately in consciousness (what is subjective). The critical philosophy, no less than the preceding dogmatic metaphysics that it opposes, is judged guilty of this dogmatism.

J. G. Fichte encounters Schulze's *Aenesidemus* as a relatively recent and particularly ardent convert to the critical philosophy. And he finds his recently acquired Kantian convictions seriously challenged by Schulze's skeptical objections to the critical program. In struggling with *Aenesidemus* in the effort to produce a review of the book, Fichte envisions key innovations to this program, which, after his review is published, he sets immediately about developing and expostulating in his *Wissenschaftslehre*.[14] Though we cannot allow ourselves to be long detained by such matters, a brief reprisal of two aspects of Fichte's response sets the scene for our discussion of Hegel's later response to Schulze's later work.

The first aspect concerns Fichte's response to Schulze's objections to Reinhold's proposed first principle for the system of critical philosophy, the so-called 'Principle of Consciousness'. Fichte claims in the first part of his review that Schulze's objections against Reinhold's principle show, not the truth of skepticism, but only the need for a yet higher principle from which the Principle of Consciousness is in turn derived (I, 2: 42–3/60–1). Schulze objects that this principle is not, as required of a first principle, 'determined completely through itself'. Schulze displays ambiguities in the principle that turn on ambiguities in its key concepts (subject, object, representation) and on ambiguities in the activities of distinguishing and relating. While Fichte acknowledges the indeterminacy of these concepts in Reinhold's principle, he takes this indeterminacy to 'point to a higher principle (which remains to be discovered)' (I, 2: 44/62). One of Schulze's criticisms in particular provides Fichte a clear direction in his search for the higher principle. The principle states, in part, that the subject distinguishes the representation from itself and relates it to itself in consciousness. Schulze notes that these

---

[14] Fichte's 'Review of Aenesidemus' occurs in part I, vol. 2 of the *Gesamtausgabe*, 41–67. It is translated by Daniel Breazeale in *Fichte: Early Philosophical Writings*, 59–77. In citing the review, I cite these two editions. For a discussion of Fichte's 'Review of Aenesidemus' in determining the direction of German Idealism, see Daniel Breazeale, 'Fichte's *Aenesidemus* Review and the Transformation of German Idealism'.

acts of the subject of relating and distinguishing its representation to and from itself must themselves be further acts of representational thinking.[15] But if so, then the analysis of these acts would in turn require appeal to the fundamental structure of representational consciousness of which they are supposed to constitute basic elements. The lesson Fichte draws from this criticism can be found already in Kant's transcendental deduction of the categories. Kant's argument teaches that representation of an object in consciousness presupposes *self-consciousness*; further, that this self-consciousness, as condition of the possibility of representation of an object, cannot be understood as representation of the special object which is oneself, on pain of a regress. This original self-consciousness must have a structure that is not in turn understood in terms of the Principle of Consciousness, but which is, rather, *sui generis*. In this way Schulze's criticism of Reinhold's Principle of Consciousness prompts Fichte to search for a yet higher principle, and directs him toward a principle that expresses the subject's self-consciousness, a self-consciousness that is also, at the same time, self-relating *activity*.[16]

Fichte also accepts Schulze's objection that, insofar as the Principle of Consciousness expresses a mere *fact* of consciousness, it cannot be understood otherwise than as based merely upon empirical self-observation and, *a fortiori*, as contingent. Again, however, Fichte draws his own conclusion from this objection: namely, not that the Principle of Consciousness is contingent, but, again, that it must be derived *a priori* from a yet higher principle. Fichte claims that the *real* first principle is founded on (or expresses) not a mere *fact* of consciousness (*Tatsache des Bewußtseins*) but rather a *Tathandlung* (I, 2:46/64). Breazeale translates *Tathandlung* as 'Act', capitalized to indicate that it is a technical term, Fichte's coinage. The word is a compound of the word for 'deed' (*Tat*) and the word for action (*Handlung*). While the controversial question of what precisely Fichte means to name with this word is one that we must mostly leave unaddressed, a couple of remarks on the question must be made here. In his transcendental deduction of the categories, Kant establishes a principle that expresses what he calls the original synthetic unity of apperception as the highest principle of all of our knowledge. Since this

---

[15] Schulze writes, in response to Reinhold's denial that these acts are representations: 'But an action of the mind which consists in relating and distinguishing is undeniably an act of thinking and therefore also an act of representing; or what else should it be?' (*Aenesidemus*, 53–4 n.).

[16] Fred Neuhouser provides a very helpful discussion of the important role Schulze's criticism of Reinhold's principle plays in Fichte's development of his conception of a first principle as expressing an act of self-positing of the subject in his book *Fichte's Theory of Subjectivity*, 68–73. See also Dieter Henrich's influential article, 'Fichte's Original Insight'.

synthetic activity of the 'I' is necessarily original, in the sense that it cannot intelligibly be referred to something higher as its source or be determined by anything outside of it, Kant describes the original activity, perhaps rather obscurely, as 'self-activity'.[17] Fichte means to name with *Tathandlung* that self-relating activity of the subject, *qua* subject, whereby it possesses the status of responsible subject of norm-governed activity. Whereas the relation of this original self-activity to the autonomy of the subject is muted at best in Kant, in Fichte it is explicit. Fichte states in his review that the critical philosophy is founded upon 'the absolute existence and autonomy of the "I"'; this absolute existence and autonomy is expressed in the first principle insofar as that expresses the I's *Tathandlung*.

We want that the first principle of the critical philosophy be *a priori*, sufficiently rich to serve as the ultimate source for the derivation of the rest of the principles constituting the critical philosophy, and known with certainty. Schulze's objections show that Reinhold fails to achieve jointly these desiderata with his Principle of Consciousness. Although Schulze himself holds that facts of consciousness are indubitable and certain, since the Principle of Consciousness, as universal and necessary, is arrived at only through a process of abstraction from such facts, it does not retain their special epistemic status. Fichte means to correct this deficiency in Reinhold's principle with his revision. For Fichte, in expressing *self-consciousness*, the real first principle is immediately certain. The first principle of the critical philosophy enjoys, in effect, the epistemic status of Descartes's *cogito*. A way Fichte has of putting the first principle of his 1794 *Wissenschaftslehre* is already stated in his review: 'I am absolutely, because I am' (*Ich bin schlechthin, weil ich bin*) (I, 2:57/70). (Fichte echoes Descartes in stating that 'I am' is 'the most immediately certain thing of all' (I, 2:62/73).) What is important here for defeating skeptical doubt is that, in asserting the existence of the 'I', there is no distance between the subject and object of thought on which the skeptical doubt would depend. But, though Fichte's principle may remind us of Descartes's *cogito* in this respect, Fichte suggests a marked departure from Descartes's procedure at the same time. Whereas the meditator in Descartes's *Meditations* immediately moves from the certainty that he exists to the determination that he is a *thing that thinks*, which immediately raises the question of the causal ground of the thing that he is, Fichte claims that the critical philosopher remains within the immediate self-certainty of the 'I' as such. Insofar as what I am immediately

---

[17] Kant, KrV, B130.

certain of through this self-consciousness, according to Fichte, is myself as self-activity, as source of my norm-governed activity, I am led, not as in the *Meditations* to query the causal ground of my being or of my ideas, but rather to query the necessary conditions of this self-activity. What remains absolute, as implicitly expressed in the first principle, is my autonomy as thinking subject, my standing as the responsible author of my norm-governed activity.

This brings us to the second of the two aspects of Fichte's response to Schulze's skepticism that bear discussion as background to Hegel's. Fichte understands Schulze's accusation that the critical philosophy itself is dogmatic to indicate merely that Schulze has failed to grasp the Copernican revolution in epistemology; the accusation only seems to have force because one conceives knowledge according to the pre-critical (hence, dogmatic) paradigm. Recall that for Schulze the dogmatism of the critical philosophy consists in its inference from our representations to the existence of a faculty of representing, as existing objectively, independently of being represented. The critical inference to the existence of the faculty of representing is an instance of the general type of inference from subjective representation to objective being, existing in itself, which Schulze identifies as 'the foundation on which all dogmatism is grounded'. Fichte writes: 'Aenesidemus cannot express sufficient amazement that Reinhold, as a Critical philosopher, should make the following inference … : "Anyone who admits a representation at the same time admits a faculty of representation".' Fichte responds:

The reviewer, or perhaps anyone very inclined toward amazement, may express no less amazement over the skeptic, for whom only a short time ago nothing was certain except that there are various representations in us, and who now, as soon as he hears the words 'faculty of representation', can think only of some sort of thing (round or square?) which exists as a thing in itself, *independently of its being represented*, and indeed, exists as a thing which *represents*. (I, 2:50/66–7)

In other words, it is the skeptic himself who imports the conception of the *task* of knowledge against the background of which alone the skeptic's denial of the knowledge claimed by the critical philosopher is motivated. Granted that the task of knowing consists in securing conformity of representations to independently existing objects or things, then the skeptical denial of such knowledge is motivated. But this conception of the task of knowledge does not belong to the critical philosopher, but is rather inherited by the skeptic from earlier dogmatic philosophy. The great contribution of the critical philosophy, as Fichte interprets it, is exactly to overturn this conception. He writes: 'But this *passage* from the external to the internal or vice versa is precisely what is in question. It is precisely the task of the Critical Philosophy to show that no such passage is required, and everything which occurs in our mind can be completely explained and comprehended on the basis of the mind itself' (I, 2:55/69). Thus, Fichte understands Schulze's skeptical objection regarding the inference to the existence of a faculty of representation to be based on a gross misreading of the teaching of the critical philosophy: 'The faculty of representation', he writes, 'exists *for* the faculty of representation and *through* the faculty of representation: this is the circle within which every finite understanding, that is, every understanding that we can conceive, is necessarily confined. Anyone who wants to escape from this circle does not understand himself and does not know what he wants' (I, 2:51/67). Fichte refers at several places in his review to this 'circle within which the human mind is enclosed'. He claims that the skeptical objection against the critical philosophy can only seem to have force to someone who has failed to grasp this circle as the primary discovery and teaching of the critical philosophy.

Insofar as Fichte evades the accusation of dogmatism by claiming that, in the critical philosophy, what exists is said to exist only *for* or *through* our representation, not independently, he may seem to erase the difference between the critical philosophy and the Humean system. Does not the Humean system—on Schulze's skeptical interpretation of it—also teach that we know only our own perceptions (representations)? Fichte explicitly addresses this question as follows:

The difference consists entirely in this: the Humean system holds open the possibility that we might some day be able to go beyond the boundary of the human mind, whereas the Critical system proves that such progress is absolutely impossible, and it shows that the thought of a thing possessing existence and specific properties *in itself* and apart from any faculty of representation is a piece of whimsy, a pipe dream, a non-thought. And to this extent the Humean system is skeptical and the Critical system is dogmatic—indeed *negatively* so. (I, 2:57/71)

There are two points here. First, even if the Humean skeptical philosophy also claims that *we in fact* know only our representations and that we are in that sense confined within the circle mentioned above, the Humean philosophy sees no *necessity* to this limit. In contrast, it is a central teaching of the critical philosophy that this limit to our knowledge is necessary. The second point is the one already indicated above. The skeptical teaching depends on claiming that we don't know that our representations conform to the independently existing objects; but, in teaching the reversal of the relation of representations to objects in knowledge presupposed by this skeptical teaching, the critical philosophy undercuts the skeptical teaching. Once one takes the point that the thought of the thing existing *in itself*, over against our representation, is itself a non-thought, then skeptical dissatisfaction with our knowledge must disappear. Again, '[a]nyone who wants to escape from this circle [the circle of the mind, the circle of our representations] does not understand himself and does not know what he wants'.

A significant tension exists between these two points: between the claim, on the one hand, that the critical philosophy specifies necessary, determinate limits to our cognition, and the claim, on the other, that the thought of that which is supposed to lie on the opposite side of this limit (the *in itself*) is 'a piece of whimsy, a pipe dream, a non-thought'. Granted the second claim, what sense can be given to the assertion of limits to our knowledge in the first? If the critical philosophy is, as Fichte claims here, negatively dogmatic, in the sense that it asserts the denial of the possibility of our knowledge of certain propositions, then those propositions must have sense; they must express thoughts.[18] Fichte would secure our satisfaction with our knowledge within the critical system of philosophy by showing the thought of the thing in itself to be a non-thought; the basis on which he does this is essentially the Berkeleyan consideration that a thought of that which exists independently of being represented is contradictory. At the same time, however, Fichte wants to assert the determinate, necessary limits to human knowledge, expressive of our finitude, that are stated by Kant in the claim that we know only appearances, not things as they are in themselves.

This tension recalls the instability in the critical philosophy expressed classically by Jacobi in his confession that, without the concept of the thing in itself, he could not enter the critical system, but with that concept, he could not remain there. It belongs essentially to the standpoint of the critical philosophy that it asserts its standpoint—the standpoint of the reflecting, criticizing, knowing subject—as self-standing or, in the words of Fichte, as 'absolute' and 'autonomous'; but, at the same time, it belongs essentially to the criticizing, knowing subject to recognize its limits, and hence to recognize itself as standing over against, and as dependent on, another standpoint that is alone absolute. The tension seems nicely condensed in the following few sentences from Fichte's review: 'Aenesidemus's objections against this procedure are all based upon his desire to make the absolute existence and

---

[18] See section 1.4, where I discuss Kant's conception of the thing in itself as a concept necessary for the critical limits to knowledge.

autonomy of the I, which is valid only *for the I itself*, into something which is valid *in itself*—we do not know how or for whom. The I is *what* it is, it is *because* it is, and it is *for* the I. Our knowledge can extend no further than this' (I, 2:57/70–1). How are we to understand the existence of the I as *both* absolute *and yet* valid only *for* the I? What does the 'for the I' restriction mean? How do we understand the restriction without at the same time qualifying the I's claim to exist absolutely, entirely through itself alone?

According to Hegel's reading of it, Fichte's *Wissenschaftslehre* does not manage to square the circle here; that is, it does not manage to make good on its opening claim, in its first principle, to the absoluteness of the I. The admission, indeed insistence, that the I exists only *for the I*, not in itself, already establishes the tension that is never resolved within the system. In the end of the *Wissenschaftslehre*, the absolute is figured merely as a necessary practical ideal for us, an object of practical *faith*, as something that *is not*, but *ought to be*. Hegel interprets this maneuver, the conception of the absolute as an object of practical faith within the critical philosophy, as a symptom of despair and self-alienation. As we will see below, Hegel regards the attempt to make ourselves satisfied within the circle of self-consciousness, within the critical limits to knowledge, as desperate and hopeless. According to Hegel's presentation in his article on skepticism, because the ancient skeptics already knew this, they sought tranquility in the skeptical annihilation of all dogmas.

3.3 ANCIENT VERSUS MODERN SKEPTICISM: HEGEL'S DIFFERENCE

The work by Schulze to which Hegel explicitly responds in his review article, namely Schulze's *Kritik der theoretischen Philosophie* (1801), makes more evident than the *Aenesidemus* (1792) that Schulze's skepticism is directed against *philosophy in general* (more particularly theoretical philosophy), not just the critical philosophy of Kant, Reinhold, and Fichte. Schulze skeptically attacks in the later work the doctrines of the 'realistic dogmatism' of both the empiricist variety (Locke) and the rationalist variety (Leibniz) before attacking the 'idealistic dogmatism' of the Kantian school. However, judged in terms of the proportions of the work dedicated to its different opponents, the most serious target of Schulze's skepticism in effect remains the Kantian critical philosophy. Given that, it can appear that Hegel's attack on Schulze's skepticism amounts—implicitly, at least—to a defense of the critical philosophy, just as

Fichte's earlier attack on Schulze's skepticism quite explicitly defends Kant's critical program. In fact, however, Hegel's case against Schulze's skepticism, far from defending the critical philosophy, actually includes it within its target. Despite the fact that some of Hegel's main points against Schulze's skepticism recall those Fichte makes in his review of *Aenesidemus*, the main features of Schulzean epistemology that Hegel finds objectionable are ones he takes it to share with (or to have borrowed from) the critical philosophy. Hegel means his attack on Schulze's 'most recent' skepticism to defend, not critical philosophy, but *philosophy itself*, as knowledge of the absolute. As Hegel sees it, Schulze's main skeptical arguments are borrowed from the case of the critical philosopher against the possibility of metaphysics and are based on the same dogmatic assumptions. Whereas Fichte's attack on Schulze's skepticism consists in his attempt to highlight and make available what he thinks of as the overlooked 'new discovery' in epistemology and philosophy that belongs to the critical philosophy, Hegel's attack consists rather in his attempt at the *recovery* of an ancient way of philosophical knowing that he sees as obscured within the contemporary 'age of criticism'.

Although Hegel sees the dogmatism of Schulze's epistemology as a reflection of the dogmatism of Kant's critical procedure, he does not rank Schulze's thought with Kant's. On the contrary. In the terms of his evaluative distinction, which he employs in his critical review essays published in the *Critical Journal*, between what he calls 'Unphilosophy' and the genuine article, Hegel categories Schulze's skepticism with the former and Kant's system with the latter. The difference between 'Unphilosophy' and genuine philosophy is that the absolute, the object of philosophical cognition, is expressed, in however obscure or distorted a form, in a system that counts as genuine philosophy, whereas 'Unphilosophy' in no way expresses the truth, but is instead pure pretension, subjectivity, or nothingness. For Hegel, though philosophy's 'Idea' is clearly expressed at points in Kant's system: 'It is the spirit of Kantian philosophy to have consciousness of the highest Idea, only expressly to destroy it again. We distinguish, therefore, two spirits that become visible in the Kantian philosophy: one of philosophy, which always destroys the system, and another of the system, which seeks the death of the Idea of reason' (Hegel, VSP, 269/352). However, importantly, this distinction Hegel recognizes between two spirits in the Kantian philosophy amounts to a distinction between the respect in which the system is *speculative* and the respect in which it is *critical*. As criticism, as a distinctive epistemological project, Kant's thought seeks the death of the Idea of reason; as such, it is subjectivism (Hegel, GW, 301/67). In his skeptical attack on philosophical cognition, Schulze holds to the letter of the 'spiritless spirit' of the Kantian philosophy, according to Hegel. Thus, Hegel's attack on Schulze's skepticism can consistently have within its scope Kantian *criticism*, even as Hegel recognizes Kantian *philosophy*, read spiritfully, as itself genuine philosophy.

One can draw from the title of Hegel's review article alone that the main point of Hegel's comparison of ancient and modern skepticisms concerns the relation of skepticism to philosophy in the various skeptical schools. According to Hegel's reading of the history of skepticism, there has been a stark (and for him, unfortunate) reversal with respect to this relation, a reversal that emerges most clearly by examining the relation of each to a third, namely, to ordinary cognition or the knowledge of ordinary consciousness. Schulze's skepticism denies philosophical knowledge in particular, but is 'one with' ordinary cognition, understanding the latter as cognition of mere appearances or phenomena. The most ancient skepticism, in contrast, is 'one with philosophy' or is merely its negative side, while it is characteristic of ancient skepticism to be turned first of all against 'the dogmatism of ordinary consciousness'. Hegel's account of the history of skeptical schools, insofar as he tells it in this article, is the story of an unremitting decline into dogmatism, culminating in the 'newest' skepticism, which grants undeniable certainty to facts of consciousness, while rejecting all philosophical or rational knowledge as dogmatic.

Before presenting Hegel's case against Schulze's skepticism and the basis of his recommendation of the ancient procedure in contrast to it, it will be helpful to present briefly the two skepticisms in immediate opposition to each other. Since we have already presented the main outlines of Schulze's skepticism in the *Aenesidemus*, it remains here only to specify how the skepticism of the later work is directed exclusively against philosophical cognition. Hegel quotes from Schulze's text the following definition of theoretical philosophy: it is 'the science of the highest and most unconditioned causes of all conditioned things the actuality of which we are otherwise certain' (VSP, 219/317). On Schulze's picture, what consciousness delivers us immediately 'in and with itself'—namely (following Reinhold) 'facts of consciousness'—cannot be doubted. According to Schulze, it would no more be possible for me to doubt the actuality of the table in front of me *as consciousness presents it to me*, that is, as a fact of consciousness, than it would be to doubt consciousness itself; such a doubt destroys itself (VSP, 220/318). However, despite the fact that the actuality of these 'things of consciousness' is indubitably certain, consciousness presents them to us as *conditioned*. In philosophy, then, we attempt to go beyond what our consciousness presents us in order to know the ground of the being of these things of consciousness, that is, their unconditioned causes. At this point, the skeptical axe falls. As in Schulze's earlier work, dogmatism here also consists in making the inference from the phenomena immediately present in consciousness to the things existing *in themselves*, external to and independently of our representation of them. According to the skeptical position Schulze advances, philosophical knowledge, conceived of as knowledge of the unconditioned causes of the conditioned things with which our consciousness presents us, as well as knowledge of the sources and, hence, limits of our cognition, is impossible for us.

What, in contrast, is ancient skepticism, according to Hegel's conception? Ancient skepticism does not constitute a monolithic school, and Hegel discusses several of its main variants, including the main division between so-called 'Academic' skepticism—the various skeptical teachings that achieved prominence and succeeded each other in the Academy—and Pyrrhonism, 'the way' that originates with Pyrrho of Elis in the fourth century BCE. Hegel relies for his discussion of Pyrrhonism mostly (though not exclusively) on the writings of Sextus Empiricus, the second-century chronicler of Pyrrhonism. As Sextus defines 'skepticism' in his *Outlines of Scepticism*, it consists in 'an ability to set out oppositions among things which appear and are thought of in any way at all, an ability by which, because of the equipollence in the opposed objects and accounts, we come first to suspension of judgment and afterwards to tranquility'.[19] For any claim presented to the skeptic, the skeptic has the ability to construct equal arguments on both sides of the question. The activity of constructing these arguments leads to suspension of judgment on the question, which in turn is followed by what is the *aim* of this activity, namely, tranquility or lack of disturbance in the soul. In his *Outlines of Scepticism*, Sextus presents and discusses each in a list of seventeen argument patterns or modes that the Pyrrhonian skeptics employ to construct their equipollence arguments. The main division in this list is between the first set of ten and the second set of five. (Sextus discusses two tropes in addition to these fifteen, but Hegel treats them dismissively.) Sextus attributes the first ten to Aenesidemus, though Hegel regards them as originating with Pyrrho. The following five, the so-called 'modes of Agrippa', are later and more abstract and are most naturally directed against foundational assertions. Although the Pyrrhonist skeptics employ their argument tropes to suspend judgment

---

[19] Sextus Empiricus, *Outlines of Scepticism*, I. 8.

on *every* question, and therefore 'come to hold no beliefs', they 'acquiesce in' appearances that are forced upon them. The skeptics 'live according to appearances', in the sense that, in their daily lives, they follow the promptings of nature within them and adhere to the social customs surrounding them. But the appearances they live by 'depend on passive and unwilled feelings and are not objects of investigation'.[20] As such, acquiescing in such appearances does not (or, anyway, is not supposed to) compromise their skeptical attitude.

An immediate difficulty confronts the attempt to regard Schulze's skepticism as representative of modern skepticism in general in the comparison of it with Pyrrhonism. Generally, what is regarded as distinctive of modern skepticism (or even of modern epistemology in general) is the problem of the 'veil of perception' or of the 'existence of the external world'. According to this familiar problem, the epistemological task is to show how we can possibly know that objects are in themselves, outside of our consciousnesses, as we represent them to be, given that the representations may be as they are in our consciousness even if the objects in themselves either do not exist at all or exist otherwise than as we represent them. Compared to the skepticism motivated by this problem, Schulze's skepticism seems quite permissive, since he attacks only our knowledge of the objects of philosophical cognition, noumena or things in themselves. On the assumption that the knowledge claims in the natural sciences of physics and astronomy are of phenomena, Schulze includes the claims of such sciences in the category of things immune from skeptical doubt. While Schulze's 'philosophical knowledge skepticism'—as we might awkwardly call it—merely confines us in our knowing to Kant's realm of possible experience—that is, to the public, shared world of Kantian phenomena, which may seem hardly a confinement at all—external world skepticism confines a person to the passing show within her own individual consciousness. Given that Schulze's philosophical knowledge skepticism is so permissive in comparison to the external world skepticism supposedly characteristic of modern philosophy, how can Hegel's targeting of the former be taken to have the broader significance of addressing the contrast of ancient and modern skepticisms in general?

Because Michael Forster in his book *Hegel and Skepticism* also takes Hegel in the review article to be criticizing modern epistemological procedure in general, he explicitly addresses this question. On Forster's interpretation, what characterizes distinctively modern skepticism for Hegel, such that his

[20] *Ibid.,* I. 11.

attack against Schulze has modern skepticism in general as a target, is that modern skepticism is founded on a cluster of epistemological *problems*; whereas ancient skepticism in contrast consists primarily in a perfectly general *method*.[21] Forster characterizes the problems of epistemology that are the basis of distinctively modern skepticism as follows: they 'concern the legitimacy of proceeding from claims about a specific kind of subject matter, the knowledge of which is assumed to be absolutely or relatively unproblematic, to claims about a second kind of subject matter, the knowledge of which is not felt to be unproblematic in the same way'.[22] Modern skeptical arguments thus typically involve attachment to a certain group of knowledge claims which form a contrast with another set of knowledge claims, which latter set, by virtue of their difference, pose the skeptical problem. He writes: 'At one time the unproblematic subject matter might be one's own (current) mental states, and the problematic subject matter the external world [as in external world skepticism]. At another time, the unproblematic subject matter might be the external physical world and the problematic subject matter the objects of religious beliefs [as in Schulze's philosophical knowledge skepticism].'[23] According to Forster, because external world skepticism shares this structure with Schulze's, Hegel's argument that ancient skepticism is superior to Schulze's amounts to a case for the superiority of ancient over modern skepticism in general. Because they press specific epistemological problems, modern skeptics perforce presuppose as valid a set of claims on the basis of which these specific problems are constructed. Because they are in contrast attached only to the method of constructing equipollence arguments, the ancient skeptics can accept the claims on the basis of which they construct their arguments provisionally from their opponents, without believing them. Hence, the ancient Pyrrhonists can withhold judgment on all questions and hence maintain a more thoroughgoing skepticism than the modern skeptic is capable of.

While not taking issue with this specific point of difference between ancient and modern skepticism, I would characterize differently Hegel's understanding of what constitutes the modern in epistemology in virtue of which he judges it dogmatic in comparison with the ancient procedure. At a minimum, Forster's characterization quoted above omits what seems essential to the commonality of the two modern skeptical problems from Hegel's point of view (that is, external world skepticism and philosophical knowledge skepticism). Insofar as both regard the essential problem of knowledge to be

---

[21] Forster, *Hegel and Skepticism*, 10–11.   [22] *Ibid.*, 11.   [23] Ibid.

the inference from what is regarded as immediately present in consciousness, hence as inner (the perception or the concept), to what is determined as external to consciousness and standing over against representation, they represent us as confined in our knowing to the circle of self-consciousness. It is at least misleading to describe what counts for Schulze as the 'unproblematic subject matter' as the 'external, physical world' since exactly what makes the subject matter of the physical world unproblematic for knowledge, according to Schulze, is that it is *not external* (that is, not external to our consciousness). Correspondingly, exactly what makes philosophical knowledge problematic for Schulze is that it consists of claims about things *in themselves*, things standing over against—external to or beyond—our representation of them. What veil of perception skepticism and Schulze's skepticism most significantly share is the conception of our epistemic situation according to which, while we have unproblematic access to things *internal* to our consciousness, since nothing justifies the inference from internal mental content to claims about things existing outside of the mind (determined as intentional objects or causal grounds of the mental content), we are confined in our knowing within the circle of self-consciousness. To put it metaphorically, the difference between Schulze's skepticism and other distinctively modern skepticisms consists only in their views regarding the length of the radius of the circle of self-consciousness within which they understand us to be confined in our knowledge. Less metaphorically, the difference consists in the precise manner in which they draw what is at a general level of description the same boundary: namely, that between the subject's knowledge of what is conceived of as subjectively determined and the problematic knowledge of that which may exist in itself, external to and independently of representational faculties of the knowing subject.

In short, what is characteristic of modern skepticism, indeed of modern epistemology in general, is subjectivism. Hegel takes the modern skeptic's denial of knowledge to presuppose as epistemologically prior and privileged the knowing subject's knowledge of its representations or of itself. As motivated principally by anxiety regarding the possibility of rational or metaphysical knowledge in particular, the characteristic move of modern epistemology is to restrict knowledge claims to that which is conceived of as subjectively determined, while attempting in some way to do without knowledge of the objective, the in itself, the absolute, conceived of as external to or other than consciousness. According to the case Hegel makes in the Skepticism article, this move characteristic of modern epistemology is symptomatic of the ascendancy of the ordinary understanding and the corresponding forget-fulness of reason's Idea in the modern period. Because Hegel takes the ancient skepticism effectively to attack the dogmatism of ordinary consciousness first of all, and thereby to raise consciousness to consciousness of the Idea, he takes it to be infinitely more skeptical than modern varieties.

First I present Hegel's case against the 'negative side' of Schulze's skep-ticism, Schulze's attack on rational or philosophical cognition; second, I present his attack on its 'positive side', the claim that facts of consciousness enjoy undeniable certainty.

3.4 AGAINST THE MODERN CONCEPTION OF RATIONAL COGNITION

Hegel implicitly accepts the claim that philosophy aims to know 'the highest and unconditioned causes of things'—or 'the rational or the in-itself'. But everything depends for him on how one understands these terms and on how one conceives the task of philosophical cognition. Schulze is gripped, Hegel complains, by the crassest picture of such cognition:

The highest and unconditioned causes themselves, however (or, better, the rational) Herr Schulze understands as yet other *things*, which transcend our consciousness, something existing, something absolutely opposed to consciousness. No other idea of rational cognition [i.e., of philosophy] is ever advanced but this (repeated *ad nauseum*) through which a knowledge of things should be acquired which lie hidden *behind* the shadows of things which the natural cognition offers us … Schulze cannot represent to himself the rational, the in-itself, otherwise than as a cliff under snow. (VSP, 219–20/317)

Besides conceiving the rational, the in-itself, as yet other things, Schulze understands these things to differ saliently from the things which they con-dition, first by virtue of being in some sense more real, and second by virtue of being *hidden* exactly by their presentation or their effects in conscious-ness. In order to acquire knowledge of them in philosophy, we would have somehow to achieve a standpoint outside of our consciousness from which the contents of consciousness could be compared with what exists externally and independently. Schulze's skepticism is predicated on such a conception of philosophical or rational cognition.

Though Hegel's objection here undoubtedly echoes Fichte's complaint that the skepticism of *Aenesidemus* depends on what Fichte calls 'the old mischief' according to which knowledge is attained exclusively through the dubious inference from inner representation to outer thing, Hegel's objection here is significantly different. Fichte finds the old mischief to be corrected by the *discovery* in the critical philosophy of the circle within which the mind is enclosed and by what goes with this, the enactment of the Copernican revolution in epistemology. For Hegel, in contrast, the relevant mischief consists in conceiving of the standards and tasks of *ordinary* cognition as those of cognition itself. Hegel attributes the mischief in Schulze's skepticism to the fact that 'the concept of a philosophy itself' escapes him (VSP, 227/323). His skepticism derives from the fact that he conceives philosophical cognition on the model of ordinary cognition or of cognition of the ordinary understanding. In this, Schulze manifests his debt to the critical philosophy.

How does Schulze's skepticism presuppose a model of the task of cognition that belongs to ordinary consciousness, and what is Hegel's model of philosophical cognition, such that it escapes the skeptical problems that Schulze raises? Schulze's skepticism essentially results from generalizing the problem of 'veil of perception' to include all representations, including supposedly *a priori* concepts. Instead of knowing the object of philosophical cognition through perception, we are supposed to know it on the basis of *a priori* concepts. But, according to the skeptical conception, concepts are no less representations in the mind than perceptions are, and so the same problem arises of how we can be sure that they conform to the really existing thing standing over against them. All we have on the basis of which to acquire knowledge of the object of philosophy, the rational or the in-itself, is 'concepts, fundamental principles, and inferences from concepts'. 'The bridge to the *hidden things* can be built out of nothing else but *concepts*' (VSP, 219/317). But such resources for knowledge are self-defeating, since the concepts themselves are conceived as constituting the veil that hides the things themselves from us. Hegel comments:

According to this latest skepticism, the human faculty of knowledge is a thing which has concepts, and because it has nothing but concepts, it cannot go outside itself to the external things. It can neither *investigate* nor *find out* about them, because [concepts and things] are different *in kind*; no rational person will claim that in *possessing* the *representation* of something, he likewise *possesses* the thing itself. (VSP, 252–3/341)

For Hegel, to use this skeptical trope (the difference between representation and thing represented) against rational cognition or philosophy shows merely that one lacks the concept of philosophy altogether.

The importance of the opposition Hegel recognizes between the standpoint of 'ordinary consciousness' (*das gemeine Bewußtsein*) and the standpoint of philosophical knowledge in the context of understanding his epistemology cannot be overestimated. 'The principle of ordinary consciousness', Hegel states, is 'non-identity', whereas the principle of philosophy is identity (VSP, 251/339). What does this mean? Ordinary consciousness conceives of itself as knowing objects that stand over against its consciousness of them. Ordinary consciousness claims knowledge of its objects through sense perception and the understanding. It knows via *representation* (*Vorstellung*). And it belongs to the very concept of representation that the thing represented is distinct from the representation of it (usually different *in kind*). The very principle of ordinary consciousness and its knowledge is in this sense 'non-identity' or the opposition between *representational* thought and thing. This opposition or non-identity 'constitutes the ground', Hegel states, 'endlessly repeated and everywhere applied, of this [Schulze's] dogmatic skepticism' (VSP, 251/339). The main skeptical argument consists in pointing out that, since the representation and the thing represented are 'different in kind', we cannot establish that things themselves are as we represent them to be.

However, the application of this ground of skepticism merely begs the question against *philosophical* cognition—it merely indicates the lack of the concept of philosophy—since the principle of philosophy, according to Hegel, is precisely the *identity* of thought and being. That is, what constitutes philosophical or rational cognition is that it expresses an identity of being and thinking. How are being and thinking identical in philosophical cognition? Hegel's own considered view is that no short answer to that question can satisfy (indeed, he maintains later that the labor of the *Phenomenology of Spirit* is required in order to comprehend philosophy's principle of identity). Still, we can draw here the abstract contrast with ordinary consciousness or representational thinking. Whereas at the level of representational thinking, the object stands over against the representation of it, different in kind, in rising to pure thought or reason, we rise to a standpoint in which thought or reason is concerned solely with itself, with its own principles. Philosophical knowledge is not *of an object* as something standing over against *our* conceptions of it, but rather the *self-knowledge of reason itself*, insofar as reason articulates its basic principles and concepts from this standpoint. At the level of philosophical thinking, pure reason knows itself as the ultimate ground of reality. This identity of thinking and what is thought characterizes philosophical thinking *alone*, which is why philosophy alone constitutes genuine knowing.

Insofar as we think of the object of rational knowledge—the unconditioned, the absolute, God—as a 'thing' to which our conceptions are to conform in knowing, we succumb to the prejudices of ordinary cognition in construing the task of philosophical cognition. Hegel points to the relation between the German words for 'thing' (*Ding*) and 'conditioned' (*bedingt*) in order to contest the assumption of the Schulzean skeptic regarding philosophical knowledge, according to which philosophy has for its objects 'other *things*, which transcend our consciousness'. *Das Unbedingtes ist kein Ding*, in this sense (the sense, that is, in which a thing is as such determined through its conditions and relations to other things).[24] Like Plato's forms or 'Ideas', the object of metaphysics for Hegel, which Hegel calls 'the Idea' after Plato, is conceived of as the ground of the being of conditioned things. 'The Idea' is conceived of as an identity of thinking and being, and hence as unconditioned, partly through the fact that its concept or its essence is not distinct from (or is identical to) its being or its existence. Thus for Hegel the process of coming to know the object of metaphysics is a matter of *elevating oneself* to the Idea, as opposed to a matter of securing conformity of a representation in consciousness to an independently existing reality.

Hegel notes that the single trope of Schulze's skepticism, applying the fixed distinction between concept and thing, is simply borrowed from Kant's criticism of metaphysics (VSP, 253/341). Kant's criticism of metaphysics expresses, according to Hegel, the making absolute of the common understanding and its presupposition of the fixed opposition between thinking and being. Metaphysics or rational cognition is not so much refuted as occluded or forgotten in Kant's critique; as Hegel reads it, Kant's critique of metaphysics expresses in highly explicit and abstract form the opposition between thinking and being that is characteristic of ordinary consciousness or understanding. In expressing this opposition in a pure form, Kant's thought expresses the spirit of the age, 'the age of criticism', which is infatuated with the common understanding and its way of knowing through experience.

Examination of Kant's alleged refutation of the so-called 'ontological argument' for God's existence, to which Hegel refers in the context of claiming

---

[24] Schelling draws out these etymological points in an early essay. See § 3 of 'Of the I as Principle of Philosophy, or On the Unconditional in Human Knowledge' (1795).

that Schulze simply borrows his skeptical trope from Kant's philosophy, illustrates how the case against metaphysics consists in implicitly absolutizing finite cognition, or in presupposing the validity of the criteria of ordinary cognition over against the criterion of rational knowledge. The proponent of the ontological argument claims that, since the concept of the supremely perfect being includes its existence, to assert its non-existence would be contradictory. Kant's refutation turns famously on the claim that being or existence is such that it cannot belong to the content of a concept: '"being" is obviously not a real predicate; that is, it is not a concept of something which could be added to the concept of a thing. It is merely the positing of a thing, or of certain determinations, as existing in themselves' (Kant, KrV, A598/B626). Or, as he also puts it: 'Whatever, therefore, and however much, our concept of an object may contain, we must go *outside* it, if we are to ascribe existence to the object' (A601/B629, my emphasis). The question of the being or existence of God, Kant points out, is the question of whether there is anything in the world ('outside' the concept) which corresponds to what is represented through the concept. Kant makes vivid this heterogeneity between existence or being, on the one hand, and concepts on the other with his memorable example of the hundred *Thalers*: 'A hundred real *Thalers* do not contain the least coin more than a hundred possible *Thalers*'. The existence or non-existence of what is represented through the concept can neither add to, nor detract from, what is represented through the concept. Granted this fundamental difference between concept and being, no judgment of existence can be justified through reflection on concepts alone.

Hegel indicates that Kant's case against the ontological argument merely expresses the presuppositions of a standpoint that is for Hegel simply as such contrasted with that of philosophy. Kant's example of the hundred *Thalers* betrays this. Kant takes a characteristic feature of finite or empirical cognition in particular to characterize cognition as such, and shows on that basis that infinite or rational cognition (i.e., metaphysics) is impossible for us. Indeed, nothing is more obvious than that representations—to use Hegel's pointed term—are different from the things represented through them. And given any *representation*, no matter its content, we can in general motivate the question whether there is anything (*outside* of it) to which it corresponds. But, from Hegel's point of view, to apply this distinction between the representation and the represented to 'the Idea', to God, simply betrays what he calls a 'fundamentally false representation of rational thinking' (VSP, 253/341). God is the traditional object of metaphysics by virtue of the fact that 'God' is the name of that in which concept and object, essence and existence, are identical. From Hegel's perspective, Kant's move against the ontological argument expresses merely the claim that we cannot know God (the unconditioned or absolute that is the object of philosophy) through *representation*. This is hardly to say more than that we cannot know God through perception. This would imply the impossibility of knowledge of God (hence of metaphysics, taking God to be the object of metaphysics) only if representation were the only way of knowing. But, for Hegel, pure thinking is exactly not representational. Kant's case against the ontological argument implicitly relies on the claim that all we have for rational cognition are representations, that is, subjective, mentalistic items, to which being is external, something other. The operative claim here, on which the denial of the possibility of metaphysics depends, is presupposed—a part of the initial starting point or orientation.[25]

Interestingly, Kant himself comments (if somewhat obliquely) on the corruption philosophy has suffered through the presuppositions of modern epistemology when he comments at the beginning of the Transcendental Dialectic of the *Critique of Pure Reason* on the fate of the word 'idea' and pleads on behalf of philosophy for the recovery of its original sense. However, looked at from the perspective of Hegel explained above, Kant advances the project of modern epistemology even at this point in which he laments it. When Kant introduces the ideas of reason in the Dialectic of the First *Critique* as the traditional quarry of metaphysical pursuit, he refers us to the philosophy of Plato. He frames his introduction of ideas (in section 1 of the first book of the Dialectic, 'The Ideas in General') with a discussion of the fate of the word 'idea', of the importance of rescuing its ancient meaning from modern distortion.

Plato made use of the expression 'idea' in such a way as quite evidently to have meant by it something which not only can never be borrowed from the senses but far surpasses even the concepts of the understanding (with which Aristotle occupied

---

[25] Hegel's objection to Kant's 'refutation' of the ontological argument should not be taken to imply that he endorses the argument as a direct proof of God's existence. Hegel's most immediate point is that Kant's refutation of the argument begs the question against the possibility of philosophical cognition through implicitly annihilating its 'highest Idea': the identity of essence and existence, of thinking and being. According to Hegel in this Skepticism article, this highest idea is 'the absolute and single principle of metaphysics' (VSP, 255 342–3). The labor of philosophy has always consisted in nothing else but 'knowing and expressing' this Idea. Since philosophy's task is just to *arrive* at the Idea—since the nature, the intelligibility, and the possibility of the Idea, of this identity, is just philosophy's task—we can't begin with it as immediately self-evident, as the proponent of the ontological argument would do. Hence, understood in a particular way, insofar as it takes the thought of God or of the Idea for granted, the ontological argument may well amount to an aversion of the work of philosophy no less than Kant's criticism of it does.

himself), inasmuch as in experience nothing is ever to be met with that corresponds to it [*damit Kongruierendes*]. For Plato ideas are the archetypes of the things themselves [*Urbilde der Dingen selbst*] ... In his view they have issued from the highest reason which, however, is now no longer in its original condition, but is constrained laboriously to recall, by a process of reminiscence [*Erinnerung*] (which is named philosophy), the ancient ideas, now very much obscured. (Kant, KrV, A313/B370)

On the Platonic conception, genuine knowledge must be of the ideas, since only they are self-identical; sensible things, in contrast, are not unqualifiedly what they are. The idealism of Plato's Doctrine of the Forms consists centrally in the claim that the ideas alone are self-subsisting reality. Plato's forms are, of course, in no sense subjective or 'dependent on the mind', as 'ideas' tend to be conceived in modern epistemology. If, according to Plato, the task of philosophy is 'to recall ... the ancient ideas, now very much obscured', as Kant claims, then that task is made that much more difficult by modern subjectivism, which threatens to erase the very meaning of the ancient 'idea' altogether. In this context, Kant's plea at the end of this section takes on special significance:

Yet, before closing these introductory remarks, I beseech those who have the interests of philosophy at heart (which is more than is the case with most people) that, ... they be careful to preserve the expression 'idea' in its original meaning, that it may not become one of those expressions which are commonly used to indicate any and every species of representation, in a happy-go-lucky confusion, to the consequent detriment of science. (A319/B376)

Kant opposes here, of course, the use in philosophy—influenced in particular by empiricism—of 'idea' as a generic term for *representations* before the mind.

However it becomes clear in the immediately following passage (if it isn't sufficiently clear already in this one) that Kant nevertheless understands 'idea' to be a species of representation (though a particular species, not 'any and every species'). Kant follows these lines with his famous *Stufenleiter* passage, in which he gives the 'serial arrangement' of the genus representation, arranged from lowest to highest, where the highest is the most pure, the least tied to experience. The penultimate rung of this ladder consists in the pure concepts, which have their origin in the understanding alone. The ultimate rung is the idea: 'A concept formed from [the pure concepts of the understanding] and transcending the possibility of experience is an *idea* or concept of reason. Anyone who has familiarized himself with these distinctions must find it intol-erable to hear the representation of the color red called an idea' (A320/B377).

For Hegel, it would be intolerable to hear an idea called a representation at all, however highly situated on the *Stufenleiter*. And, indeed, Kant's placing ideas in a series of representation types is in some tension with what he himself emphasizes regarding Plato on 'idea'. Kant's account here of an idea as a concept formed from the pure concepts which have their source in *our* understanding, *our* subjectivity, runs directly counter to Plato's account of the idea as the archetype of the things themselves. Read from the standpoint of Hegel, Kant betrays his subjectivism here in giving an account according to which an idea is an idea *of that* which transcends all experience (e.g., God). It belongs to Kant's account that the idea is ours in the sense that it is a mental representation; in contrast, the object of the idea, that which is represented through it, although it by its nature cannot be given in any way through experience, is nevertheless something else, something distinct from, or external to, the idea of it. Kant further betrays this subjectivist conception of 'idea' in the rest of the Dialectic, which he structures around the question of the objective reality of the ideas; that is, the question whether there is something corresponding to the content represented in the representation. Hegel's point against this subjectivism can be put, crudely and quickly, as follows: the idea, as the traditional quarry of metaphysical pursuit, is not an idea *of* God (or *of* anything at all). 'God', taken as the name of a traditional object of metaphysics, is another name for the Idea, as the archetype of the things themselves. Hence, the Idea is neither itself a representation nor the object of one, but rather the ontological ground of that very opposition, the opposition between representational thinking and its objects.

Whereas a 'serial arrangement' or hierarchy of species of representations belongs to Kant's epistemological idealism, a hierarchy of *being* belongs to the ancient idealism that Hegel opposes to it. The Idea is at the top of this hierarchy as well (just as it is in Kant's *Stufenleiter*), while representations rank very low. The degree or level of being is largely a matter of degree or level of ontological dependence on some other being. Following traditional notions, Hegel holds that to be fully real is not to depend on anything other than oneself in any way for one's being. (Hegel's favored term for this quality is 'self-standing' (*selbständig*).) According to this measure, representations (as the very word confesses) fare poorly. A representation depends in multiple ways on what is other than it for its being. Whereas the modern subjective idealism, for which Hegel has no sympathy in this early period, consists in asserting the dependence of the being of things on representations, Hegel's idealism consists in asserting that the one self-subsistent reality, which depends on nothing else for its being and on which all else ultimately depends, is the Idea.[26]

To be the source of one's own being is to be defined and caused through oneself alone. Showing again his debt to the ontological tradition (here to Spinoza in particular), Hegel finds a tension between self-definition, self-causation, and self-identity on the one hand, and relation to some other being, on the other. For Hegel, the self-defined being atop the hierarchy of being cannot be related to what is other than it, since to 'stand over against' an opposite is to be defined negatively in relation to that other, hence to be dependent on it and limited by it. Hence, if what philosophy aspires to know, what Hegel calls 'the rational', is to be 'eternally and everywhere self-identical' (as it must be), then it must not stand over against anything. As Hegel frankly puts it: 'The rational has no opposite' (VSP, 247/336–7). Hegel's idealistic

---

[26] The question of whether, or in what respect, Hegel advances an idealism was reanimated recently by the nearly simultaneous publication of two discussions which present sharply opposed interpretations of the question. Kenneth Westphal argues in *Hegel's Epistemological Realism* (1989) (as well as in more recent publications) that 'Hegel defends the view that there is a way the world is that does not depend on our cognitive and linguistic activity and that we can know the way the world is' (p. x). Robert Pippin develops an interpretation in his book *Hegel's Idealism*, published the same year, according to which, Hegel's adoption of the principle of apperception from Kant implies that he accepts Kant's idealist conclusion, the conclusion that 'human reason can attain non-empirical knowledge only *about itself*, about what has come to be called recently our "conceptual scheme", and the concepts required for a scheme to count as one at all' (8) (despite his rejection of Kant's restriction of our knowledge to mere phenomena). Though I do not advance a developed interpretation with regard to the question of whether or in what respect Hegel's system is idealism, since the question arises here and elsewhere in this study, I indicate here the stand this study takes with respect to the interpretive contrast defined by the approaches of Westphal and Pippin. My approach agrees with Westphal's, and opposes Pippin's, in highlighting the impetus of Hegel's epistemology to overcome subjective idealism. If a position is a realism by virtue of claiming that knowledge is absolute, unrelativized to the standpoint of the human knower or to our conceptual scheme, then Hegel's position is in that sense a realism (according to the view taken here). However, this study follows Pippin's in finding Hegel's epistemology to be in this respect Kantian: the knowledge expressed in the metaphysical system is possible only through an epistemological inquiry in which we reflect on our capacity for such knowledge. Insofar as Westphal's epistemological realism denies this relation between the knowing and the being of the absolute, it is denied here that Hegel's position is an epistemological realism in Westphal's sense. According to the interpretation offered in this study, Hegel attempts in his *Phenomenology of Spirit* to meet distinctively modern epistemological demands while overcoming subjectivism. I attempt here to show the project and its method as the result of this ambition. In the Preface to the *Phenomenology* Hegel announces that the key to success in the attempt is the construal of the metaphysical reality (the absolute or the Idea) also as subject. That the absolute is subject means that it realizes itself through a process of development at least partially constituted through its developing self-knowledge, as that is revealed in the history of philosophy. While it is relatively easy to see that the idealism Hegel strives to articulate is neither merely an ontological holism (pace Westphal) nor merely subjectivism, it is much more difficult to provide a full and detailed interpretation of his interpretation such that his position is philosophically compelling, as both Westphal and Pippin attempt to do.

thesis is that *reason* or *thought* (what he later comes to characterize as 'spirit') exhibits the self-relating structure by virtue of which it, in particular, is the supreme reality that both underlies and transcends the opposition character- istic of finitude. When in thinking we've risen to the level of pure thought, we think thinking itself; pure thought is thought relating to itself alone. Hence in pure thought alone we know the Idea that is the identity of being and thinking. An important obstacle to elevating oneself to pure thought is exactly the representational thinking characteristic of the ordinary standpoint.

From the transcendental standpoint of the critical philosophy, the Coper- nican revolution reverses the direction of conformity of representation to object in our knowing, relative to the direction supposed in the ordinary conception. But this revolution remains within the dualist framework of representational thinking. Hegel takes Kant's formulation of the epistemolo- gical problem to which his critique is addressed to betray the representational thinking that must be overcome in rising to the standpoint of philosophy. The epistemological problem of how to relate the pure representations, the pure concepts of the understanding or the ideas of reason, to their objects, standing over against them, presupposes the dualism of representation and represented, subject and object. Hence, attainment to the philosophical Idea is methodo- logically precluded. As Kant calls to our attention in the passage quoted, Plato conceives of the task of philosophy as a task of *recovery* (reminiscence) of ideas 'very much obscured'. Plato's 'upward journey of the soul to the intelligible realm', to the ideas, requires liberating ourselves from the representations, which we are prone to mistake for reality. But in Plato, the copies or images of the real by which we are transfixed are the things presented to us through the senses, the vast visible world lying wide around us. Our modern condition is worse, according to Hegel in this early article. After the Cartesian event and empiricism, that is, after subjectivism has taken hold of our conceptions, it has become possible for us to take the mental representation (what we call 'ideas') of what is for Plato already merely a representation—that is, the shadow of a shadow—as the true object of our knowledge.

How does one rise from the standpoint of ordinary consciousness, char- acterized by its principle of non-identity, to the standpoint of philosophy, characterized by its principle of identity? In the following passage from the Skepticism article, which is characteristic of those from the early Jena writings that may seem dogmatically to dismiss the task of justifying metaphysical knowledge altogether, Hegel indicates how he conceives the transition from ordinary consciousness to the standpoint of philosophy.

In daily life, says Herr Schulze, we *presuppose* that identity [of thinking and being, of concept and thing]; that it is *presupposed* in daily life means that it is not present in consciousness. '*The recent metaphysics seeks to ground* [*ergründen*] *the possibility of this identity*'; but that the recent philosophy seeks to ground the possibility of the identity *presupposed* in ordinary life is no true saying, for this metaphysics does nothing but express and know that presupposed identity. Just because that identity is presupposed in daily life, the ordinary consciousness posits the object always as an other relative to the subject ... ; metaphysics brings this identity, which is for ordinary consciousness merely presupposed and unconscious, to consciousness; this identity is its absolute and only principle. (VSP, 255/342)

The work of metaphysics, then, relative to the suspicions and doubts and ignorance of ordinary consciousness, consists not in the demonstration or proof or justification of its principle to ordinary consciousness, but in *expressing* that principle in consciousness, which already resides therein (*implicitly*, *unconsciously*, or it is *presupposed*). Hegel implies that this work of raising (ordinary) consciousness to the Idea (or, what seems to be the same, raising the Idea to consciousness) is the work of skepticism, in particular, the *ancient* skepticism that is but the negative side of philosophy. The epistemological demand of Kantian criticism that the possibility of metaphysical knowledge be justified *to us*, standing over against the standpoint of metaphysics, as a condition of its possibility, is characteristic of distinctively modern epistemology; such an epistemological demand is characteristically modern in essentially presupposing as fixed and unbridgeable the ontological and epistemological gulf across which subject and object are supposed to face each other in the tradition of modern skepticism. As such, the procedure of philosophical critique ends predictably in skepticism with respect to philosophical knowledge. The arguments of the ancient skeptics, in contrast, are directed first of all *against* the claims and criteria of ordinary consciousness and gradually bring to consciousness the Idea as their presupposition.

3.5 AGAINST MODERN SELF-CERTAINTY

Complementing his attack on 'the negative side' of Schulze's skepticism, Hegel also objects strongly to its 'the positive side': namely, that this skepticism grants to 'facts of consciousness', or whatever is given within the field of consciousness, 'undeniable certainty'. From the point of view of this skepticism, that which is immediately present to consciousness cannot sensibly be doubted. The attempt to doubt it amounts to attempting to doubt consciousness itself, but since doubt itself cannot occur without consciousness, the attempt undercuts itself and is self-defeating (VSP, 220/318). In expressing the positive side of his skepticism, Schulze alludes to the alleged positive discovery of Cartesian doubt, namely, the discovery of the indubitability of the *cogito*. Thus, the larger issue raised here is whether there is such a self-discovery at the origin of modern philosophy, and whether modern skepticism (or modern epistemology generally) takes its distinctive shape (as determined by the problem of the possibility of knowledge of the *external* world) through such a discovery. On the interpretation I develop in this chapter and the next, Hegel *rejects* in his early Jena writings the claim that there is a distinctively modern self-discovery (the *cogito*) which transforms the tasks and procedures of epistemology, relative to the ancient; but Hegel *comes to recognize* while at Jena such a self-discovery as justifying the distinctively modern epistemological project of critique. How exactly does Hegel challenge in the early Jena article Schulze's characteristically modern claim that the contents of consciousness are indubitable and undeniably certain? And how does he contrast ancient skepticism with the modern on this question of the skeptic's supposedly indubitable knowledge of her own subjective states?

As noted above, Hegel finds the attempt to *secure* one's knowledge claims in the face of skeptical challenges by restricting them to what is (in some sense conceived as) subjective, inner, or relative to the standpoint of the subject to be a hopeless maneuver. Hegel sees Schulze's skepticism as having this maneuver at its core, and as such he regards it as distinctly inferior to ancient varieties of skepticism. In the case of Schulze's skepticism, the maneuver consists in restricting the content of one's assertions to that which is immediately present in the relevant state of mind, on the assumption that the relevant skeptical arguments are effective only against the inference from the state of mind to something beyond it as its intentional object or causal ground. If one refrains from venturing such an inference, if one restricts one's claims to immediate 'facts of consciousness', then one's claims are supposedly immune from skeptical arguments. But for Hegel the failure of this attempt at self-limitation, limitation *by* the self of its claims to claims *about* itself (about what appears to it), is shown by its failure to respond satisfactorily to the demand that the knowing subject define the limits of its knowledge. The knowing subject cannot define the objects of its immediate certainty *as limited* within the confines of its self-limited stance, and thus its stance does not withstand self-criticism. The claim to special epistemic status for these knowledge claims, their immunity from skeptical attack, depends on the conception of their objects as in some sense limited (that is, as being subjective or relative to the subject). But then the subject's allegedly immediate knowledge of these essentially subjective (conditioned, relative) objects turns out to depend on the subject's knowledge of the objects *as* subjective (or as conditioned or as relative), which knowledge is not likewise immediate, not likewise contained immediately in the relevant state of mind. Validation of this knowledge requires going outside the immediate state of mind, which destroys the immediacy and undermines its claim to special epistemic status. In short, skeptical reflection on such allegedly immediate knowledge destroys its alleged immediacy and thereby undermines the claim that it possesses self-certifying status.

Ancient skepticism, as Hegel conceives it, proceeds characteristically by manifesting the tension or instability that inheres in the claim to know with certainty any conditioned thing. One is supposed securely to know some conditioned thing, but, under skeptical pressure, it turns out that securing the knowledge requires knowledge of the conditions of the thing (insofar as those conditions enter into its definition). Such skeptical reflection leads us ultimately to what alone can be genuine, secure knowledge for Hegel: knowledge *of the unconditioned.*

Let me illustrate the abstract point here with a brief discussion of the order of discovery and of justification in that text which is supposed to contain the paradigmatic, trendsetting performance of the distinctively modern epistemological maneuver. The mediator in Descartes's *Meditations* is supposed to defeat skeptical doubt by restricting his claims (initially anyway) to claims about his own mind. The meditator gradually scales back his claims, in response to the increasingly hyperbolic doubt that he generates, until he reaches the position at which he attempts to suppose that nothing at all exists; there he discovers that, even if nothing *else* exists, he cannot doubt that *he* exists, so long as he is thinking. The certainty or indubitability of the proposition 'I am, I exist' seems to depend on the thinness of what it asserts: the proposition attests merely to what is immediately presented in consciousness. Insofar as we take it that the meditator has arrived with the *cogito* at a piece of secure knowledge in defiance of the arsenal of skeptical arguments, while making particularly pressing the knowledge of the existence of anything else besides the 'I' and the immediate contents of its thinking, then we take it that the *Meditations* performs the relevant epistemological maneuver.

However, on closer inspection, the *Meditations* does not obviously contain an enactment of the relevant maneuver after all; moreover, the meditator prominently employs the epistemological principle that Hegel employs against the modern epistemological maneuver. The first point to note in explanation of this is that knowledge of the proposition 'I am, I exist' depends on knowledge of *what* I am, which the meditator acknowledges through turning immediately to that question. But the question of what this 'I' is the existence of which I am allegedly immediately certain of is not likewise known immediately in self-consciousness. Second, and more importantly, the meditator tells us at the beginning of the Third Meditation that he cannot be certain of anything at all, (*a fortiori* not even that he exists as a thinking thing), until he knows himself as the creation of a non-deceiving God.[27] That he cannot doubt a proposition does not prove that it is true if he is by nature so faulty and defective a thing that even what he perceives clearly and distinctly could be false. Therefore knowledge of his nature and source is a condition of the possibility of trusting his clear and distinct perceptions as a guide to truth. In what follows in the Third Meditation, the meditator takes himself to prove the existence of an infinite and perfect being and that this being is the cause of his own finite and limited being. In the context of that proof, the meditator articulates, employs, and briefly defends the crucial principle that knowledge of the finite, as finite, depends on knowledge of the infinite. In response to the possibility—threatening to his proof for God's existence—that his idea of the infinite substance may have been arrived at by negating his idea of the finite, the meditator says: 'On the contrary, I clearly understand that there is more reality in an infinite substance than in a finite one, and hence that my perception of the infinite, that is of God, is in some way prior to my perception of the finite, that is myself. For how could I understand that I doubted or desired ... and that I was not wholly perfect, unless there were in me some idea of a more perfect being which enabled me to recognize my own defects by comparison?'[28] So the initial self-knowledge of the *cogito* is in fact not immediate, as it initially seemed to be; in the course of the inquiry, it turns out that the meditator's knowledge of himself as a finite, thinking thing is mediated by knowledge of the unconditioned condition of his own being, namely, God.

Hegel subscribes to the abstract principle that the success of the attempt to secure knowledge of what is finite and conditioned requires achieving knowledge of its unconditioned conditions, hence, metaphysical knowledge. This is the basis of the dim view he takes of modern epistemology (modern skepticism and subjectivism), insofar as the latter regards the knowing

---

[27] Descartes, AT, vol. 7, 35–6.   [28] Descartes, AT, vol. 7, 45–6.

subject's knowledge of itself as epistemically privileged relative to knowledge of what exists in itself or absolutely.

In his review article, Hegel makes this general point against Schulze's specific brand of skepticism. He claims that Schulze's skeptical philosophy cannot adequately account for the need or desire to know the absolute. He writes: 'One cannot query this philosophy, which places undeniable certainty in facts of consciousness and which, just like the most common Kantianism, restricts all knowledge of reason to the formal unity brought to such facts, regarding how it understands that the human being cannot satisfy itself with this undeniable certainty ...' (VSP, 220–1/318). What is the basis of the want for any other knowledge, in particular knowledge of the unconditioned (metaphysics), given that the facts of consciousness are undeniably certain? Hegel quotes Schulze appealing at this juncture to yet another fact of consciousness: 'Owing to an original constitution of our mind we have a yearning to seek out the final and unconditioned ground of all that which *according to our insight* exists in a *merely* conditioned way'.[29] However, Hegel recognizes a contradiction between saying of a fact of consciousness that it is immediately certain and saying of it that it exists merely in a conditioned way: 'If however every fact of consciousness has immediate certainty, the insight that something exists merely in a conditioned way is impossible; for to exist in a conditioned way and to be for itself nothing certain [*für sich nichts Gewißes*] is the same.' It appears that Hegel articulates here a principle of ontology: namely, that 'to be for itself certain' and 'to exist in a conditioned way' are incompatible predicates (or that 'to be for itself nothing certain' and 'to exist in a conditioned way' say the same thing). However, the point can also be construed epistemologically. That by virtue of which a fact of consciousness is supposed to be immediately certain is its immediate presence to the mind—this is announced in its being a fact *of consciousness*. But this state of mind is supposedly known to exist as something conditioned. Otherwise there would be no impetus to inquiry; otherwise no skeptical conclusions regarding knowledge of the unconditioned would be in the offing. But how is the thing (the fact of consciousness, the state of mind) known as conditioned separate from consciousness of its conditions, however obscure and indistinct that consciousness may be? Presumably consciousness of the conditions is not likewise immediately present in the state of mind, or such consciousness would already be of the unconditioned. Hence the

---

[29] Schulze, *Kritik der theoretischen Philosophie*, I, 56.

subject is forced out of its immediate state of mind, its fact of consciousness, in order to account for the supposedly indubitable knowledge, and this just shows that the fact of consciousness is not immediately certain after all.

We can see that the general point Hegel applies here against Schulze's skepticism applies also against the subjective idealism of Kant and Fichte. As we have seen above, Fichte in his review of *Aenesidemus* aims to reformulate the first principle of the critical philosophy, relative to Reinhold's Principle of Consciousness, in order to make it invulnerable to Schulze's skeptical attack. He replaces Reinhold's principle, which expresses the fact (*Tatsache*) of consciousness, with a principle expressing the original self-activity of the knowing subject (its *Tathandlung*). Here I merely recall the tension we noted above in Fichte's presentation of this principle in his review. Fichte means to secure the principle from Schulze's skeptical attack by relativizing it: 'Aenesidemus's objections against this procedure [of the critical philosophy] are all based upon his desire to make the absolute existence and autonomy of the I, which is valid only *for the I itself*, into something which is valid *in itself* — we do not know how or for whom. The I is *what* it is, it is *because* it is, and it is *for* the I. Our knowledge can extend no further than this' (I, 2: 57/71). The assertion of the I's self-activity as a principle is supposed here to be safe against skeptical attack exactly because the assertion does not transcend the subject's self-consciousness. The assertion that 'I am' is 'the most immediately certain thing of all' exactly because it asserts something that is only valid 'for the I', not *in itself*. The application of Hegel's general point here would consist in demanding that the knowing subject define this limitation, which is the ground of the supposed immediacy and certainty of the assertion. The problem of defining in a determinate and stable manner the boundary between what is 'for the I' and what is 'in itself' such that knowledge of phenomena within that boundary is well-founded and secure merely *as knowledge of phenomena*, is the persistent bugbear of the critical philosophy in general.

3.6 THE HISTORY OF SKEPTICISM: DECLINE INTO DOGMATISM

Hegel understands ancient skepticism to attack primarily and first of all our knowledge of that which is presented immediately in consciousness, hence the same knowledge, roughly speaking, which is apt to be regarded as 'undeniably certain' in the context of modern epistemology. This is for Hegel one of the major defining differences between ancient and modern skepticisms and one of the major bases for his judgment that the former are superior to the latter. But how exactly does Hegel understand ancient skeptical procedure such that it attacks (and *successfully* attacks) that which the moderns regard as indubitably certain?

Pyrrhonist skepticism claims to be fully general, in the sense that Pyrrhonists claim to suspend judgment on *every* question. At the same time, however, these skeptics unapologetically assent to claims of the form 'such and such appears to me now thus and so', just as if this were no restriction at all on their skepticism. Whereas Hegel holds that this apparent restriction on ancient skepticism is merely apparent, Myles Burnyeat has recently developed an interpretation according to which it is genuine.[30] Burnyeat develops an interpretation according to which Descartes's *cogito* amounts to a refutation of ancient skepticism, understood as the activity of suspending judgment on *all* questions or as a way of holding *no* beliefs whatsoever. According to his interpretation, Cartesian skeptical doubt, which is radicalized relative to the ancient, pushes the Cartesian meditator up against the indubitability of the *cogito*, and thereby establishes the special problem of the relation of the contents of thought to what is external or other to consciousness as the dominating epistemological problem. In this section, I employ Burnyeat's interpretation of the relation of modern skepticism to the ancient as a sharp counterpoint to Hegel's.

Supposing that there is a real conflict between the Pyrrhonists' assent to appearances and their claim to hold no beliefs, the pressing question for Burnyeat is why or how ancient skeptics fail to see this restriction as a restriction. Why do the ancient skeptics not understand their ready assent to appearances as in fact beliefs, in opposition to their ambition to suspend judgment on *every* question? According to Burnyeat's account, the ancient skeptics' understanding of knowledge and truth implies an implicit commitment to realism, a commitment which hides from their view the possibility that they know how things appear to them. How something appears or seems to them is not for them a candidate for being true or false, hence for being known, since for the ancients 'true' always means 'true of a real objective world'. 'In the skeptic's book, to say that an appearance, or the statement expressing it, is true is to say that things really are as they (are said to) appear to be'.[31]

Burnyeat understands this dramatically to change with Descartes's *Meditations*. In this text, Descartes employs the traditional skeptical materials to

---

[30] Myles Burnyeat, 'Idealism and Greek Philosophy: What Descartes Saw and Berkeley' Missed.
[31] *Ibid.*, 26. See Myles Burnyeat, 'Can the Skeptic Live His Skepticism?' 119–22.

'support a doubt more radical than the traditional skeptic himself had dared suppose'.[32] In particular, Descartes employs the hypothesis of the deceiving evil demon, a skeptical hypothesis used by ancient skeptics to call into question the truth even of luminously clear and distinct perceptions, in a more radical way to call into question *all* the deliverances *both* of the senses and of the reasoning faculties. 'This is the "hyperbolic" doubt [unthought of by the ancients] which alone poses in an absolutely general way the problem of the existence of the external world where that ... includes the existence of one's own body'.[33] According to Burnyeat, this radicalized skeptical doubt backs one up against the truth of the *cogito*, which is secure against the skeptical arguments employed by the Pyrrhonists and the Academics. This truth, as the fundamental truth of epistemology, then solidifies the new epistemological problem as that of the existence of an *external* world, a world of things existing outside one's thoughts in correspondence to them.

Interestingly, Hegel likewise accounts for the fact that ancient skeptics do not consider their ready assent to appearances as constituting knowledge—further that they do not consider assertions stating what appears to them so much as *candidates* for knowledge—by appealing to the fact that for these skeptics such appearances have no *reality* or *being*. The fact that the standard of skepticism is the appearance (as Sextus writes) does not violate the skepticism, because for the skeptics appearances are *as such* not held *as true* or *objective* or *real*.[34] But, whereas for Burnyeat, this assumption is a *dogmatic* presupposition—the presupposition of realism which is effectively overturned by Descartes's inquiry—for Hegel, it is not.[35] Why or how not?

The difference in attitudes to appearances between the ancient and the modern skeptics can be at least approximately captured as the difference between (1) asserting that something *appears* thus and so, meaning thereby exactly to withhold judgment on whether the thing is really or objectively thus and so, and (2) asserting that it *is the case* (objectively, in reality) that

[32] Burnyeat, 'Idealism and Greek Philosophy', 37.   [33] *Ibid.*, 37.

[34] Hegel writes that the ancient skeptics were far from elevating the consciousness that assents to appearances 'to the rank of a knowledge that is an objective assertion' (Hegel, VSP, 225/321). See also, VGP, *Werke*, vol. 19, 361; Haldane and Simson, vol. II, 332. Forster discusses this feature of ancient skepticism, in relation to both Hegel's interpretation and to Burnyeat's, in *Hegel and Skepticism*, 15–17.

[35] I ascribe to Burnyeat the view that the ancient skeptics are in fact guilty of dogmatism by virtue of their presupposition of realism on the basis of the fact that he characterizes their presupposition of realism as 'an unquestioned, unquestioning *assumption*' and then goes on to argue that Descartes's *cogito* in effect refutes this assumption (see 'Idealism and Greek Philosophy', 33–4.). Burnyeat argues in 'Can the Skeptic Live his Skepticism?' that the ancient skeptic cannot successfully live without beliefs, in part because he cannot fail to believe what appears to him (140–1).

something appears thus and so (to me, now). That ancient skepticism does not so much as engage statements of the latter sort, whereas such statements belong among the first, foundational thoughts of modern skepticism has everything to do, obviously, with the contrast in their *aims and purposes*. The aim of Pyrrhonist skepticism is tranquility or lack of disturbance in mind or soul (*ataraxia*). While assertions of the latter sort are incompatible with the tranquility of soul at which the ancient skeptic aims, the assent of ancient skeptics to appearances in the sense of (1) is supposed necessary in order for them to act. Because tranquility of mind is supposed to follow upon suspension of judgment, Pyrrhonists strive to hold no beliefs. But they must act in order to live; and belief would seem to be necessary as a guide to action. The solution within Pyrrhonism to this problem is to live according to appearances; Pyrrhonists let themselves be guided by the promptings of nature within them and the laws and customs of the society surrounding them. But, crucially, they act in accordance with such promptings *without attachment* to such ways of acting; that is, they do not believe that such laws and customs mark the way of virtue, the right or good way of acting.[36] The ancient skeptics relate to appearances in the way they do as necessary in order to live in a detached state of mind, hence in order to achieve tranquility; in contrast, modern skeptics relate to appearances in their way as part of a strategy for defeating skeptical arguments and providing a foundation for knowledge.

For Hegel the distinctively modern strategy for evading the negating power of thought displayed in skeptical arguments by restricting one's assertions to what is confessed to be merely subjective, to that which merely seems or appears, attests to an attitude of desperation exactly opposite to the attitude of tranquility. The critical, negating power of thought, if allowed free reign, is bound to unfix or dissolve one's supposed self- or sense certainties. Ancient skepticism in contrast, as the *active* negation of every assertion, exactly consists in giving free reign to the critical, negating power of thought. One achieves tranquility of soul, according to this ancient skepticism, exactly through detaching oneself thereby (that is, by the skeptical negation of beliefs or dogmas) from everything finite and limited. Ancient skepticism, Hegel says, 'has its positive side solely in character', which character consists in an attitude of indifference in the face of the passing away of everything finite, in particular

---

[36] In his argument that the ancient skeptic cannot live his skepticism, Burnyeat argues that the project of achieving tranquility through suspension of belief requires a stance of detachment from self that is ultimately impossible to maintain. (See 'Can the Skeptic Live his Skepticism?' 129 and 137–8.)

of one's own life (VSP, 239/331). In the context of explaining this, Hegel recounts the story according to which, when Pyrrho was traveling on a ship in the midst of a violent storm with companions who were made frightened and anxious by the storm, he pointed to the pigs on board which simply ate meanwhile, undisturbed, and said to his companions: 'the wise must stand in such tranquility'. The implication is that the source of anxiety and trouble is our own attachment to, or identification with, that which as finite will pass away. Hegel writes earlier in this paragraph that the application of the first ten modes of the ancient skeptics effects 'the tottering of everything finite' with which the ordinary consciousness unconsciously occupies itself. In making everything finite totter, one detaches oneself therefrom; one achieves an elevation of consciousness such that the passing away of the finite is no longer perceived as a threat. This elevation of the soul above finitude constitutes the philosophical caste of mind. Hegel sees ancient skepticism in this way as essentially one with the philosophical attitude. He sees distinctively modern skepticism, insofar as it is directed against knowledge of the unconditioned in particular, in contrast, as essentially a desperate and hopeless ploy to evade the negating power of thought by restricting claims to 'objects' that are defined as merely subjective (appearances, phenomena, mental states).

As Hegel tells it in his article on skepticism, the history of skepticism is a story of step-by-step descent into dogmatism, culminating in the extreme dogmatism of Schulze's work. The steps of this descent are distinguished according to the relation of each of the successive varieties of skepticism to philosophy. I will summarize Hegel's conception in this early Jena period of epistemology and its relation to philosophy, a period in which he simply rejects the epistemological project of Kantian critique, by way of briefly describing the stages of the decline of skepticism, as Hegel presents it.

Originally skepticism is 'in its most inward nature' one with philosophy (VSP, 227/322–3). Hegel writes that philosophy, as cognition of the absolute, 'necessarily has at the same time a negative side, which is turned against everything limited and thereby against the pile of facts of consciousness and their undeniable certainty … against this entire ground of finitude, on which this newer skepticism has its essence and its truth'. A true philosophy is therefore 'infinitely more skeptical than this [newer] skepticism' (VSP, 227–8/323). Hegel cites Plato's *Parmenides* as exemplifying a truly 'authentic' skepticism, which as such has its positive side in cognition of the absolute or the Idea. Hegel suggests that Plato's *Academy*, the *old* Academy, at least—or anyway, Platonic philosophy itself—escaped the general opposition between

dogmatism and skepticism by managing to be *philosophy*, in which knowledge
of the absolute and skeptical negation of claims about finite things are united
as two sides of a single presentation.

At some point, however, *pure* skepticism emerges; skepticism breaks off
from philosophy and establishes itself on its own account. Hegel distinguishes
two historical stages of this pure skepticism, again in terms of the relation
of each to philosophical knowledge. The first ten tropes define the earlier
stage, associated in particular with Pyrrho. These tropes are directed 'like all
philosophy generally, against the dogmatism of the ordinary consciousness'
(VSP, 238/330). This shows in the content of the tropes, which generally
exploit the conflicts that arise among ordinary empirical claims about finite
objects from such sources as diversity of points of view, differences in sense
organs, differences in customs and laws, etc. Far from its being the case that
the first ten tropes provide instruments for skeptical attack against rational
knowledge, the most general of the tropes, the eighth, which has to do with the
relationship of things, nearly expresses a principle of reason itself, according
to Hegel. Every actual thing, as finite, is conditioned through another, which
constitutes its defining limit. This relation to another is the ground of its
negation, insofar as it is asserted as existing through itself, absolutely. In
general, the equipollence arguments, constructed on the basis of the first set
of ten patterns of argument, simply effect that negation for each assertion
in turn. Thus, this skepticism is turned 'against the ordinary consciousness,
which holds fast to the given, the fact, the finite ... and sticks to it as certain,
as secure, as eternal' (VSP, 240/332). This skepticism is therefore, Hegel says,
'the first stage of philosophy; for the beginning of philosophy must, of course,
be the elevation above the truth which ordinary consciousness gives ...'[37]

Although this skepticism of the ten tropes is not directed against philosophy, it differs from philosophy in having its positive side *solely* in character,
rather than in reason's knowledge of the absolute (VSP, 242/333). But this
difference at the same time is the denial of one. In insisting that their path is
not defined as a *school*, but as 'an education to a way of life, a *Bildung*', these
ancient skeptics in effect insist that they do not define themselves over against
philosophy, in opposition to and competition with it. Moreover, as we noted
above, the character or inward being of the skeptic that is the positive side of
this skepticism 'is not alien to any philosophy. The "apathy" of the Stoics and

---

[37] Hegel, VSP, 240/332. Accordingly, Hegel refers the skepticism of Schulze, which holds facts
of consciousness to be 'indubitably certain', to the skeptical arguments of this ancient skepticism.

the "indifference" of the philosophers generally must recognize themselves in the "ataraxia" [of the skeptics]' (VSP, 242/333). Hegel emphasizes this in order to make the point that, in this second stage in the history of skepticism, after it has quit the condition of being merely philosophy's negative side, skepticism remains inwardly one with it.

As Hegel tells the history here, *originally* philosophies were, and were recognized to be, one. 'It is a contingency of the time [*eine Zufälligkeit der Zeit*]', he writes, 'that later on the diverse philosophical systems completely separated out from each other and that the 'apathy' became opposed to 'ataraxia', and the dogmatics of the Stoa counted for the skeptics as their most decisively opposed opponents' (VSP, 243/334). That this differentiation is 'a contingency of the time' implies that it is external to reason and its Idea. In fact that this development expresses differentiation (as opposed to unity and identity), is contingent, and belongs to time all mark its alienation from reason and its Idea, in accordance with the Platonic idealism strongly intimated in Hegel's early Jena writings. Ancient skepticism turns against the claims of philosophy, Hegel suggests, only when philosophy itself becomes dogmatic. This happens when philosophers define their principles *in opposition to* those of other philosophers, which is itself in opposition to the very idea of philosophy. Hegel writes that: 'The essence of dogmatism consists in positing something finite, something ensnared in an opposition [*ein mit einer Entgegensetzung Behaftetes*] ... as the absolute' (VSP, 245/335). A principle defined over against another is a mere dogma; it has its limit or negation outside of itself, and hence it is susceptible to skeptical attack. One can always confront such a principle with its necessary relation to its opposite, which undermines its claim to assert what is unconditioned and absolute.

The second historical stage of *pure* skepticism, then, employs both the first ten tropes against the ordinary empirical claims about ordinary empirical objects and the second later set of five, attributed to Agrippa, against the dogmas of the scientists and the philosophers. Hegel claims that, although Sextus employs the five later tropes with great success against the dogmas of the physical sciences, when he turns the tropes against reason and its self-knowledge in philosophy, his arguments are lame. Because Hegel interprets all five of Agrippa's tropes to have their source in reason's own need to negate that which is defined over against another by means of showing its relation to the other through which it is defined, he holds that the tropes are bound to be ineffective when turned against reason itself and its self-knowledge in philosophy. Recall that for Hegel here 'the rational has no opposite—it encloses those finite things, the one of which is the opposite of the other, both within itself' (VSP, 247/336–7). Agrippa's tropes can be thought to work against genuine philosophy only insofar as 'they pervert it [their target, the rational] into something finite; they give it the itch of limitedness, as an excuse for scratching it'.

While Hegel does not provide in this essay (or in any of those of his early Jena period) a detailed, determinate solution to the difficult philosophical problem of how 'the rational' is to be made intelligible given that it has no conditions by means of which it could be defined, he discusses briefly the form of a 'rational proposition', that is, a proposition which, unlike 'a proposition of the understanding', articulates rational knowledge (VSP, 229–30/324–5). Such propositions do not consist in making ordinary predications. If one were to predicate something of the Idea in an ordinary way, one would thereby define it in relation to something else—one would thereby limit it—which is to say that one would betray its claim to be the ultimate identity in which all difference, hence all finitude, has its source. Hence, Hegel claims, an expression of philosophical or rational knowledge must express the absolute exactly through more or less explicitly contesting itself.[38] It must contain its negation *within* itself, not through being opposed to another. Hegel illustrates the rational proposition here as elsewhere with an example of a proposition from Spinoza's *Ethics*. Part I, Proposition 18 of the *Ethics* reads: 'God is the immanent, not the transient, cause of the world'. However, a cause is a cause, as Hegel goes on to explain, only through being opposed to the effect. If we say that cause and effect are one and the same, as we say in claiming that God is the immanent cause of the world, then we undermine the very application of the concepts we are trying to apply. All expressions of rational knowledge, of philosophical knowledge beyond the understanding, must display in their form this identity of opposites, since the rational, the Idea, is exactly the ultimate identity of opposites.

This example is telling because it shows that it is as true of Hegel's absolute as of Spinoza's God that it must not be conceived as something (some particular *thing*) which exists beyond the world—or, to take Schulze's picture, something which is *hidden* by the world, by its appearances. Rather it must be understood as at one with its manifestation or appearance. This identity of the Idea and appearance (of infinity and finitude) is the ontological expression of the epistemological identity Hegel claims between genuine skepticism and

---

[38] Hegel makes a similar point in the Preface to the *Phenomenology*, when commenting upon the form of what he calls there the 'speculative proposition' (PhG, 57–60/¶ ¶ 60–3).

genuine philosophy. The path of ancient skepticism is not a path that leads us to cognition of something else, some other thing beyond this realm of finitude or opposition—that is, of something beyond or behind the realm of appearance. If it were, the path of skepticism would be, though perhaps a necessary propaedeutic to philosophy, distinct from it nevertheless. However, Hegel in this article does not conceive skepticism as a necessary propaedeutic to philosophy. Rather, he claims that the truth of skepticism, properly understood, is identical with the truth of philosophy. This inward identity of skepticism and philosophy is required by the 'identity philosophy' that Hegel advocates at this period. The Idea would not be an ultimate identity in which all being has its source—it would still be, as Hegel puts it, ensnared [*behaftet*] in an opposition—if it stood over against, or were itself opposed to, opposition itself.[39]

Because propositions of reason contain negation within themselves, because they are not, like propositions of the understanding (whether ordinary or not), defined as asserting something in particular, they are not vulnerable to arguments constructed on the basis of the skeptic's tropes. That ancient skepticism is by the time of Sextus attempting to defeat propositions of reason by employing the skeptical tropes against them indicates that the very Idea of philosophy, in its original (Platonic) sense, has been progressively lost hold of (forgotten, obscured) through the march of time and culture. But there remains a good distance yet to fall from this still ancient skepticism of Sextus to the 'newest' skepticism of Schulze. As Hegel tells the story, the stepwise descent of skepticism bottoms out in the skepticism of Schulze, in which, in direct opposition to the original skepticism, skeptical attacks are directed *exclusively* against the claims of philosophy, while facts of consciousness are supposed undeniably certain. Hegel remarks on the final step of this 'degeneration' in the following passage:

[Skepticism's] turn against [philosophy], as soon as philosophy became dogmatism, shows how it has kept step with the general degeneration of philosophy and the world, until skepticism in the most recent times falls finally so far with dogmatism that for both facts of consciousness have undeniable certainty and truth resides in temporality [*in die Zeitlichkeit*]; so that in these happy times, because the extremes meet each other, the great goal is attained again from their side, in the sense that dogmatism and skepticism come together *down below* and offer each other the most fraternal hand. (VSP, 237–8/330)

---

[39] As we will see below, that the Idea and its expression in philosophy must not stand opposed to anything poses a problem for Hegel's idealism in this period, insofar as he sees the standpoint of philosophy to be opposed by the standpoint of ordinary consciousness.

Hegel presents here the history of skepticism, of philosophy, and indeed of the world as a general degeneration. We must take note of the implications of this for Hegel's understanding at this period of the relation of epistemological procedure to philosophy.

3.7 PHILOSOPHY COUNTER CULTURE AND TIME

As careful reading of several of the passages quoted above reveals, the position Hegel takes in the comparison of modern with ancient skepticism in this article is significantly underwritten by his metaphilosophy, by his conception more particularly of the relation of philosophy to history and to time in general. In a section at the beginning of his essay on the difference between Fichte's and Schelling's systems explicitly concerned with 'the historical view of philosophical systems', Hegel denies that philosophy as such has a history. The Idea is as such, as the unconditioned condition of all conditioned things, 'eternally one and the same'. Because philosophy, as the expression of the absolute, as reason's knowledge of itself, is itself identical with the Idea, philosophy too is 'eternally one and the same'. Hegel writes that 'there is in regard to the inner essence of philosophy neither predecessors nor successors' (Hegel, Diff, 17/87). Hence there is, in regard to its inner essence, neither modern nor ancient philosophy as such; insofar as skepticism is bound up with the inner essence of philosophy, there is neither an ancient nor a modern version of it. Hegel opposes modern skepticism in this article, not as modern as opposed to ancient, but as temporally conditioned in the first place—moreover, as a view that finds truth in what is temporally conditioned. Likewise, he affirms ancient skepticism in contrast, not as ancient, but as one with philosophy, and hence as timeless, as independent of temporal and spatial determinations.

In accordance with his conception of philosophy and its Idea in this period, Hegel refuses to recognize a *discovery* as marking the onset of the alleged event of distinctively modern philosophy. He refuses to recognize Descartes's *cogito* as an epoch-making *self-discovery*, and he refuses to recognize the alleged reformulation of the age-old problems of knowledge that is supposed to follow upon this alleged discovery. He refuses to recognize the validity of the allegedly new epistemological demand contained in Kant's criticism. For the Hegel of the early Jena essays, all this is vanity, and there is nothing new under the sun. (Or, rather, all this is subjectivism, and there is nothing new in the Idea.) In opposition to the modern conception of the path to or of philosophy, according to which it consists in bridging the gulf that has recently opened between the 'I', the self-certain knowing subject, recently discovered in reflection, and the things in themselves external to the realm of the subject's ideas, Hegel conceives the path of philosophy rather as one of *recovery* of the ancient (or, better, eternal) Idea, *now* very much obscured—obscured now in particular by the events and culture that characterize the 'modern' in time and the 'northwestern' in space. The temporal developments in culture serve rather to cover up than to reveal the Idea; they make its recovery and expression, always difficult, more so.

According to Hegel's interpretation, the culture of the modern (north-western) world is characterized by the assertion of the 'rights' of the ordinary understanding and, what goes with this, the assertion of the individual subject as self-standing, as existing on its own account. The expression of the cultural development in religion is principally the various forms of Protestant revolt against the authority of the Roman Church; its expression in the realm of political authority is the articulation and expression of the Enlightenment political ideals of the dignity and the autonomy of the individual rational being as such; a main expression in the realm of the sciences is the ascendance of the tribunal of experimentation and experience at the expense of the tribunal of pure reason; and the expression in the realm of ontology is the Cartesian dualism of mind and body. Of most relevance for us is the expression in the realm of epistemology. As I have characterized it here, there is a characteristically modern epistemological demand which expresses the assertion of the claim of the ordinary consciousness to be self-standing: the individual knowing subject, from a standpoint in which it claims to be immediately certain of itself, as existing on its own account, independently of its relation to the absolute, demands legitimation of reason's claims regarding the absolute as a condition of recognizing their validity.

In 'Faith and Knowledge', the essay for the *Critical Journal of Philosophy* in which Hegel criticizes the philosophical systems of Kant, Fichte, and Jacobi as subjectivism, Hegel writes: '[According to the idealisms of Kant, Fichte and Jacobi] the single certain thing [*das an sich und einzige Gewisse*] is that there exists a thinking subject, a rational being affected with finitude, and the entire philosophy consists in determining the universe for this finite reason' (GW, 298/64). These systems are alike, and like Schulze's too, in posing the problem of the possibility of metaphysics as the problem of the relation of the finite subject, which, though finite, is allegedly immediately certain of itself in reflection, to the unconditioned or the absolute, which cannot be conceived otherwise than as finally and ultimately other. In the polemic he mounts in the early pages of 'Faith and Knowledge' against what he calls there 'the all-powerful culture of our time', characterizing it as 'a culture of the ordinary human understanding', Hegel says that the philosophy of his time, insofar as its principle is the finite subject's self-certainty, 'cannot aim at cognition of God, but only at what is called cognition of human beings' (GW, 299/65). It follows, then, that if philosophy is to be philosophy, if it is to achieve its original aim of knowledge of the unconditioned or of God, it must be radically counter-cultural, radically counter to the prevailing *Zeitgeist*. Philosophy must attain its end through the laborious recovery of its Idea, as always from the obfuscation it suffers from ordinary conceptions, but *now* in addition from the implicit *banishment or exile* it suffers in modern times, in these times in which the self-assertive individual renders the absolute an inaccessible object of infinite longing.

In Chapter 2, I reconstructed and provided a limited defense of Hegel's objection against Kant's project of philosophical critique, according to which the latter presupposes subjectivism and the skeptical denial of the possibility of rational knowledge of the unconditioned. In this chapter, I have placed Hegel's rejection of Kant's project of critique within the context of Hegel's conceptions of epistemology, of metaphysics, and of their relation in his early Jena writings, in particular in his essay on the varieties of skepticism. The once-common conception of Hegel as a thinker who blithely dismisses epistemological concerns has been supported largely by appeal to passages from the early Jena essays. Placing such passages in context shows Hegel to be rejecting, not epistemological demands in general, but a distinctively modern epistemological demand in particular. In particular, the context shows Hegel to reject the epistemological demand of philosophical critique. He rejects the demand as itself *dogmatic*, in the sense of dogmatism that he defines in the Skepticism article: the demand implicitly asserts something finite, something 'ensnared in an opposition' (namely, the self-certain knowing subject) as absolute. As such the demand implicitly presupposes as fixed and final the dualism between thought and being, between subject and object, between those apparently opposed terms the identity of which is expressed in philosophy's Idea.

As I will discuss more fully in the following chapter, Hegel's rejection of the validity of this new epistemological demand in effect amounts to accepting, with Schelling, the status of philosophical knowledge as esoteric. The claim that philosophy is esoteric means that its principle cannot be justified or made intelligible to the ordinary consciousness through the provision of reasons that the ordinary consciousness is capable of recognizing the validity of. Schelling expresses the esotericism of philosophy in the following passage from his work, 'Further Presentations from the System of Philosophy' (1802):

It is inconceivable why philosophy should be obliged to be considerate of incapacity, it is rather appropriate to cut off the way to [philosophy] sharply and to isolate it on all sides from common cognition in such a way that no path or pavement can lead from [common cognition] to [philosophy]. Here begins philosophy, and whoever is not already there or is afraid to reach this point—let him stay away or flee back.[40]

Looked at from Hegel's point of view, the incapacity of ordinary consciousness for rational cognition consists simply in the fact that the standpoint of ordinary consciousness is characterized by employing a principle of non-identity in its cognition, whereas the criterion of rational cognition is the principle of identity. Granted this opposition in their standards or their principles, what constitutes rational cognition from the standpoint of philosophy is unintelligible or false, judged by the standards of common cognition. Because what it is to recognize the truth of a philosophical proposition or theory is to recognize the expression of the identity of being and thought in it, if one lacks consciousness of the Idea (as ordinary consciousness does), then one is not in a position to begin philosophy. Hence, the beginning of philosophy presupposes that one already occupies the standpoint of philosophy, that is, that one already possesses philosophy's criterion, the principle of identity or the Idea.

Whether one perceives this position as dogmatic will depend on whether one takes the relevant epistemological demand to be valid. The position is, in any event, not cavalier with respect to epistemological demands, since there are principled reasons for rejecting the validity of the relevant demands. However, Hegel himself comes to see the position he advances in the early Jena writings as dogmatic. And there are already strong hints of his later views in the earlier articles. Hegel already strongly suggests in the Skepticism article that he recognizes a *discursive* path from the standpoint of ordinary consciousness to that of philosophy, from the principle of non-identity that characterizes the former standpoint to the principle of identity. Hegel suggests that this path consists in a path of skepticism, in particular the ancient skepticism that attacks with its ancient tropes the dogmatism of ordinary consciousness and is but the negative side of philosophy. This process is the construction of the absolute *for*

---

[40] Schelling, *Fernere Darstellungen aus dem System der Philosophie*, 414. Paul Franks discusses this passage in the context of his enlightening discussion of Schelling's esotericism in general, in his Ph.D. dissertation, *Kant and Hegel on the Esotericism of Philosophy* (Harvard, 1993).

consciousness, which ordinarily is unconscious or presupposed (VSP, 251/339). But insofar as Hegel hints at a discursive path from the standpoint of ordinary consciousness to the standpoint of philosophy, he resists at the same time the idea that this is in response to a valid epistemological demand and that such a path constitutes a demonstration or justification of philosophy's principle.

While the seeds of the project of the *Phenomenology of Spirit* are clearly visible in the early Jena writings, a significant change occurs in Hegel's conception of epistemology and of the justification of the possibility of philosophy after these essays, a change that renders the project of the *Phenomenology* necessary for him. I present the view in the following chapter according to which this change consists in Hegel's coming to recognize as valid the epistemological demand of Kantian critique, the demand he rejects in these earlier essays, together with distinctively modern epistemological demands generally. One significant point of tension in the early Jena writings is that, in conceiving of epistemological procedure as recovery, via ancient modes, of the timeless Idea, in opposition to historical advances in culture, Hegel sets himself against Enlightenment claims on behalf of the individual rational being for autonomy and dignity, independently of its relation to God or state. Hegel recognizes that the demand of philosophical critique, as well as other epistemological demands, expresses the new aspirations and assertions of the modern individual subject; and since he recognizes the validity of these aspirations, he cannot remain long in the position of simply rejecting those epistemological demands. In the following chapter, I demonstrate how the project of the *Phenomenology* emerges through Hegel's recognition of the validity of the epistemological demand of Kantian critique, against the background of his rejection of it in the early Jena writings.

4

The Return to Kantian Critique: Recognizing the Rights of Ordinary Consciousness

Hegel's project of the *Phenomenology of Spirit* constitutes a dramatic shift in his relation to the Kantian project of critique from that expressed in his first philosophical publications, which are published under the strong influence of Schelling in his first couple of years after he arrives in Jena. Instead of *rejecting* the epistemological demand as expressed in Kant's critical project as inherently subjectivist and therefore dogmatic, Hegel recognizes the legitimacy of that demand and undertakes to meet it. In this chapter I document and characterize this shift in Hegel's relation to Kantian critique; I show that the shift turns on Hegel's coming to recognize as valid the claim of the subject to be self-standing, a claim the validity of which he had previously rejected.

As we have seen in the previous chapter through examining Hegel's early article on skepticism, Hegel initially *rejects* or dismisses the modern skeptical crisis as resting on a mistake or misconception. The modern skeptical crisis is framed by the opening of the alleged ontological and epistemological gulf across which the subjective and objective are supposed to face each other. According to the diagnosis in the article on skepticism, the modern crisis appears compelling only given the dogmatic prioritizing of the criteria and conceptions of 'the ordinary consciousness' over the criteria of rational or philosophical cognition. In opposition to the modern procedure of addressing this crisis by attempting to work out from a position of self-certain subjectivity to knowledge of the objective, Hegel advocates the procedure of ancient skepticism, which he interprets as elevating the soul to the intelligible realm through the skeptical negation of ordinary criteria and conceptions. The turn in Hegel's thought consists in his coming to recognize as legitimate the epistemological demand expressed in Kantian critique, insofar as this demand is backed by a modern self-discovery, the discovery of self-standing subjectivity. This recognition renders untenable the dismissal or avoidance of the modern skeptical crisis; the crisis must be entered into. As I argue in the final chapter, the methodology of the *Phenomenology* puts self-standing subjectivity (ourselves) at stake together with our relation to the opposed objects of knowledge, and thus addresses the crisis by intensifying it.

Though it is widely recognized that Hegel's *Phenomenology* constitutes a break with the dogmatism of Schelling's identity philosophy and, correspondingly, some sort of concession to the critical philosophy of Kant, no account of which I am aware does justice to the significance of this turn. Recent commentary tends to underestimate the significance of the development in Hegel's orientation to Kant's critical program between his earliest writings, which contain some of Hegel's most extensive discussion of Kant's positions, and the *Phenomenology of Spirit.*[1] In older commentaries on Hegel, one commonly finds the claim that Hegel is blithely indifferent to fundamental epistemological issues, and one finds this claim supported by appeal to passages from the early writings in particular. As Michael Forster argues, these interpreters mistake Hegel's rejection of *modern* epistemological demands for a neglect of epistemological issues altogether.[2] But, as I will argue, these interpreters make a second error that Forster shares with them: they fail to see that this rejection of modern epistemological demands, of modern skepticism, is itself temporary. Hegel's return to critique consists in coming to recognize these demands, and the shape of his *Phenomenology* is determined by his attempt to meet them.

4.1 TWO CONCEPTIONS OF PHILOSOPHICAL CRITIQUE

In this chapter I document and characterize the dramatic shift in Hegel's thought by contrasting the view on philosophical critique articulated in Hegel's Introduction to *The Critical Journal of Philosophy* (entitled, 'On the Essence of Philosophical Critique Generally, and its Relationship to the Present State of Philosophy in Particular') with the view he expresses in central passages in the Preface and Introduction to the *Phenomenology.*[3] The essay on

[1] The most important example of this, I think, is Robert Pippin's important and influential study *Hegel's Idealism: The Satisfactions of Self-Consciousness.* He advances an elaborately developed interpretation of Hegel's idealism based on Hegel's discussion of Kant's transcendental deduction of the categories in *Faith and Knowledge.* As I understand Hegel's development, Hegel *replaces* the account of *Faith and Knowledge* with the project of the *Phenomenology.*

[2] Forster, *Hegel and Skepticism*, ch. 6.

[3] Please see 'Abbreviations' for information about how I cite the Criticism article and other works by Hegel and Kant. The pieces for *The Critical Journal* were unsigned, and so the question

criticism is interesting in part because it can be seen as a sort of preliminary sketch of the magisterial productions of the Preface and the Introduction to the *Phenomenology*, even though the conception of philosophical criticism expressed in it is in salient respects diametrically opposed to that advanced in the later texts. In the Criticism article, Hegel articulates the conception of the activity of philosophical criticism that belongs to the period in which he rejects *distinctively Kantian* philosophical criticism. The fundamental difference between the conception of philosophical criticism articulated in the Criticism article and the conception in the Preface and Introduction to the *Phenomenology* can be briefly characterized. Recall from Chapter 2 that Kant's critical project combines (uneasily) a task of assessment or examination (i.e., a task of assessing the *legitimacy* of candidate claims to rational knowledge) with a task of founding (i.e., a task of establishing the justified criteria of assessment for the first time). In rejecting *Kantian* critique, Hegel rejects the foundational task. In this early article, he outlines a conception of the task of philosophical criticism according to which it consists in the activity of assessing candidate claims of philosophy, of bringing them before the tribunal of pure reason. From the orientation from which the Criticism article is written, the project Hegel explains and justifies in the preliminary material to the *Phenomenology* is both unnecessary and impossible. By comparing passages from the early article with passages from the later works, one can see Hegel justify his completely reoriented project of philosophical criticism, but with terms, tropes, and even arguments borrowed from the earlier article.

Many of the most important elements of Hegel's early conception of philosophical critique are expressed in the first paragraph of the Criticism article. So I quote it in full.

Criticism, in whatever part of art or science it is practiced, demands a criterion [*Maßstab*] ... which is derived neither from the singular appearance nor from the particularity of the subject, but rather from the eternal and unchangeable archetype of the thing itself. As the idea of fine arts isn't first created or invented through art criticism, but is absolutely presupposed by it, so the Idea of philosophy itself is the condition and presupposition of philosophical critique, without which we would have in all eternity only subjectivities placed up against subjectivities—never the absolute placed up against the conditioned. (Hegel, WdpK, 171/275)

of authorship is sometimes controversial. H. S. Harris discusses the question of the authorship of the pieces published in *The Critical Journal* in his *Hegel's Development: Night Thoughts*, pp. xxxiii–xlviii.

Most saliently, for our purposes, Hegel's conception of philosophical critique here is such that it *presupposes* the criterion.[4] Hegel conceives of critique here, primarily, as an activity of judgment.[5] The activity of critique consists in the *application* of a criterion; or, as he puts it later in the article, 'all critique is subsumption under the Idea' (WdpK, 173/276). The objects judged are *appearances* of philosophy, by which I take Hegel to mean systems of thought which claim to present philosophical truth. The judgment consists in deciding whether and to what extent the appearance of philosophy really is philosophy. (Hegel evidently takes the claim to be genuine philosophy at all to depend on the truth of the claims presented within the philosophical system.) The criterion applied in such judgments is, then, the 'Idea of philosophy' or the absolute itself.

In his presentation of philosophical criticism in this early article, Hegel hearkens back to a broadly Platonic model. His reference to 'the eternal and unchangeable archetype of the thing itself' recalls Plato's forms. Appearances are to be judged according to the degree to which they approximate (or 'measure up') to the Idea or the archetype: the closer the approximation, the greater their participation in reality. Thus, Hegel claims, we must already possess the criterion or the standard—hence the Idea or the absolute—if our judgment is to be *objective*: otherwise 'we would have in all eternity only subjectivities placed up against subjectivities'.

One sees the shift in Hegel's conception of philosophical critique by comparing the above passage from the Criticism article with the corresponding passage from the Introduction to the *Phenomenology*, in which Hegel begins his discussion of the method of that work:

It seems that this presentation [the *Phenomenology*], regarded as a *relating* of *science* [i.e., philosophy] to knowledge as it *appears*, and as the *investigation* and *testing of*

---

[4] Hegel uses *Maßstab* consistently in this context, which is translated both with 'criterion' and with 'standard'. One might object to translating this word both with 'criterion' and 'standard' on the grounds that these two words do not mean the same in English. As Stanley Cavell shows in his discussion of Wittgenstein's use of 'criteria' in the *Philosophical Investigations*, criteria are the bases on which we judge, whereas we employ standards to measure the extent to which the criteria we employ in judging are fulfilled. (See Cavell, *The Claim of Reason*, ch. 1.) One might argue then that *Maßstab*, which literally translates as 'measuring stick', ought to be translated exclusively with 'standard'. However, the *Maßstab* is for Hegel the basis of judgment. In Hegel's discussion, the fate of our knowledge is at stake in the fate of our relation to the *Maßstab* in a way similar to that in which our knowledge is at stake in our relation to criteria, according to Cavell and Wittgenstein and the skeptical tradition generally.

[5] According to *Webster's Third New International*, the English word 'critique' derives from the Greek work '*kritikos*', which is an adjective meaning 'able to discern or judge'. The adjective derives from the verb '*krinein*' meaning 'to judge' or 'to separate'.

the reality of cognition, cannot take place without some criterion [*Maßstab*], which can be laid at the basis as *presupposition*. For the testing consists in the application of an assumed criterion, and in the decision of correctness or incorrectness based on the resulting agreement or disagreement with the criterion. The criterion in general, and likewise science, if it is the criterion, is thereby assumed as the *essence* or as the *in-itself*. But here, where science first comes on the scene, neither it, nor anything else, has yet justified itself as the essence or as the in-itself. (Hegel, PhG, 75–6/¶81)

Here again Hegel presents the task as that of judging the validity or the truth of what appears or claims to be philosophical knowing. As above, such judgment (critique) seems to presuppose a criterion as its basis; it presupposes that we already possess knowledge of the principle of philosophy, what he calls in the earlier article 'the Idea of philosophy', and here 'science'. The fundamental shift in Hegel's conception of philosophical critique, his return to the standpoint of Kantian critique, is marked by Hegel's acknowledgment that we exactly *lack* the justified criterion. In Kant's words, metaphysics does not yet exist.[6] Hegel mentions this lack in a sentence on the way toward posing the problem which occupies him for the next several paragraphs in the Introduction: granted that our condition is exactly that we do not yet possess the justified criterion, that metaphysics (science) does not yet exist, how then do we begin? How then do we proceed?

In acknowledging that we do not yet possess the criterion on the basis of which judgment would be possible, Hegel acknowledges that our condition—the condition of critique—is one of *crisis* for metaphysics.[7] If the criterion on the basis of which just claims are distinguished from unjust claims in this field is itself in question, then the whole science is in question. The possibility of metaphysics is at stake in the critical reflection. Critique is the reflection to determine the criterion out of this condition in which nothing has yet justified itself. What is to be determined through critique is the basis on which anything can be determined in philosophy. In finding that we lack a justified, shared criterion, we find ourselves *before the beginning of metaphysics*. Critique is thus the prior, foundational inquiry with respect to metaphysics. Supposing a favorable outcome, which would consist in the institution or

---

6 Kant, Prol, 4: 257.

7 The etymological derivation of 'critique' relates it directly, not only to the concept of judgment, but also to the concept of crisis. Both 'critique' and 'crisis' derive from the same Greek verb '*krinein*' meaning 'to separate' or 'to judge'. 'Crisis' originally refers to the decisive turning point in a sickness or a fever. Interestingly, 'criterion' also has the same Greek root. However, as noted, Hegel does not use *Kriterium* but *Maßstab*. Nevertheless, it is clear from comparing the two passages above that the second recognizes an epistemological crisis, the problem of the criterion, that the first denies.

constitution of a justified criterion, the critical inquiry would found the science or bring it to be.[8] Whereas Hegel conceives of the task of philosophical critique in the Criticism article as the task of judgment, as the application of the presupposed criterion, he conceives of the task of the *Phenomenology* as including the task of founding the science, that is, as the prior process of *arriving at* the criterion, of determining it or of constituting it as common, out of the critical condition in which *nothing* has yet justified itself. Since Kant originally specifies critique as this prior, founding act or process of instituting the criterion (or criteria), in response to the recognition that the bases of metaphysical judgment have never yet been determined, in this sense the *Phenomenology* represents Hegel's return to the standpoint of Kantian critique.

That Hegel himself undertakes in the *Phenomenology* a reflection on knowledge in order to determine the criterion through which alone metaphysical judgment would be possible does not imply that he has withdrawn his objection to Kantian critique. However, it does indicate that the objection has undergone a significant reorientation. Whereas initially the objection is directed against the epistemological demands of critique, later Hegel accuses Kant's procedure of failing fully to meet those very demands. In the early articles, Hegel objects to the demand that we determine the criterion in advance of the science itself in reflection. Hegel protests that the attempt to begin before the beginning, in a presuppositionless reflection on the presuppositions, presupposes *self-reflection*, rather than the unconditioned, as ultimately authoritative in our knowing. Initially, Hegel objects to *what* is presupposed in Kant's critique, rather than to the fact that it *presupposes* anything at all.[9] But with Hegel's recognition of the crisis and the epistemological demands, Hegel objects that Kant's critique *presupposes* something—namely, self-reflection as the ultimate authority in our knowing—and, hence, fails to meet its own demand to begin before the beginning in a reflection in which *nothing* has yet justified itself and in which everything is, accordingly, at stake. Kant's critique is not fully critical, since, in Kant's reflection, the standpoint of self-reflection, our standpoint, is not equally at stake with the possibility of metaphysics. Kant's critique does not allow the skeptical crisis

---

[8] As we will see below, it turns out that the *way* in which critique brings the science to be is an important part of the difference of Hegel's critique from Kant's. What I am emphasizing here is that Hegel returns to Kantian critique to the extent that he recognizes that, insofar as we lack shared criteria, there is a sense in which the science does not yet exist; and there is a sense in which it will come to exist only through achieving shared criteria.

[9] Recall Hegel's denial in VSP of the need to justify or ground the principle of philosophy; the task is simply to bring the presupposed principle to consciousness (255/342).

fully to flower. The difference between the early view and the *Phenomenology* is the difference between rejecting (Kantian) critique and radicalizing it.

Hegel's return to critique poses two prominent questions for us. First, what motivates Hegel's return to critique? If Hegel had earlier been content to reject the project of critique and its epistemological demands as inherently subjectivist or dogmatic, how does he come to see the *need* for the *Phenomenology*? Why is critique *necessary*? Second, Hegel's objection, according to which Kantian critique is inherently subjectivist or skeptical, renders the possibility of fulfilling the epistemological demands of the critical turn problematic. How does Hegel propose to undertake the prior, reflective investigation into the criterion without presupposing subjectivism (or anything else)? How is critique *possible*? The latter question concerns what becomes of the methodology of Kantian critique under the pressures to which Hegel submits it. I address this in the last chapter by providing a reading of Hegel's paragraphs on methodology in the Introduction. The former question concerns the justification of the need for the project of the *Phenomenology*. I will present Hegel's reply in this chapter.

4.2 THE RETURN TO CRITIQUE AND THE RELATION OF PHILOSOPHY TO ITS HISTORY

Hegel's return to critique implies a significant change in his conception of philosophy's 'Idea' and, hence, a change in the sort of idealism that he advances. Through this development in his thought, Hegel comes to see philosophy's Idea as itself *historical*, as itself something that develops and becomes what it is.

I have argued in the previous chapter that Hegel's rejection of the epistemological demand expressed in Kant's critical project belongs to a general rejection of distinctively modern epistemological demands and procedures. According to Hegel's diagnosis, the distinctively modern in philosophy is an expression of the valorization in modern European culture of the 'self-standing' subject, the ordinary consciousness, over against the absolute. Hegel conceives the epistemological project of bridging a gap between the merely subjective and the objective as an expression of this valorization; he judges the project to consist in the dogmatic application of the principle of ordinary consciousness (the principle of non-identity). According to the view Hegel presents in the article on the relation of skepticism to philosophy, we achieve the expression and cognition of the Idea (the principle of identity) through a procedure that skeptically attacks ordinary criteria of knowledge. Hegel presents the ancient skeptical practice as a *via negativa* that takes us out of the realm of appearances and elevates us to the intelligible realm through the destruction of ordinary consciousness and the construction of philosophical consciousness. We rise to the philosophical Idea along this skeptical path only through the annihilation of our natural attachment to self. The energy with which I cling to the dogmas or beliefs which ancient skeptical procedure attacks derives from regarding my particular, finite existence as at stake in the validity of the finite existences that are the objects of my belief. In shaking and dissolving my natural certainties, ancient skeptical practice threatens my existence. However, according to Hegel's interpretation of the highest end of the ancient skeptics, tranquility, I achieve genuine existence only through the destruction of these natural certainties—these identifications with finite exist-ences—along the skeptical path. In the philosophical knowledge achieved at the end of the skeptical path, I achieve the unification or identification with the infinite. From this perspective, distinctively modern epistemological demands look to be a sort of entrenchment of the age-old insistence on individual or particular subjectivity against the claims of philosophy. With the modern claim that the subject is self-certain or self-standing—that is, the claim that I am immediately certain of my own being independently of my relation to anything external or other to me—the dogmatic insistence on self is elevated to a first principle and the defense against philosophy becomes particularly entrenched.

Hegel's conception of philosophy and of the Idea in this period has import-ant consequences for his conception of how various systems of philosophy must be related to each other. Philosophy is knowledge of the Idea. The Idea is an ultimate principle of identity between being and thinking, subject and object. Since philosophy expresses this identity, it must not be conceived according to the model of ordinary cognition: we (as subjects) know an object (the Idea, in this case) that stands over against us. Rather, philosophy is alone genuine knowing exactly because in philosophy alone thinking and what is thought are identical. Thus, philosophy is reason's knowing of itself, which we rise to and participate in through the *via negativa*. An implication of this for Hegel is that the various manifestations of philosophy in different systems must themselves be identical. Hegel writes in the Criticism article:

That philosophy is and can be only *one* rests on the point that reason is only *one*. Just as there cannot be diverse rationalities, so too a wall cannot be established between reason and its self-knowledge, through which its self-knowledge could become essentially distinguishable from its appearance. For reason absolutely considered and reason as object of itself in self-knowledge (hence, as philosophy) are again just one and the same and throughout identical. (Hegel, WdpK, 172/275)

Accordingly, Hegel denies the possibility or coherence of the notion of a *particular* philosophy, of a philosophy tied to a particular person or culture or restricted to a particular time and place. The ambition of philosophy must be to know and to express the Idea, the eternal and unchangeable archetype, as the ground of all difference and particularity.

The implication for the conception of the history of philosophy is clear, and Hegel draws it explicitly. There can be no history of philosophy, in the sense, anyway, of an historical development *within* philosophy, since, granted the relation between the Idea and its expression in philosophy, this would imply an historical development in the Idea as well. Since the Idea has no history, but is eternally one and the same, unchangeable, philosophy has no history either. Hegel writes in the Difference Essay:

If however the absolute, along with its appearance, reason, is eternally one and the same (as it indeed is), then every rationality which has directed itself onto itself and known itself, has produced a true philosophy and solved the problem of philosophy, which is, along with its solution, in all times the same. Because in philosophy reason knows itself and has only to do with itself, there resides in reason itself its whole work and activity, and in regard to the inner essence of philosophy, there are neither predecessors nor successors. (Hegel, Diff, 17/87)

Hegel's conception of the object of philosophy at this time, hence of philosophy itself, mandates that, if some system manages to be philosophy at all, then to that extent there can be no before and no after with respect to it. As he puts it a couple of pages later in the same work, recurring to the comparison of philosophy with art which is much on his mind in this period: 'Every philosophy is perfect in itself and has, like a genuine work of art, the totality in itself' (Hegel, Diff, 19/89). As noted in the previous chapter, it follows that whatever is distinctively modern in systems of philosophy does not genuinely belong to philosophical truth. Just as there is no before and no after from the perspective of the standpoint of philosophy, so there is no ancient and no modern either. Just as the standpoint of philosophy must transcend (through unifying) any difference between the standpoint of *my* philosophy, say, and yours, between my truth and your truth, it must transcend any difference between a modern truth and an ancient one. Any philosophical discovery that Descartes, say, (or Kant) manages to express must also be present in Plato's system as well, granted that Plato's system expresses the Idea at all. This implies not that there can be no discovery in philosophy, but rather that philosophical discovery must always be recovery of truth that has been discovered and expressed before—and will be again.

How does this point bear on Hegel's conception of philosophical critique in this period of his thought? This essential identity—the identity of what counts as philosophical truth in Plato's system, say, with what counts as philosophical truth in Spinoza's or in Kant's—is not visible to the naked eye, as it were; differences are what we immediately see. Hence, the *appearance* of a history of philosophy. The recognition of the eternal and unchangeable Idea as expressed in some particular system of philosophical thought requires the labor of recovering the Idea through philosophy itself. Philosophy cannot be, by its nature, simply manifest on the face. It takes philosophy to know philosophy, as it were.[10] The work of making manifest the Idea as expressed in some particular system of thought (be it Plato's, Kant's, or some other) recovers the identity of that thought with all true philosophy; it recovers its universality, as it were, from the particularity of its expression. What passes for the history of philosophy is but different expressions and articulations, decked out in the dress befitting the particular time and place, of the one eternal and unchangeable Idea. Hence the appearance of a history of philosophy disappears exactly through the work of making manifest the eternal and unchangeable Idea as expressed in the particular work before us. This work elevates us above historical change to the eternal Idea.

Philosophical criticism, as Hegel presents it in this early article, consists precisely in this work. As noted, philosophical critique is the relating of philosophy to some *appearance* of philosophy. As in criticism of a work of art, the work of philosophical critique consists in recognizing the universal expressed in this particular, or in showing how the particular, singular representation, despite its various time- and place-bound elements, nevertheless manages to express 'the totality in itself', i.e., the Idea. 'When the Idea of philosophy is really present [in some work under consideration], it is the business of critique to make distinct the manner and degree in which it emerges freely and clearly, as well as the extent to which it organizes itself into a scientific system of philosophy' (Hegel, WdpK, 174/277).

---

[10] This is *part* anyway of what Hegel means in the striking claim he makes in this article (which will be discussed below): 'Philosophy is by its nature esoteric'.

Thus, the characterization in Section 4.1 of this early conception of critique as judgment is not complete. This characterization misses the dynamic quality of the process. Through critique, the Idea, as implicitly present in some object work, is made manifest or explicit. This process has two sides: the positive side of showing the *truth* expressed in the work, and the negative side of showing the *nothingness* of the particular, individual, and subjective features of the object work. Thus, we can perhaps describe the work of criticism, as Hegel conceives it in the early article, not only as judgment and not only as manifestation of the Idea, but also as the work of purification of the object, since through this process the truth hidden in the particularity of the work is, for lack of a better word, distilled out, and the falsehood (that is, the particularity or subjectivity) refined away.[11]

Indeed, Hegel in this article seems to conceive of a work of philosophy as a sort of mixture or factor of two opposing forces. We can describe these as the tendency toward the objective, on the one hand, and the tendency to preserve subjectivity, on the other. In this article, Hegel revealingly describes the Idea as 'the objective' (*das Objektive*) (WdpK, 175/277). Hegel claims here that there is a genuine need (*Bedürfnis*) that seeks and can find satisfaction only in the Idea or the objective. The counter-tendency is to preserve, or to express as true or as universal, what is merely subjective. Thus, despite the fact that expression of the objective satisfies a genuine need, the objective is nonetheless threatening, insofar as rising to it requires a sort of self-surrender or self-annihilation. The particular expression of philosophy represents a compromise between these forces. The philosophical critic must side with the tendency to express the objective against the tendency to preserve individuality or subjectivity.[12]

---

[11] The reader may detect a tension in Hegel's view on criticism at this period, as I have presented it. If the Idea can be more or less manifest in some particular expression—emerge more or less freely and clearly, as he writes in the quotation above—then can it not in principle be fully explicit, hence exoteric? There is, *prima facie*, a conflict between the view (1) that the Idea is, when present, always completely present, though the recognition of it and its completeness always requires the work of recovery; and the view (2) that the Idea, though perhaps completely present whenever it is expressed at all, is expressed in differing degrees of explicitness, thus implying the ideal, at least, of perfect explicitness. I do not attempt to resolve this tension here; as I discuss below, internal tension in the view Hegel expresses on criticism in this early article in part motivates his moving beyond this view to the project of the *Phenomenology*.

[12] Hegel writes in WdpK: 'When it shows itself here that the Idea of philosophy is really present [*wirklich vorschwebt*], critique can cleave to the demand and to the need which expresses itself, and to the objective in which the need seeks its satisfaction, and critique can refute the limitedness of the form [*Gestalt*] out of its own genuine tendency towards complete objectivity' (175/277). I am struck by the similarity between Hegel's conception here of the work of the philosophical critic and Freud's

In the Criticism article, Hegel catalogues types of such compromise and characterizes the specific work of critique that each type calls for. That Hegel here depicts philosophy as pitched in a battle against subjectivity is significant for our purposes. For Hegel here, to achieve philosophy is to annihilate one's subjectivity, since subjectivity is in itself *nothing*. Hegel associates the expression of subjectivity with what he calls here 'Unphilosophy', which, as the opposite of philosophy, is nothing at all, pure pretension. But this nothing that we individually are can seem to us, standing over against philosophy, everything; and thus Hegel offers an account—not very elaborated, but suggestive nonetheless—of our *resistance* to philosophy. If the achievement of philosophy requires the surrender of ourselves, then our efforts to evade philosophy, even in counterfeit expressions of it, have intelligible motivation. The dynamic Hegel describes here between the objective and subjectivity is not distinctively modern, but as old as philosophy itself. What is distinctively modern is the insistence on individual subjectivity as self-standing, as having an irrefutable claim to its own being independently of its relation to the absolute.

Among the types of compromise (between the expression of the objective and the expression of subjectivity) that Hegel catalogues, one is recognizably the type exhibited by Kantian critical philosophy. Hegel describes it in the following passage, together with the critical method of dealing with it.

Or it is evident [in contrast to the previous case] that the Idea of philosophy is more distinctly known, but that subjectivity has striven to defend against philosophy to the extent necessary to save itself. —The task is not to set the Idea of philosophy in relief, but rather to reveal the nooks and crannies which subjectivity employs in order to evade philosophy, and to make the weakness for which any limitation offers a secure foothold visible *both for* its own sake and for the sake of the Idea of philosophy which is here associated with a subjectivity; for the true energy of the idea and subjectivity are incompatible. (WdpK, 175–6/278)

In Kant's philosophical system, the Idea of philosophy is fairly distinctly expressed as the autonomy of reason. However, it is the distinctive feature of the Kantian philosophy, Hegel claims, that, at the point where the Idea

---

conception of the therapeutic work of the psychoanalyst. The particular expression of philosophy is the result of a more or less compromised attempt to gain satisfaction for a genuine need. The satisfaction is not complete, and the expression is distorted, since we oppose the satisfaction we at the same time seek. We fear the satisfaction of this need; we fear the objective. The expression of philosophy is, consequently, a compromise between two opposing forces. The philosophical critic must, like the psychoanalyst, side with the satisfaction of the need, against the inhibiting, defensive, self-protective tendency.

is on the tip of reason's tongue, so to speak, thought shrinks back, reverts to subjectivism: the Idea is merely for us, not in itself; reason is supposedly autonomous, but then autonomous reason is set over against an external reality from which it must borrow its content, but into which it can have no insight (VSP, 269/352). Accordingly, the criticism of Kant's philosophy must consist in convicting and condemning the subjectivism by cleaving to the Idea of philosophy it itself expresses, though obscurely. In the process of recovering or expressing 'the truth of Kant's philosophy' from what is merely subjective in it, the articulation of subjectivity it contains must be refined away. Hegel's rejection of the subjectivism of Kant's thought is, at first, the rejection of the articulation of subjectivity within it.

However, as I discuss in detail below, Hegel comes to recognize that the subjectivism of Kant's idealism is closely bound up with a distinctively Kantian discovery and articulation of a principle of subjectivity (which is, in turn, a sort of refinement of a general discovery of the subject in modern philosophy, a discovery which backs distinctively modern epistemological projects in general). Hegel's return to Kantian critique turns, in great part, on his recognition that its epistemological demand is backed by a modern self-discovery. Hegel's belated recognition of Kant's articulation of subjectivity as a particular *development* or *advance* in philosophy (which, accordingly, belongs to the truth of Kant's system) accompanies a change in Hegel's conception of the nature of the truth of philosophy itself. Hegel's previous conception of the Idea precluded the possibility of development in philosophy. Given the identity, as Hegel conceives it, between the Idea and reason's self-knowledge in philosophy, the recognition of development in philosophy requires recognition of development in the Idea as well. Whereas Hegel had previously conceived of a philosophy as essentially complete in every expression, with no before and no after, essentially without a history, now he conceives it, along with the truth known through it, as essentially historical. The Idea of philosophy is now no longer an 'eternal and unchangeable archetype', but something essentially historical, something which *becomes* what it is. 'In my view', Hegel writes, famously, in the Preface to the *Phenomenology*, 'everything turns on grasping and expressing the true, not only as *substance* but equally as *subject*' (PhG, 22–3/¶17). Hegel's discovery of the principle of subjectivity as a modern discovery requires the reconception of the Idea or the absolute as itself also subject, in the sense that the philosophical Idea itself, like a human, rational being, becomes what it is through a process of self-development. The claim that the absolute is subject implies not merely that it becomes what it is, but also that its becoming is in relation to knowledge of itself (in philosophy). Not only does reason have a past, but its past is constitutive of it, so that reason's knowledge of itself (that is, philosophy) must also be knowledge of its development.

How Hegel conceives 'the true' or the Idea as also subject, and how this requires the conception of the true as essentially historical and as essentially determined through its knowledge of itself in the history of culture, lies outside of our focus. I wanted here merely to show the scope of the change in Hegel's philosophy signified by his return to critique and give some sense of its nature. Hegel's act of 'taking on subjectivity', if I may put it that way, has significant consequences throughout his thought, not just in epistemology. Through this turn, Hegel's relation to philosophical idealism becomes much more complicated; he no longer elevates an ancient (or, for him, eternal) model against modern, subjective, epistemological idealisms, but rather he attempts to conceive an idealism that reconciles the predominant ancient and modern models. This requires conceiving and expressing an 'Idea', a 'truth', that becomes what it is.

4.3 THE RIGHTS OF ORDINARY CONSCIOUSNESS AND THE NEED FOR CRITIQUE

We turn now to the question of the motivation of Hegel's return to Kantian critique. Hegel addresses this question (though not under this description) in his justification of the need for the project of the *Phenomenology* in the Preface and Introduction of that work. Hegel's answer turns on his belated recognition of *our right* (the right of ordinary consciousness) to demand of philosophy or of metaphysics that its claims be demonstrated (their intelligibility and necessity) to us, with reference to our criteria of justification and truth. This epistemological demand is itself backed by a self-discovery, a self-discovery that is distinctively modern. We have discovered ourselves as *self-standing*; we have discovered in self-reflection that we are immediately certain of our own being, which implies that we are certain of ourselves independently of our relation to the absolute. With his recognition of our right to demand, Hegel recognizes the condition in which we stand over against metaphysics, lacking shared criteria by which to assess its claims, as a condition of crisis for metaphysics. The *Phenomenology* is a response to this crisis. The *Phenomenology* presents the process of constituting a mutually recognized criterion out of this condition of opposition in which nothing has yet justified itself as authoritative. The possibility and the existence of metaphysics are at stake in this prior reflection on criteria.

I will proceed by comparing prominent ways in which Hegel, early and late at Jena, stages what I will call 'the scene of criticism'.[13] What I mean by 'the scene of criticism' is best communicated by quoting Hegel's most important staging of it. This occurs in the Preface in the context of Hegel's justification of the need for the *Phenomenology*:

> The standpoint of consciousness, which knows objects [*gegenständliche Dinge*] opposite itself and itself in opposition to objects, counts for science as the other [*das Andere*] to its own standpoint. The condition in which consciousness knows itself to be at home is for science marked by the loss [*Verlust*] of spirit. Conversely, the element of science is for consciousness a transcendent beyond, in which it no longer possesses itself. Each of these two standpoints appears to the other to be the inversion of the truth [*das Verkehrte der Wahrheit*]. (PhG, 30/¶30)

This is a scene of criticism by virtue of the fact that consciousness is represented as standing over against the standpoint of metaphysics, in a scene of opposition in which common criteria of justification are exactly lacking. To borrow Kant's figure, ordinary consciousness and philosophy or metaphysics encounter each other in a *state of nature*.[14]

In this condition, we stand *opposed* to each other. This means that, according to the criteria of truth that characterize each party, the criteria of the other party have no truth. 'Each of these two standpoints appears to the other to be the inversion of truth.' Thus, from the standpoint of philosophy or of science, the standpoint of ordinary consciousness is 'marked by the loss of spirit'. The standpoint of consciousness is oppositional in the sense that ordinary consciousness knows itself to stand over against the realm of objects which it knows. (Hegel's word choice is significant here. What 'objects' translates in the above passage is *gegenständliche Dinge*: literally, 'things which stand over

---

[13] I find it helpful to characterize Hegel's various depictions of philosophy standing over against its 'other', namely ordinary consciousness, as 'the scene of criticism', adapting a device employed by Stanley Cavell in another context. In the context of discussing Kripke's 'solution' to Wittgenstein's supposed skeptical problem regarding rule-following, Cavell claims that the picturing of what he calls 'the scene of instruction' is essential to the debate. (See Cavell, *Conditions Handsome and Unhandsome*, ch. 2.)

[14] Kant employs this figure in the Transcendental Doctrine of Method in the First *Critique*: 'Without this [critique of pure reason], reason is as it were in the state of nature, and it cannot make its assertions and claims valid or secure them except through war' (Kant, KrV, A751/B779). (I quote the passage at greater length, and comment on it, in Ch. 2)

against'.) But achieving the standpoint of philosophy—that is, of reason or spirit—implies achieving insight into the ultimate principle of identity from which derive the oppositions which characterize this standpoint. In this sense, from the standpoint of philosophy, the oppositions that structure cognition as conceived from the standpoint of ordinary consciousness have no truth.

Hegel insists here that the alienation is mutual. From the standpoint of ordinary consciousness, the element of science, the standpoint of metaphysics or of philosophy, is a transcendent beyond [*eine jenseitige Ferne*] in which the individual no longer possesses himself. In the period of Enlightenment philosophy, the concepts, claims, and questions which constitute the field of metaphysics are, relative to the standpoint of the ordinary rational subject, distant and devoid of meaning. Hegel here acknowledges the condition of disorientation in which ordinary consciousness is cast by metaphysical inquiry, the condition of disorientation that Kant diagnoses and aims to address in his critical inquiry. Inquiries into the nature or existence of God, the origin or cause of the world, or the nature of the human soul seem *ungrounded* above all. We speak of 'flights' of metaphysics, because it seems from the standpoint of ordinary consciousness that in order to pursue such questions we must surrender our firm footing and abandon ourselves to an element in which we are disoriented and dispossessed. Hegel further illustrates our sense of self-dispossession in metaphysics in the continuation of the above passage:

For natural consciousness to entrust itself straightway to science is for it to make the attempt, attracted by it knows not what, to go about on its head once too. The force to assume this unwonted position and to move about in it is apparently a violence it is expected to do itself, without preparation and without necessity. Whatever science may be in itself, in relation to immediate self-consciousness, it presents itself as something inverted [*als ein Verkehrtes gegen es*]. (PhG, 30/¶26)

The question why the project of the *Phenomenology*, or why Kantian critique, is necessary is the question of why this condition of mutual opposition and alienation constitutes a crisis for metaphysics. Why is this condition intolerable for philosophy? Why must philosophy come to terms with this opposed standpoint, with ordinary consciousness and its criteria?

It belongs to Hegel's earlier view that philosophy need not—indeed cannot—come to terms with this opposed standpoint. One sees this by comparing Hegel's staging of the scene of criticism in the above passage with Hegel's presentation of this stand-off between philosophy and the ordinary understanding in the Criticism article:

Philosophy is by its nature something esoteric. It is neither made for the vulgar nor capable of being spread to the vulgar. It is philosophy only through being exactly opposed to the understanding, and hence even more to the healthy human understanding, by which one means the limitedness in space and time of a race of human beings. In relation to this, the world of philosophy is in and for itself an inverted world [*eine verkehrte Welt*]. (WdpK, 182/282–3)

Hegel here addresses the question whether the truths of philosophy can or ought to be made common or ordinary (*gemein*); that is, whether they can be made available to what Hegel calls in this period 'the ordinary consciousness' (*das gemeine Bewußtsein*). Hegel's claim that 'the world of philosophy'—what Hegel calls in the Preface to the *Phenomenology* 'the element of philosophy'—represents 'an inverted world' relative to our ordinary or common world, the world of ordinary consciousness, is here employed to a purpose exactly counter to its employment in the Preface passage above. In the Preface, the purpose is to specify an epistemological crisis to which the *Phenomenology* responds. In the Criticism article, the purpose is to reject as unjustified the demands of ordinary consciousness to understand philosophy. If it seems that philosophy demands that the aspirant to philosophy dispossess herself of herself in order to achieve its standpoint, well philosophy does indeed demand this, and *must* demand it by its own nature. 'Philosophy is by its nature something esoteric.' Because philosophy's Idea is attained only through the ancient skeptical *via negativa* along which the criteria of ordinary consciousness are shown to be inadequate for genuine knowledge, philosophy's Idea is inaccessible to ordinary consciousness as such.

The revolution in Hegel's thought, his return to critique, turns on his recognition of the epistemological demands that he here rejects. According to the Preface of the *Phenomenology*, the claims of philosophy *must* be made commonly intelligible (*verständlich*) as a condition of the existence of philosophy as a science. We can see this turn made by following further Hegel's staging of the scene of criticism in the Preface. Hegel reiterates there the demand that philosophy must make on us in our encounter with it: 'The beginning of philosophy makes the presupposition or the demand that consciousness find itself in the element [of science]' (PhG, 29/¶26). Or, a few sentences further: 'Science from its side demands of self-consciousness that it have elevated itself [to the standpoint of philosophy]'.[15] But here Hegel recognizes *our right* to make a

---

[15] I have substituted 'to the standpoint of philosophy' here for 'into this aether', in order to keep the parallelism clear and not to confuse. It is clear from the way in which Hegel characterizes this

corresponding demand on philosophy as well: 'Conversely', Hegel continues, 'the individual has the right to demand that science at least extend to him the ladder to this standpoint, or show him the ladder in himself.' This is exactly the demand of critique which Hegel earlier maintains is incompatible with the truth of philosophy: the demand that philosophy justify and make intelligible its claims to us, who occupy a standpoint apparently external or opposite to that of philosophy.[16] The project or journey of the *Phenomenology* is founded on the right of the individual or ordinary understanding to demand this of philosophy. The work of the *Phenomenology* consists in meeting this demand. Independently of the individual's right to demand, the *Phenomenology* is not necessary. On Hegel's earlier position, according to which this demand is inherently subjectivistic, the work of the *Phenomenology* is not possible.

It is clear both in the Criticism article and in the relevant passages in the Preface and Introduction to the Phenomenology that Hegel's stance with respect to the right of the individual or of ordinary consciousness to demand of philosophy that it makes its claims intelligible to him reflects his stance with respect to the ideals and claims of the European Enlightenment. This is indeed a pivot on which Hegel returns to the stance of philosophical critique. In the Criticism article, Hegel follows his assertion of the esotericism of philosophy with the following passage:

In these times of freedom and equality however, in which a great public has formed itself that will not stand to know itself excluded from anything, but rather holds itself as good for everything—or everything as good enough for it—in these times,

---

'aether' or this 'element of philosophy' that it is to be identified with what we have been calling the principle of philosophy: 'This *pure* self-knowledge in absolute being-other, this aether *as such*, is the ground and soil of science [*Wissenschaft*] or of *knowing in general* [*das Wissen im Allgemeinen*]' (PhG, 29/¶26).

[16] In the Criticism article, Hegel writes, in the context of claiming that philosophy is by its nature esoteric, that 'philosophy must certainly recognize the possibility that the people [*das Volk*] will elevate itself to it, though it must never lower itself to the people' (WdpK, 182/283). Hegel's claim here that philosophy must recognize the possibility that people will elevate themselves to the standpoint of philosophy is perhaps to be set over against Schelling's comment in his *Fernere Darstellungen*, written about the same time, which implies that philosophy ought to 'cut off the way to [philosophy] sharply and isolate it on all sides from common cognition in such a way that no path or pavement can lead from [common cognition] to [philosophy]' (Schelling, *Fernere Darstellungen*, 414). But Hegel's recognition in the Criticism article that philosophy must recognize that people *can* elevate themselves to philosophy is far short of his recognition in the Preface to the *Phenomenology* of the right of the individual to demand that philosophy demonstrate its principle by constructing the path from the standpoint of ordinary consciousness to the standpoint of philosophy. It is this recognition that the possibility of philosophical knowledge is at stake in the task of justifying its criteria to the opposed ordinary consciousness that constitutes Hegel's return to the standpoint of philosophical critique. (See discussion at end of Ch 3.)

the highest beauty and the greatest good cannot escape the fate of being mishandled by commoners [*die Gemeinheit*] … until it is made common enough [*gemein genug*] for it to be appropriated … . The Enlightenment already expresses in its origin, and then in its realized essence, the commonness [*die Gemeinheit*] of the understanding and its vain exaltation above reason. (WdpK, 182–3/283)

In affirming the esotericism of philosophy in the Criticism article, Hegel dismisses the aspirations of the ordinary understanding to appropriate for itself the truths of philosophy. Hegel recognizes and allows that this dismissal puts him at odds with 'these times of freedom and equality', presumably because he supposes that the aspirations of subjectivity in this period manifest the 'vain exaltation' of the understanding above reason. Given the young Hegel's enthusiasm for Enlightenment ideals and for the French Revolution, one might wonder whether the position he takes in the early Jena writings is a completely stable one. And, indeed, we see Hegel take a completely opposite stance in the *Phenomenology* to the question of the esotericism of philosophy. His passage concerning the esotericism of philosophy in the Preface occurs in the context of his famous claim that 'our time is a time of birth and transition to a new period' (PhG, 18/¶11). Hegel alludes with this claim to the French Revolution, and its aftermath, then shaking Europe. However, given the context of Hegel's justification of the need for a particular epistemological project, I take Hegel also to allude with this claim to Kant's characterization of our age as an age of criticism.[17] Among the points Hegel is concerned to make with his remarkable comparison of 'our' time of transition, revolution, and crisis with the birth of a child is the point that the first appearance of the new or the novel remains distant from what it will be in its complete development and articulation. 'But this new world is no more a complete reality than is a newborn child; it is essential to bear this in mind' (PhG, 19/¶12). This brave new world, this world that has just come on the scene, is still, like a newborn baby, nine-tenths promise. This promise is realized only through the work of what Hegel calls here *Ausbildung*.

A lot of meaning is packed into *Ausbildung* as Hegel employs it. A natural initial rendering would be 'education'. However, given the containment of *Bildung* in the word, it also connotes cultivation, formation, or the activity of taking definite shape. Hegel's point about the newborn infant is that the

---

[17] 'Our age is, in especial degree, the age of criticism, and to criticism everything must submit. Religion through its sanctity, and law-giving through its majesty, may seek to exempt themselves from it. But then they awaken just suspicion, and cannot claim sincere respect which reason accords only to that which has been able to sustain the test of free and open examination' (Kant, KrV, Axi n.).

inherent potentialities of a newborn are realized only through the long labor of
forming and developing them. To give form to these inherent capacities is not
to impose on them a form initially alien to them (as, say, in the ancient example
of the sculptor and the formless lump of bronze), but rather to undertake the
labor which enables the form already implicit to emerge (as in the ancient
example of the acorn and the oak tree, to which Hegel in fact explicitly
refers here). This new world, or this new human being, must become what *it*
specifically already is, but as yet only potentially. The work of making explicit
the implicit form is importantly for Hegel the work of specification, or better
perhaps, as *Ausbildung* is in fact translated here by Miller, of articulation.
This work is also the work of *realization*. When the newborn first comes on
the scene [*das erste Auftreten*], it has the form of mere *appearance*. It achieves
complete *reality* [*eine vollkommene Wirklichkeit*] only through this labor.

What does this have to do with esotericism, on the one hand, and with
criticism on the other? The allusion to political developments and the analogy
with child development serve here merely as an illustration of Hegel's primary
concern, which is with the development of the science of metaphysics. When
Hegel writes here that 'that which first comes on the scene is present only in
its immediacy or in its concept', he refers primarily to philosophy: 'Science,
the crown of a world of spirit, is not complete in its beginning.' Hegel applies
the points he has made intuitive with the case of the newborn child to the
case of metaphysics:

Without such articulation [*Ausbildung*], science dispenses with universal *intelligibility*
[*Verständlichkeit*], and has the appearance of being an esoteric possession of a singular
few: an esoteric possession since it is present at first only in its concept or in its
inwardness; of a singular few, since its undiffused appearance renders its existence
something singular. Only that which is completely determined is at the same time
exoteric, comprehensible, capable of being learned and of being the property of all.
The intelligible form [*die verständige Form*] of science is the path to it offered to all and
made the same for all. And to arrive at rational knowledge [philosophy] through the
understanding is the just demand of any consciousness that confronts [*hinzutreten*]
science. For the understanding is thinking, or the pure I in general ... (PhG,
19–20/¶13)

This passage, like the later one in the same text, marks Hegel's return to critique through his acknowledgment of our right to demand in this encounter
that science or metaphysics make itself intelligible (*verständlich*) to us,
'through the understanding'. But since the topic here is explicitly the esotericism of philosophy, the contrast with the position of the early article could not

be starker. When science first comes on the scene, it is or appears to be something esoteric, something not generally intelligible. But it *must become* exoteric, it must become intelligible generally, it must be made publicly available.[18]

Though I postpone to the next chapter the question of how Hegel now understands critique to be possible (without presupposing subjectivism), I must say more about why he now regards it as necessary. If the project of the *Phenomenology* is founded on the right of the individual to make its demand vis-à-vis philosophy, then what is this right itself based on, the right that Hegel had earlier refused to recognize? Hegel addresses this question very briefly in the Preface in the context in which he recognizes the right.

[The individual's] right is based on his absolute independence [*Selbständigkeit*], which he knows himself to possess in each configuration [*Gestalt*] of his knowledge. For in each, whether recognized by science or not, and whatever the content may be, the individual is the absolute form, that is, he is the *immediate certainty* of himself, or should this expression be preferred, unconditioned *being*. (PhG, 29–30/¶26)

In claiming that the individual or self-consciousness 'is the immediate *certainty* of himself, or should this expression be preferred, unconditioned *being*', I take Hegel to refer to Descartes's *cogito* argument. Later in the paragraph, affirming the need from science's own point of view to recognize and to meet the individual's demand, Hegel claims that the individual or self-consciousness 'has the principle of its actual existence in the certainty of itself'. In such passages, Hegel seems to recognize that the individual has in immediate self-consciousness certainty of its own existence, independently of its relation to another, in particular, independently of its relation to the absolute. But this immediate self-certainty of the finite subject is just what Hegel rejects as the starting point of philosophy in his commentary on the subjective idealisms of Kant and Fichte in his early Jena writings. In a passage from the article on skepticism attacking the modern skeptic's claim that facts of consciousness are immediately certain (a passage quoted and discussed above in Chapter 3), Hegel writes that 'to exist in a conditioned way and to be for itself nothing certain [*für sich nichts Gewißes*] is the same' (VSP, 221/318). But now he seems to claim that the self has immediate certainty of its existence, as finite thinking thing, independently of relation to the absolute. How are we to understand Hegel's recognition here of a distinctively modern self-discovery as making necessary a distinctively modern epistemological project?

---

[18] For an account of the theme of esotericism of philosophy in the transition from Kant to Hegel, see Franks, *Kant and Hegel on the Esotericism of Philosophy*.

This question deserves a fuller treatment than I can give it here. Despite appearances, Hegel does not surrender his claim that secure knowledge of what is finite or conditioned depends on knowledge of the unconditioned or the absolute (insofar as the former is determined finally as grounded in the latter). Thus, what consciousness is certain of, in immediate self-reflection, is not, despite Hegel's allusions to Descartes's *cogito* argument in the passages quoted above, its existence as a finite (conditioned) thinking thing. Instead, what is claimed in immediate self-consciousness is the normative standing of *subject*, that is, the standing of determining for oneself the good and the true through the giving and taking of reasons. Accordingly, the better reference for understanding Hegel's new recognition of the right of the individual to make its epistemological demand of philosophy (in preference to that of Descartes' *cogito*) is the claim of the individual rational being within Kant's critical philosophy to autonomy. In Chapter 2 above, I attempt to show that the epistemological demand of Kantian critique expresses the subject's claim to autonomy, insofar as the latter is contained in its claim not to be bound by an external authority, or, positively put, to be bound only by principles the authority of which can be legitimated in the process of its reflection on norms or principles. I noted that this claim is bound up with its claim to being a rational subject at all, a subject who as rational is responsible for the conformity of its judgments to the norms of reason. I noted that, though Kant does not make explicit the relation of the epistemological demand of critique to autonomy, he does indicate that relation in the following passage from the *Groundwork*: 'Now, one cannot possibly think of a reason that would consciously receive direction from any other quarter with respect to its judgments, since the subject would then attribute the determination of his judgment not to his reason but to an impulse' (Kant, GMS, 4: 448). Our very conception of ourselves as rational implies that nothing determines our judgment except insofar as it is mediated by our *recognition* of it as a (sufficient) reason, as justifying that which we come to hold on its basis. This implies our right, as rational subjects, to demand justification of the claims of metaphysics in reflection as a condition of our recognition of their authority or validity for us. Interestingly, in the context of discussing (Kantian) morality in his later *Philosophy of Right*, Hegel explicitly recognizes 'the right of the subject not to recognize that which I lack insight into as rational', and calls it 'the highest right of the subject' (Hegel, PhR, §132A).

Though the *Philosophy of Right* appears many years after the *Phenomenology*, the above-quoted passages show that Hegel comes to recognize this right of the subject while at Jena and, on its basis, the need for the project of the

Phenomenology. What remains unclarified is how the assertion of this right, or, correlatively, the standing as rational being, is grounded in immediate self-consciousness. Here I will merely remark that Hegel's assertion of the relation between the normative standing as subject and immediate self-consciousness is an inheritance from the philosophies of Kant and Fichte. I have argued in Part I that Kant's principle of apperception, which he puts at the head of all human knowledge, expresses our normative standing as sources of judgment. Fichte develops this more explicitly. It would be a mistake to suppose that self-consciousness is appealed to in this context as a source of immediate evidence on the basis of which the right to make the relevant epistemological demands is justified. Rather the assertion of the relevant demands for justification implies the assertion of a normative standing (the standing as subject) that is *expressed* by a principle of self-consciousness. If this is the correct reference for understanding Hegel's remarks in the Preface, then we should not expect that the relation between self-consciousness and the right of individual self-consciousness to make its epistemological demand is that between evidence and assertion.

However exactly we are to understand Hegel's claim here regarding the basis of the individual's right to make the epistemological demand, we have seen that Hegel's project in the *Phenomenology of Spirit* comes to be through his coming to recognize the standing of individual self-consciousness, the claiming of which is characteristic of the Enlightenment, and with it the validity of the epistemological demand of Kantian critique.[19]

4.4 CRITIQUE AS THE REALIZATION OF THE SCIENCE OF METAPHYSICS

Not only does the individual make the epistemological demand upon science (metaphysics) that its claims be validated, justified, and made intelligible to it, as a condition of their claim to authority, but science must make this demand upon itself, since, in the absence of this 'critique'—as I think we

---

[19] In support of this interpretation, according to which Hegel himself comes to recognize the claim of the individual to the status of subject, I note that Hegel's rejection of the epistemological demand of critique in the early articles is accompanied by a denigration in those articles of subjectivity. 'Subjectivity' is virtually a *Schimpfwort* in the early articles. In the Criticism article in particular, subjectivity, standing over against 'the rational', or *das Objektive* is characterized by Hegel, not as something which must be reconciled to the standpoint of philosophy, but as nothing, as pure pretension, as a mirage to be dispelled.

may call it—philosophy *does not yet exist* as a science; or rather, it exists only potentially, as something yet unrealized, as something private and singular and inward. Philosophy's coming to terms with ordinary consciousness, out of an initial situation in which the two standpoints stand over against each other without common terms, is, according to Hegel, the *realization* of the science of philosophy, its coming to be. Hence, the work of critique, as Hegel conceives it here, is the work of *articulating* philosophy, of bringing philosophy's Idea, as something initially private and inward, to outward expression. What is initially the private and inward possession of a few must become the public possession of all. This work, which is the making of the Idea completely determinate, is at the same time the realization of the Idea.[20]

So, besides the demand for critique coming from the self-standing individual, over against the standpoint of metaphysics, there is also an internal demand for critique coming from within the standpoint of metaphysics itself. In this section, I address the question of how Hegel comes to recognize this internal demand, over against his earlier rejection of it.

Hegel presents the scene of criticism in the Preface as essentially a scene of opposition. Our standpoint, or the standpoint of natural consciousness, is opposed to the standpoint of philosophy: the truth of the one is the negation of the truth of the other.[21] The opposition consists in the absence of shared or common criteria. We noted in the previous chapter that Hegel's conception of the object of philosophical knowledge, of what he calls 'the Idea', requires that it not stand in a relation of opposition to anything else. As he puts it in the Skepticism article, 'the rational has no opposite' (VSP, 247/336). To find that what we know as the rational or as the Idea is caught in a structure of opposition signifies that we haven't yet attained insight into the rational after all, according to Hegel. The principle of reason is for him a principle of

[20] This is the point at which Hegel's break with Schelling is most immediately manifest. Schelling foregoes the work of criticism. He fails to recognize its necessity. He is willing to let philosophy (as knowledge of the Idea or of the absolute) remain the private possession of a few singular individuals. (He thinks it must be, as Hegel himself previously thought.) According to Hegel, the price he pays is that the Idea, according to his system, is completely indeterminate. The absolute is, on his conception of it, according to Hegel's famous accusation, 'the night in which, as the saying goes, all cows are black'. Schelling's principle is an empty formula which means nothing since, in abstaining from criticism out of a false sense of the purity of the Idea, he abstains from the work of articulating its meaning.

[21] That Hegel hammers on the oppositional structure of this scene of criticism is more obvious in the German original than in the English translation: *Wenn der Standpunkt des Bewußtseins, von gegenständliche Dingen im Gegensatze gegen sie zu wissen, der Wissenschaft als das Andre gilt ... so ist ihm dagegen das Elemente der Wissenschaft eine jenseitige Ferne, worin es sich selbst nicht mehr besitzt* (PhG, 30/¶26).

an identity from which all opposition, and hence all determinacy, ultimately derives. Since Hegel continues to hold this view at the time of the *Phenomenology*, in emphasizing the oppositional structure of the scene of criticism in the Preface, Hegel expresses a *problem* for philosophy or for science. The *Phenomenology* is the response to this problem. Since philosophy's criterion is such that it cannot bear to be opposed, on Hegel's view, the truth of philosophy depends on the work of eliminating this (apparent) opposition to its standpoint. Hence philosophy must come to terms with the apparently opposed standpoint of ordinary consciousness.

We must pause to note the emergence of a new determination of the work of critique: critique as the process of eliminating (apparent) opposition between standpoints through constituting common criteria. We have seen that Hegel represents critique in the Criticism article as *judgment*, and hence as the *application* of the criterion or as subsumption under the Idea. Philosophy relates to some appearance of philosophy. The critic judges the extent to which the Idea is present in the object work through comparison with the standard. We have further determined this early conception of critique as the *discrimination* of the Idea and the *manifestation* of it, and hence as the *purification* of the object work through demonstrating its ultimate unity with the one true philosophy. The work of the philosophical critic eliminates the appearance of difference between systems of metaphysics. Hegel's return to (Kantian) critique consists in his recognition that we exactly lack a justified criterion that can be applied. The condition of critique is exactly that nothing has yet justified itself. The criteria of metaphysics haven't yet been determined or established for us; criteria of metaphysical judgment are not yet shared. Critique is the process of *arriving at* common or justified criteria. Thus, it is the process of quitting the state of nature with respect to metaphysics and of entering a realm of recognized law. Critique is the process of constituting unity (or community), or of removing opposition, through constituting criteria as common out of a condition in which shared criteria do not yet exist. As Hegel puts it in the Preface, science must, lest it forego its own realization, 'posit as one with itself [the apparently opposed] self-consciousness' (PhG, 31/¶26).

But given that Hegel's early view already prominently contains the thought that opposition to its principle is intolerable for the true philosophy, it may seem, perhaps, that he should recognize already there the need for philosophy to come to terms with the standpoint of ordinary consciousness. We have seen that he already in the early article characterizes the standpoint of philosophy and the standpoint of ordinary consciousness as opposed: '[Philosophy] is only philosophy precisely through being opposed [*entgegengesetzt*] to the understanding, and even more to the healthy human understanding ...' (WdpK, 182/283). Given that philosophy cannot brook standing in a relation of opposition with anything, does this not already imply the need, from philosophy's side, to come to terms with ordinary consciousness?

This doesn't constitute an inconsistency in the early position, since Hegel has a reply to this challenge. Another important element of Hegel's early view is that the individual subject has no claim to its own being independent of its relation to the unconditioned. Subjectivity is in itself nothing; the criteria of ordinary consciousness, insofar as they are insisted on for their own sake, independent of their relation to the rational, are pure vanity. One rises to philosophy only via insight into their vanity as self-grounded principles. Exactly for this reason, we must rise to philosophy; it cannot descend to us. Accordingly, this opposition between the standpoint of philosophy and the standpoint of the ordinary consciousness is but the *appearance* of an opposition. What is in truth nothing does not stand over against anything. It seems, then, that Hegel's recognition of the demand of ordinary consciousness *vis-à-vis* philosophy turns not on any inconsistency in the earlier position concerning the oppositional structure of ordinary consciousness and philosophy, but on his coming to recognize the validity of the claims of the individual subject to his own being independently of the relation to the Idea: '[the individual] has in the certainty of itself the principle of its own reality'.

Though this is substantially correct, there are complications. We can't say that, while the opposition portrayed in the early article is merely apparent (since subjectivity is in itself nothing), the opposition portrayed in the Preface is *real* (since individual subjectivity is there recognized as self-standing). By the principle of Hegel's idealism, if what we know as the unconditioned turns out to be in a real structure of opposition, then what we know as unconditioned is not unconditioned after all. From the standpoint of science or philosophy, the project of the *Phenomenology*, as the process of reconciling these (apparently) opposed standpoints, is exactly necessary in order to show that this opposition is not real (or rather, as we will see, not *final*).

The important thought here is the following. According to Hegel's early view there are only two options: the opposition between ordinary consciousness and philosophical consciousness is either apparent or real. If the opposition is real, then what appears as the Idea is not the genuine unconditioned after all. If the opposition is merely apparent, then there are again two options: either the apparent opponent implicitly expresses the Idea, in which case critique, through manifesting the Idea, can show the identity of the apparent opponent with philosophy; or, alternatively, the apparent opponent lacks relation with the Idea, in which case it is nothing at all, and hence cannot stand over against philosophy. In the early article, the relation of philosophy to ordinary consciousness is depicted as the last of these cases. But *none* of these cases fits the relation as depicted in the *Phenomenology*. In the Preface and Introduction, Hegel claims that there is *at least the appearance* of opposition, and he claims that philosophy must not merely dismiss this opposition as apparent but must undertake the work of coming to terms with this opposite. (We will examine his reasoning a bit further below.) Through Hegel's return to critique and his recognition of subjectivity, Hegel has provided himself with another option for conceiving how appearance and reality are related in the context of critique. The work of critique overcomes the opposition through *constituting* a common standpoint; it institutes common criteria. This process is the *becoming*, the *realization*, of the unconditioned and of science. Through Hegel's recognition of subjectivity, he recognizes the unconditioned as *also* subject, in the sense that, like a newborn, it must become what it is. Philosophy's coming to be consists exactly in the critical process of coming to terms with ordinary consciousness, which stands over against it.[22]

So far, there is no inconsistency in the Criticism article, since, by virtue of the distinction between a real and an apparent opposition, Hegel can escape the demand of coming to terms with the opposed ordinary consciousness, despite the view, held consistently throughout, that philosophy cannot, on its own terms, brook opposition. However, a further point Hegel insists on in the Criticism article does present a difficulty for the dismissal of the demand of ordinary consciousness to have philosophy's Idea demonstrated to it. Hegel insists in the earlier article—indeed it is one of his main points there—that the appearance of opposition to philosophy renders philosophy or philosophy's Idea itself a mere appearance or a mere *party* in a dispute. The mere appearance of opposition to philosophy unseats philosophy's claim. Part of Hegel's later justification of the need for the *Phenomenology*, hence for coming to terms with ordinary consciousness, relies on this same claim and proceeds by essentially rehearsing the reasoning in the earlier article.

---

[22] Hegel writes in the Preface: 'It is this becoming of *science in general*, or of *knowing* [*dies Werden des Wissenschaft überhaupt, oder des Wissens*] which this *phenomenology* presents' (PhG, 31/¶27).

Recall that, according to Hegel's conception in the Criticism article, a philosophical work is essentially a compromise between 'the energy' of the Idea/objective on the one hand, and subjective or particular or individual elements on the other. The Idea may be more or less consciously or clearly recognized in the work, making for the different cases of critique that Hegel catalogues and discusses. However, the general task of the critic is always to make manifest the Idea so far as it is present or to discriminate the eternal and necessary from the time-bound or subjective. At the limit is the case in which the objectwork bears no relation to the true, in the sense that the Idea is completely absent from it. In this interesting case, there is only the appearance of opposition, not because there is implicitly an identity (to be made explicit through critique) between what is expressed in the work, albeit obscurely, and philosophy's Idea, but because the work lacks any relation to the Idea and is, hence, nothing at all. Lacking any relation to the Idea, the work is pure pretension or subjectivity. Hegel claims, interestingly, that, in this case, critique is impossible. 'The business of critique is thoroughly lost on those works which have dispensed with the Idea' (WdpK, 173/276). His reason, it seems, is the same as his reason for claiming in this article that we must already possess the criterion in undertaking philosophical critique: critique, as (objective) judgment, presupposes at least implicitly shared terms. Critique is not possible in this case because the object of critique lacks the resources to be able to *recognize* the basis of judgment. The judgment of the work that wholly lacks the Idea must appear to the other, he writes, as a 'one-sided despotic decree [*ein einseitiger Machtspruch*]' (Hegel, WdpK, 173/276). The judgment in philosophical critique must be by way of appeal to the Idea of philosophy, 'which, however, because it isn't recognized by the opponent, is for the other a foreign tribunal [*ein fremder Gerichtshof*]' (WdpK, 173–4/276). Hegel evidently holds already in this early article that philosophical criticism consists in arriving at a *mutually recognized* judgment, at a mutually recognized agreement, from an initial position of *apparent* disagreement or difference. But he also holds that critique presupposes that the parties *already share* (at least implicitly) the criterion. Whereas philosophical critique occurs, originally for Kant and later for Hegel, exactly in the condition of finding ourselves in a state of nature with respect to one another—confronting one another, lacking common terms by which to negotiate our mutual claims—here Hegel explicitly maintains that philosophical critique, as objective judgment, exactly presupposes that we have already quit that condition, that the common terms of judgment have already been instituted. The condition that for Kant constitutes the condition of philosophical critique is explicitly for Hegel in this early article a condition in which philosophical critique is impossible.

However, the significant point is that Hegel recognizes *already* in this early article that this state of nature, this condition in which philosophy faces off with that which in no way recognizes the Idea—'Unphilosophy' as he calls it—is a state of *crisis* for philosophy. Thus the germ of his mature view is already evident here. When the Idea is lacking and the condition of an eventual mutual recognition, hence of critique, is revoked, philosophy falls into embarrassment (*Verlegenheit*), according to Hegel. In this case, in the case in which *judgment* is not possible, it seems that nothing is left to philosophy but repudiation [*Verwerfung*].

In repudiating, however, critique breaks completely all relation of that which lacks the Idea to that in the service of which criticism functions. Because the mutual recognition is hereby negated, there appear merely two subjectivities opposite each other. Things which have nothing in common come on the scene with equal right for that very reason. (WdpK, 173/276)

In the condition in which philosophy faces off with its opposite (the condition in which the criterion of judgment, and with it philosophy's judgment or truth, is itself undermined), philosophy's right to claim has itself been revoked. Philosophy has neither more nor less right than that which stands over against it, since the precondition of having any right at all has been revoked. This is merely to repeat that they encounter each other in a *state of nature*, in which the question of right cannot be determined. Hence Hegel claims that, in the absence of at least implicitly shared criteria, the two parties appear merely as two *subjectivities* opposite one another.

When philosophy stands over against another, it gives the *appearance* of being merely a *party*, a one-sided point of view, in a dispute (WdpK, 186/285). But philosophy, given its own conception of its truth, cannot advance one particular position among other possible particular positions. In the case in which philosophy is opposed by pure pretension, by that which wholly lacks the Idea, it cannot remove this appearance of opposition by uniting this other standpoint with itself through critique, since the condition of critique (namely, at least implicitly shared criteria) is not met. So what remains for philosophy to do in such a condition?

Since the condition of critique, of objective judgment, is revoked in this situation, philosophy is tempted merely to *repudiate* the other, to declare it to be 'nothing for the true philosophy'. Hegel ends the Criticism article arguing that philosophy must not succumb to this temptation to rely on its unrecognized criterion, but must abandon its criterion and submit itself to the struggle for recognition with its apparent other.[23] (I quote in full because the points I aim at here rely on noticing resonances between Hegel's expressions in this passage and in corresponding passages in the *Phenomenology*.)

Now if one group stands over against another group, each is called a party; but when one ceases to appear as anything, the other also ceases to be a party. Each side must find it unbearable, then, to appear only as a party and must not avoid the momentary illusion of partisanship (which disappears of itself), which it gives itself in the struggle. On the other hand, should a group want to save itself from the danger of the struggle and of the manifestation of its inner nothingness through simply declaring the other to be a *mere* party, it would have thereby recognized the opposite as something, and renounced for itself the universal validity in respect to which what is actually a party must not be a party but nothing at all. In so doing it has at the same time confessed itself to be a party, that is, as nothing for the true philosophy. (Hegel, WdpK, 186–7/285–6)

If philosophy would evade the struggle with its opposite through merely repudiating this other, if it would refuse to recognize the crisis through declaring the other to be a mere party (that is, to be nothing for the true philosophy), philosophy would thereby institutionalize this oppositional structure, as it were. To say, merely, that the other is nothing for philosophy in effect recognizes it as something and renders oneself *in fact* (permanently) a mere party in a dispute, and, hence, 'nothing for the true philosophy'. If philosophy would save itself through refusing to surrender its criterion, hence, its claim to truth, in the engagement with its opposite, it *in fact* surrenders its claim to truth—against itself.

Hegel's prescription, then, if philosophy would save itself, is to surrender its criterion, to get down on all fours with Unphilosophy, so to speak. It must submit itself 'to the danger of the struggle and of the manifestation of its inward nothingness'. Philosophy must submit itself to the crisis—it must submit itself to what I would call, though Hegel pointedly does not, *critique*.

---

[23] As Harris remarks in his notes to the translation, this is the first appearance of Hegel's famous life-and-death struggle which is a centerpiece of the master-slave dialectic. (See BKH, 290, n. 34.) Paul Franks made the compelling suggestion in a public presentation that Hegel's discussion at the end of his article on criticism of the act of 'repudiating' is meant to comment on Kant's famous open letter repudiating Fichte's philosophy (repudiating, in particular, Fichte's claim to be a Kantian).

If what apparently opposes it is indeed pure pretension, Unphilosophy, then this cannot fail to become manifest in the struggle. As he puts it earlier in the article: 'It cannot fail that that which is nothing in the beginning will appear ever more as nothing in the process [of the struggle], so that it can be generally recognized as such' (WdpK, 174/276). Then, when it is so recognized, when the other ceases to appear as anything, philosophy is no longer a party in a dispute either. Its truth, the Idea, is restored. Thus, Hegel ends this article describing what can seem a sort of paradox: philosophy in order to preserve itself must surrender its truth; that is, philosophy must, in order not to confess itself against itself as a mere party, let go of that through which it is in fact philosophy and, hence, not a mere party—namely, its Idea or its criterion—and engage in a struggle with its opposite. In this way alone philosophy can establish itself in this confrontation as philosophy.

This reveals the tension in the earlier position. If, according to Hegel here, philosophy cannot complacently let itself appear in an oppositional position, even if (especially if) what opposes it is nothing in itself, then how can philosophy be explicitly esoteric? Hegel's justification of the esotericism of philosophy in the Criticism article is the mere repudiation of demands of 'the healthy, human understanding'. There he is content simply to reject or to dismiss the ordinary consciousness's demand that philosophy's claims be justified according to its criteria. Ordinary consciousness has no right to demand that the claims of philosophy be made intelligible because '[philosophy] is only philosophy precisely through being opposed to the understanding, and even more to the healthy, human understanding ...' However, this point stands in some tension with the claim that philosophy, by its own principle, *must* reconcile itself to its opposite through foregoing its criterion and engaging in a struggle for recognition.

That Hegel himself comes to recognize the tension is evident in the fact that he comes to recognize the need to make philosophy intelligible (*verständlich*) to the ordinary consciousness 'through the understanding', together with the fact that his justification of undertaking that project in the *Phenomenology* is based in part on the reasoning of the earlier article according to which philosophy cannot bear even apparent opposition to its principle. Hegel is able to overlook the tension as it exists in the early article, I assume, because he doesn't treat the relation of philosophy to the ordinary understanding as a question of critique there. In this article, the question of critique concerns the relation of philosophy to other would-be works of philosophy (or *appearances* of philosophy). The question of the relation of philosophical knowledge to the ordinary understanding (or, as he also says, to the people) is the different question of whether philosophy can be made popular or common (*gemein*). But, as we've already shown above, Hegel comes to regard the question of philosophy's relation to the ordinary understanding as a question of philosophical critique. We've examined Hegel's claim in the Preface, as against his earlier view, that philosophy must become *verständlich* or common. What remains to be shown is how his justification of the need for this project, as Hegel presents it in the Introduction to the *Phenomenology*, virtually repeats the reasoning of the Criticism article regarding the need to engage in the struggle with Unphilosophy.

Hegel opens his Introduction to the *Phenomenology* by rehearsing his general objection to Kant's way of beginning the task of metaphysics. He attacks the 'natural idea that, before proceeding in philosophy to the thing itself (namely, to the actual knowledge of that which truly is), it is necessary first to come to an understanding about knowledge'. We have dwelt at length in Part I on the question of how to understand the objection against Kant's critical procedure that Hegel hardly does more here than merely mention. After rehearsing this objection, Hegel reflects on the line of objection he has just advanced and notes that it too, like Kant's critical turn itself, makes various essential presuppositions. In objecting that the critical turn implicitly presupposes the transcendence of the in-itself relative to our cognition—hence, the subjectivity of all our knowledge—we must mean certain things by 'absolute', 'objective', 'subjective', 'knowledge', meanings we cannot suppose are shared by our opponent. Hence the objection will appear merely polemical, partisan or dogmatic. Hegel writes: 'For the pretension [*Vorgeben*] that their meaning is universally known or that one has their concept oneself looks rather like the attempt to spare oneself the main problem, which is precisely to give [*geben*] the concept' (PhG, 71/¶76). Since the task is exactly to *arrive at* the determinate meaning and application of these concepts through the philosophical investigation itself, the argument before or outside of philosophy about how to begin philosophy is bound to be hopelessly arbitrary or partisan or dogmatic.[24] We could decide this prior question authoritatively only through the criterion the establishment of which constitutes the founding of philosophy.

Hegel then suggests an essential possibility in this dialectic: 'With more right we could spare ourselves the effort of taking any notice of such pictures

---

[24] This recalls Hegel's claim in the Difference essay that it is hopeless to attempt to begin philosophy before its beginning, by discussing its presuppositions. (See Diff, 25/94.)

[*Vorstellungen*] and manners of speaking, through which science itself would be warded off. For they constitute only an empty appearance of knowing, which must disappear immediately in the face of science, as it comes on the scene.' That is, we do best simply to dispense altogether with preliminaries, exactly because we do not occupy the common ground on which to decide these prior questions authoritatively and objectively. The assumption that we occupy that ground before, or outside of, philosophy is simply the presumption of subjectivism. We can decide whether or how metaphysics is possible as a science only through the work of science itself; accordingly, we ought to begin metaphysics straightway, without preliminaries. I take Hegel to mark with this sentence his earlier position, his wholesale rejection of the project of Kantian critique.

But here he turns immediately against this suggestion, in words that recall the reasoning of the Criticism article. 'But science, in coming on the scene, is itself an appearance: in coming on the scene, it is not yet science in its developed and diffused truth'. We have already encountered in the Preface—there also in the context of justifying the need for the *Phenomenology*—Hegel's claim that when science first comes on the scene, it is present 'only in its immediacy or its concept' (PhG, 19/¶12). Hegel claims in the Preface passage that science, when it first comes on the scene, has the appearance of being esoteric, since 'its undiffused appearance renders its existence something singular', that is, the private possession of a few singular individuals (PhG, 20–1/¶13). Here, however, the emphasis is on the point (closely related, of course) that science comes on the scene *next to other* points of view, and that this oppositional position is unbearable for philosophy. After claiming that science, when it first comes on the scene, is itself merely appearance, Hegel continues: 'It is here indifferent whether we suppose that *science* is the appearance, because it comes on the scene *next to others*, or whether we call the other untrue knowing the appearance of science.' The point I want especially to call to attention is the implication that science or philosophy itself exists only as appearance just insofar as it stands over against other points of view, just insofar as it is (apparently) opposed. Science isn't present in its reality or in its truth, but only in the form of appearance, when it is (apparently) opposed. Hence, philosophy cannot bear to be (even apparently) opposed. It *must* come to terms with apparent difference or disagreement.

In the paragraph from the Introduction quoted above (¶76 in Miller's translation; pp. 70–2 in the German), Hegel continues to elaborate this, continually recalling the earlier article: 'Science must however liberate itself from this illusion [*Schein*—that is, the illusion of being one point of view next to others]; and it can do this only through turning against it.' Philosophy must turn against this (apparent) opposition, because if it were to let it be, it would consign *itself* to existing in the form of an opposite or of appearance, which is not a form consistent with the claim of philosophy. In the earlier article, such reasoning demands that philosophy surrender its criterion, its Idea, and get down on all fours with Unphilosophy in order to make manifest its nothingness. Here, however, Hegel applies the point, as he exactly neglects to do in the earlier article, with reference primarily to the standpoint of ordinary consciousness. 'For, when confronted with a knowledge that is without truth, science cannot [] merely repudiate it as an ordinary perspective on things [*eine gemeine Ansicht der Dinge*] while assuring us that science is a quite different sort of cognition, for which that ordinary knowing is of no account at all'. Isn't this exactly what we have seen Hegel himself do in the early article in making and specifying the claim that philosophy is by its very nature esoteric? And why, according to Hegel here, cannot philosophy do what Hegel was content to do there in the Criticism article? 'Through such assurances, science declares its power to lie simply in its *being*; but the untrue knowledge likewise appeals to the fact that *it is* and *assures* us that for it science is of no account. One bare assurance is worth just as much as another'. I take this to be the later transcription of the passage from the earlier article that we have already quoted: 'Because the mutual recognition is hereby negated, there appear merely two subjectivities opposite to each other. Things which have nothing in common come on the scene with equal right for that very reason' (WdpK, 173/276). If the standard of objective judgment isn't shared between them, then the two 'parties' are in a symmetrical relation to each other. Accordingly, philosophy can't let itself be fixed in this oppositional position. Hegel ends the paragraph from the Introduction to the *Phenomenology*: 'For this reason the presentation of knowledge as it appears should be here undertaken' (PhG, 72/¶76). That is, the prior critique of knowledge, which is the phenomenology of spirit, is necessary; the existence of science, of philosophy, of philosophy as science, depends on it.

However, as claimed earlier, the sense in which the being of philosophy depends on the reconciling of opposition is different in the *Phenomenology* by virtue of Hegel's recognition of subjectivity. In finding philosophy opposed, in the sense that ordinary consciousness stands over against it with no common criteria, we find ourselves *before the beginning* of metaphysics as science. Science or metaphysics does not yet exist; or, rather, it exists, but *in the form of appearance*. Metaphysics comes to exist through the work of constituting criteria as common out of the critical condition of opposition. Thus, Hegel will understand the beginning of metaphysics in critique not as its sudden institution, but as its *realization* through the prolonged, arduous process of constituting agreement on criteria. As argued above, given Hegel's conception of the necessary relation of the unconditioned to knowledge of it in philosophy, this implies that the unconditioned itself becomes what it is or realizes itself through this process. Hegel's reoriented conception, according to which philosophy's Idea—and the science of metaphysics—comes to be through the critical procedure is brought about through his recognition of the modern self-discovery and the corresponding recognition of the legitimacy of the epistemological demand of Kantian critique.

5

Hegel's Self-transformational Criticism

Finally we arrive at Hegel's characterization of his own method of criticism in the Introduction to the *Phenomenology*. Hegel's objection to Kantian critique, discussed in Part I, together with his belated recognition of the need for Kantian criticism documented in the previous chapter, constitute the formative philosophical pressures that shape the method of the *Phenomenology of Spirit*. Hegel claims that the method of Kantian critique, the prior self-reflection to determine the authoritative norms of reason, implicitly presupposes subjectivism. Now he finds that this critical inquiry, this prior self-reflective inquiry in which the possibility of metaphysics is at stake, is necessary. With this acknowledgment, the question becomes: how is the inquiry possible? How is it possible to determine in a prior self-reflection the authoritative norms of reason without presupposing subjectivism, without presupposing that the object must conform to the subject rather than the subject to the object and, hence, the impossibility of metaphysical knowledge, the possibility of which one set out impartially to investigate in the first place? I will show that the distinctive feature of Hegel's method, the feature by virtue of which Hegel means to avoid presupposing subjectivism even while addressing the modern epistemological demand arising from the modern subject's self-certainty, is that the method manages to put the reflecting subject at stake in the inquiry, together with its relation to the object. Unlike Kantian critique, which fixes the self-standing subject in opposition to the original object of inquiry, Hegelian critique is self-transformational. The critical procedure is a process through which the reflecting subject becomes what it is, and in so doing, reconciles itself with the initially opposed other.

With his return to the standpoint of Kantian critique, Hegel's objection against Kant's critical philosophy must be formulated differently. Whereas Hegel in the early Jena writings rejects the apparent epistemological crisis to which Kant's criticism responds as itself based on dogmatic assumptions, through his return to the standpoint of Kantian critique, he enters into the crisis for the possibility of metaphysics that Kant displays. Now Hegel's objection against Kant's system is not that as criticism it is dogmatic, but rather that it fails to be sufficiently critical; the standpoint of Kant's critical philosophy fails to be fully critical in the sense that it fails to let the skeptical crisis regarding knowledge reach fever pitch. Kant's criticism presupposes the standpoint of the critic as self-standing, over against metaphysics; it does not put that position at stake with the possibility of metaphysical knowledge; hence it presupposes subjectivism. Through his recognition of the right of ordinary consciousness to make its epistemological demand upon metaphysics, Hegel sees the need for a more radical critical procedure, a critical procedure that manages to put *everything* at stake: not only the possibility of metaphysics, but our standpoint as critics of that possibility as well, self-assured in the possession of our criteria of knowledge.

But how is such a radical critical inquiry possible? How do we test knowledge claims in self-reflection without presupposing a standard, even the formal standard of self-reflection? If our condition is the critical one that nothing has yet justified itself as the criterion (as Hegel says in the Introduction to the *Phenomenology*), then how is critique possible at all, granted (as Hegel also says in the same context) that the activity of testing knowledge claims seems to presuppose that we are already in possession of some standard? How can we investigate without presupposing anything at all?

5.1 PRESUPPOSITIONLESS PHILOSOPHY

The suggestion that Hegel's struggle is to define an inquiry that is without presuppositions will strike many interpreters of Hegel as exactly missing the difference between Hegel's method and Kant's. The question whether philosophy ought or ought not to strive to be presuppositionless divides the partisans in discussion of Hegel's relation to Kant. On the one hand, Kant is sometimes defended against Hegel's critique on the grounds that, contrary to Hegel's interpretation of his epistemological project, Kant thoroughly renounces the old ambition of philosophy to begin without presuppositions and to construct the edifice of our knowledge from a position in which nothing is taken for granted. On the other hand, proponents of Hegel's thought sometimes predicate their advocacy on an interpretation of Hegel according to which his methodology strives to get beyond this old ambition, whereas

Kant is supposed to remain captive to it. [1] I maintain, in contrast, that neither Kant nor Hegel simply renounces the old ambition of philosophy to begin without presuppositions. However, it is also importantly correct that neither attempts, with his distinctive methodology, simply to meet inherited epistemological demands. As I have argued above (Chapter 2), critique is essentially a foundational project, but it is a *distinctive* foundational project. We gain a better sense of its distinctiveness through tracing how the relation of philosophy to presuppositions acquires a distinctive shape through the critical turn and how Hegel's critique of Kant bears on this relation. This should provide us a clearer sense of the specific respect in which Hegel's method aims to be presuppositionless and of the specific problems this ambition gives rise to. [2]

---

[1] For an example of the former, see Ameriks, 'Hegel's Critique of Kant's Theoretical Philosophy', 14. (In Ameriks's discussion, as often, this point is accompanied by the claim that Kant does not attempt to refute skepticism.) For examples of the latter, see Smith, 'Hegel's Critique of Kant', 444; and Richard Norman, *Hegel's Phenomenology: A Philosophical Introduction*, ch. 1.

[2] William Maker argues in his *Philosophy Without Foundations: Rethinking Hegel* that Hegel's *Phenomenology* ought to be understood as systematically critical of the foundationalist tradition in epistemology, but as a critique of foundationalism that, far from recoiling to the relativism fashionable among contemporary anti-foundationalists, establishes the standpoint of reason as autonomous with respect to its norms. Richard Dien Winfield develops a similar view on Hegel's *Phenomenology* in his recent *Autonomy and Normativity: Investigations of Truth, Right and Beauty*. (See chs. 2 and 3 of this work, as well as his article 'The Route to Foundation-Free Systematic Philosophy', in id., *Overcoming Foundations: Studies in Systematic Philosophy*, 13–33.) This recent work on Hegel is like Onora O'Neill's on Kant in the respect that it argues that the articulation of the autonomy of reason that they find in Hegel enables avoiding the unhappy choice between (in O'Neill's words) the futile attempt to achieve 'a transcendent vindication of reason', on the one hand, which is characteristic of the tradition of foundationalism in epistemology, and 'the whirlpools of relativism', on the other, which is the plight of contemporary anti-foundationalism—though they differ of course in maintaining that Kant's project belongs to the foundationalist tradition. My interpretive position may seem diametrically opposed to these, since I present Hegel as inheriting and trying to fulfill—if also transforming—the foundational ambitions of modern epistemology. But in fact the opposition is less sharp than it initially appears to be. Maker characterizes 'the modern project of foundational epistemology' as seeking to 'show that the ultimate foundations for determining truth lay, not in certain privileged texts or institutions, as the tradition would have it, but rather within the thinking-rational subject, in its possessing access to certain privileged, knowledge-foundational and criteriological givens, be they sense impressions, innate ideas, or *a priori* forms of judgment' (27). (O'Neill likewise characterizes foundationalism as the attempt to found knowledge on something 'given'.) So conceived, foundationalism is indeed alien to Hegel's project, and the disagreement is more verbal than real. But I believe that this conception of foundationalism does not display much sympathy for the enterprise. Maker maintains that Hegel's *Phenomenology* 'introduce[s] the standpoint of autonomous reason and philosophical science through a radical and consummately destructive critique of foundational epistemology and transcendental philosophy' (13–14, and chs. 3–5). I can agree even here. According to the interpretation I present, the question regarding foundationalism in epistemology that is *internal* to Hegel's development at Jena, culminating in the project of the *Phenomenology*, is the question of whether metaphysics (philosophy, science) depends for its possibility (or actuality) on a prior inquiry in which reason's principles are instituted and legitimated or not. Hegel's coming to accept the legitimacy of the epistemological

According to Hegel's conception of it, Kant's critical turn consists in reflecting on the presuppositions of metaphysics. Previous metaphysicians are dogmatic insofar as their thinking is based on presuppositions that must first be reflected upon and validated (principally, of course, the presupposition of the objective validity of the philosophical concepts). Thus, the critical turn consists in backing up to a position before the beginning of metaphysics, as it were, to determine through reflection the possibility of this science. In this way, Kant's critical inquiry is explicitly a prior and foundational inquiry, though with respect to the science of *metaphysics* in particular, not with respect to our knowledge in general.

Some passages in Hegel's early Jena publications support the claim that Hegel rejects the ambition of philosophy to be presuppositionless. He objects in these publications to the attempt, which he ascribes to critical philosophy, to begin philosophy before the beginning, in what he calls the 'vestibule' or 'ante-room' (*der Vorhof*) of philosophy. He claims that such a procedure essentially condemns us forever to this vestibule, unable ever to cross the threshold.[3] The absolute is projected into an inaccessible beyond relative to our knowledge. In opposition to the critical procedure, Hegel claims that philosophical knowledge can be grounded only in and through philosophy itself, not in a prior reflection. In this context Hegel can seem to claim that the absolute must be presupposed in metaphysics; it cannot be approached or arrived at from some position supposedly outside or before it.[4]

demand of critique is his coming to accept the validity of a demand for a sort of foundationalist justification of rational knowledge, against his earlier rejection of this demand. But, of course, Hegel's reasons for rejecting this epistemological demand remain alive for him: most importantly, that the attempt to validate or determine the normative principles of rational knowing *in advance* of such knowing leads inevitably to (or implies) skepticism or subjectivism. Accordingly, as I discuss below, it is very important for Hegel that the phenomenology is determined in the end *not* as a *prior* inquiry relative to science or metaphysics, but as belonging to it as its first part. More exactly, the phenomenological inquiry is, as Hegel explicitly characterizes it, the *coming-to-be* of science (*das Werden des Wissenschafts*). I can agree with Maker's characterization of the *Phenomenology* as a radical critique of foundational epistemology in the sense that rational or absolute knowing comes to be in it only through overcoming the opposition between the standpoints of ordinary consciousness and of metaphysics which the relevant epistemological demand presupposes. But clearly my interpretation differs from those of Maker and Winfield insofar as I understand Hegel to mean with the *Phenomenology* literally to establish the science of rational knowing for the first time through the epistemological justification of reason's claims, a process of justification in which the criticizing subject, the individual self-consciousness, standing outside and over against metaphysics, is 'posited as one with' philosophical consciousness. (See Hegel, PhG, 30–1/¶26.)

3 Hegel, Diff, 24–5/93–4.
4 I recall here Hegel's claim in VSP that metaphysics does not recognize the need to justify its principle or its Idea. Rather, it does nothing else but bring its principle, unconscious and presupposed in ordinary life, to consciousness. (See Hegel, VSP, 255/342.)

However, if my claim regarding Hegel's return to critique is correct, then the view expressed in these early Jena writings must be complicated by that return. And, indeed, it is not difficult to find texts in Hegel's mature writings that express his commitment to 'presuppositionless thinking' in philosophy. The best text for this purpose, so far as I know, is the *Vorbegriff* to the *Encyclopedia Logic*, the so-called 'Three Attitudes to Objectivity'.⁵ Hegel assesses the three attitudes in terms (among others) of whether or to what extent each represents 'free thinking', where 'free thinking' amounts to presuppositionless thinking. For example, he writes the following in commenting on the first attitude, which is, essentially, the old (i.e., pre-critical) metaphysics: 'This metaphysics was not free and objective thinking since it did not let the object determine itself freely out of itself, but rather presupposed it as finished' (EL, § 31Z). He continues in this passage to specify a bit what he means by 'free thinking', and who in the history of philosophy best practices it. In comparing the ancients with the moderns in this respect, he says of the ancients that

[they] had no further presupposition than the heaven above and the earth about, for mythological conceptions had been jettisoned. Thought is in this concrete environment [*in dieser sachlichen Umgebung*] free and withdrawn into itself, free from all material, purely with itself. This pure being-with-self belongs to free thinking, to the setting out into the open sea, where nothing is under us and nothing above us, and we are there in solitude with ourselves alone. (EL, § 31Z)

Though it may not be very clear what this free, presuppositionless thinking exactly amounts to, for Hegel, that it represents for him an ideal that philosophy must strive to meet is clearly implied in his discussion of the three attitudes. Hegel is most explicit when he discusses the attitude of the critical philosophy. Earlier in the same passage in which Hegel makes his famous cryptic objection that the critical philosophy consists in wanting to know before knowing or in not wanting to enter the water before one has learned to swim, he writes: 'It was already remarked earlier that free thinking is characterized by not having presuppositions. The thinking of the old metaphysics was not free for the reason that its determinations were simply presupposed, or supposed as valid *a priori*, without being submitted to the test of reflection' (EL, § 41Z1). Such a passage shows Hegel's aim not to be that of getting beyond the ambition of Kantian philosophical procedure to test everything in critical reflection as a condition of granting it authority,

⁵ Hegel, EL, §§ 19–82.

but rather that of *inheriting* that ambition, over against the 'old metaphysics', which took up and applied concepts without subjecting them to the critical procedure of reflection.

While making these claims on behalf of presuppositionless thinking, Hegel remains aware, of course, that there is a way of assuming a supposedly presuppositionless position before the beginning of our knowing that in fact presupposes essentially everything (since this remains the thrust of his objection to the Kantian reflection). Hegel is also aware that thought may have presuppositions (or, better perhaps, conditions) that we abstract from only at the cost of destroying the possibility of knowledge (since something like this remains his view regarding the relation of thought to the absolute). If we make clearer the nature of Hegel's commitment to presuppositionless thinking, we see that it represents, not a return to a Cartesian methodology, but a development of the critical turn.

In order to see this, we need to distinguish two ways in which thinking may be related to presuppositions. We may take, as the model of the first way, the relationship of the transcendental unity of apperception or the categories to our knowledge of objects, according to Kant's epistemology. According to Kant, all our knowledge, and indeed all our thought of objects, is necessarily conditioned by (presupposes) the transcendental unity of apperception and the functions of this unity, the categories. The transcendental unity of apperception and its concepts are a sort of ground of our thought of objects. But what is essential here is that we can, through transcendental reflection, gain insight into the necessity of these conditions, into their role in conditioning and making possible our knowledge of objects. Though we are, in the actual activity of knowing, unaware of these pre-conditions—these 'prepositings', as the German word *Voraus-setzungen* literally says—we can, through reflection, posit (*setzen*) them for thinking. The demand of critique is that we must. What is implicit (*an sich*) in thought and knowledge must become explicit (*für sich*).[6]

We should understand Hegel's claims in his early writings that the absolute must be presupposed according to this model, I think. The absolute is the ground of all thinking, the unconditioned condition of all thought, and thus all thinking presupposes it, though not consciously. When Hegel claims in the Skepticism article, for example, that the absolute is presupposed in daily life, he means minimally that the relation of ordinary thought, the thought of ordinary consciousness, to its ordinary objects presupposes as

---

[6] I do not claim that this is Kant's conception of the demand.

its unconditioned condition the absolute, though ordinary consciousness is unconscious of this presupposition of its thought (VSP, 255/342). However, if we grant this, then it may seem that Hegel continues to hold, up to and through the project of the *Phenomenology*, that all thought presupposes the absolute, since, in this sense of 'presuppose', our reflection at the beginning of the *Phenomenology* also presupposes the absolute, according to Hegel; otherwise, we could never arrive at cognition of it through the path of the *Phenomenology*. What, then, of my claim that the *Phenomenology* marks Hegel's return to critique as a sort of first philosophy, as a sort of prior, foundational, and presuppositionless inquiry?

At this juncture, it helps to introduce a second model of the way in which thinking may be related to presuppositions—a model which, like the first, is a peculiar development of the critical turn. In the course of discussing the method in the Introduction to the *Phenomenology*, Hegel refers at one point, famously, to something that goes on essentially 'behind the back' of the configurations of consciousness (Hegel, PhG, 80/¶87). With this conception of something going on *essentially* behind the back of a configuration of consciousness, we have an importantly different model of the relation of thinking to presuppositions. If a presupposition determines thinking essentially behind its back, then this presupposition cannot become explicitly posited through reflection—at least not by the particular configuration that it determines. The making of such a presupposition conscious inevitably changes the shape of thinking that it determines. Such a presupposition determines thinking externally, from outside the particular configuration it determines. A 'pre-positing' that occurs essentially behind the back of the shape of thinking that it (partially) determines cannot be self-posited.

The difference between these two senses of 'presupposition' is that, in the first sense, the pre-positing of a configuration of consciousness can be posited by that consciousness without thereby transforming the configuration, whereas in the second sense, to become conscious of the pre-positing is thereby to move beyond the configuration. We can best illustrate the second sense of 'presupposition' by Hegel's charge that Kant's critique presupposes subjective idealism. In Kant's critical reflection, reason reflects back on itself in order to determine in a prior and independent inquiry whether or how its object knowledge is possible. According to Hegel's objection, this reflection presupposes (unconsciously, as it were) that the ultimate authority for us inheres in self-reflection. Hence the Kantian critical inquiry, which means to be 'free and open', in fact presupposes the impossibility of metaphysics. This presupposition of Kantian critique determines the shape of Kantian philosophy necessarily 'behind its back'. If the transcendental philosopher becomes conscious of this presupposition, she transcends thereby that particular project of critique, just as the dogmatic metaphysician passes over into critical philosophy through becoming conscious of the fact that his investigation simply presupposes the objective validity of the philosophical concepts.

When Hegel implies in the Introduction to the *Phenomenology* that philosophy must have no presuppositions, he must mean 'presupposition' in this second sense. Kant's critical philosophy, despite its reflectiveness, still has a presupposition in this sense. According to Hegel's view in the early writings, all attempts to begin philosophy in reflection in effect preclude or foreclose the possibility of having the absolute come into view for thinking. The criteria or standards of knowing that are implicitly instituted in the critical reflection are incommensurate with those that must determine philosophical knowing. According to the early Jena publications, there is an unbridgeable gulf, a hiatus, between the standpoint of reflection and the standpoint of philosophy. We are confronted with an either-or structure: either we begin with subjectivity in self-reflection, in which case we implicitly confine ourselves to a subjectively constituted realm in our knowing, or we begin in what Hegel later calls 'the element of philosophy', an element in which 'the Idea' or 'the absolute' is at least implicitly present, in which case we work to make the absolute as explicit for thinking as possible. There can be no mediation, no path, between the two standpoints (since the basis for this, terms of judgment which are at least implicitly shared, is lacking). Hegel's claim in the early writings, then, that the absolute must be 'presupposed' means not that philosophical claims cannot be arrived at or demonstrated, but only that such a demonstration must begin from a position which has in place criteria or standards which allow the absolute to come into view. In making these claims, Hegel expresses opposition to critical philosophy, since, as he understands it, critical philosophy prescribes a way of beginning that does not let the absolute come into view.

However, the *Phenomenology* is exactly the path from the standpoint of ordinary consciousness (reflecting on its criteria of knowledge) to the standpoint of philosophy, i.e., the very mediation that Hegel had earlier thought impossible. Hegel comes to hold that such mediation *must* be possible if philosophy is to be possible; such mediation must be enacted if metaphysics (what Hegel calls 'science') is to be actual. Hegel remains conscious that there is a way of undertaking the critical reflection that exactly precludes that we ever arrive at philosophy, and he means to protect against that way of conducting critique. The demand implicit in the Introduction to the *Phenomenology* that the critical reflection be presuppositionless must be heard in this context. Hegel reopens the critical inquiry, the prior inquiry concerning the criterion, but he means it to be *fully* open, in contrast to Kant's critical inquiry, on his conception of it. This means that everything—in particular both the impossibility and the possibility of metaphysics—must be possible so far as the reflection itself is concerned. The methodology of reflection must allow us to discover (if it is true) that there can be no prior and independent reflective inquiry into the possibility of metaphysics, since, in some sense, the absolute is a condition of (presupposed by) all knowledge. The critical reflection must be such that nothing is pre-posited behind the back of thinking; everything must be open to be posited through the reflection itself.

In the quotations above, Hegel associates presuppositionless thinking with free thinking. We took note in Chapter 3 that Hegel in his article on skepticism describes the ancient skepticism that is the negative side of the genuine philosophy as its 'free side', by which we took him to mean that philosophy requires uninhibited, unrestrained thought, since thought so uninhibited negates all limitations and thereby arrives at the absolute (Hegel, VSP, 229/324). But now, after his return to the standpoint of Kantian critique, Hegel's association of presuppositionless thinking with free thinking takes a Kantian twist. Kant's critical turn contains, according to his own description of it, the demand that the positive claims of religion, political law, and metaphysics demonstrate themselves before the tribunal of reason, constituted by its (or our) self-reflection, as a condition of their claim on our assent. Reason does not acknowledge as valid any claim that is not validated according to its own standards; reason produces its laws out of itself, and that constitutes at least part of what is meant by the Kantian idea of the autonomy of reason. Hegel's objection to Kant's critical system is that, insofar as its shape is determined by a presupposition (a pre-positing), behind its back, it does not attain to its own ideal of autonomous reason. Hegel means with his reflection to attain that ideal. Thus, neither Hegel's nor Kant's reflection simply re-enacts a Cartesian methodology of first philosophy, but it is also true that neither simply rejects as unjustified the traditional demand of philosophy to be free of presuppositions. Each reinterprets that demand and seeks to fulfill it within the context of the critical turn.

As we turn now to Hegel's characterization of his method in the paragraphs at the end of the Introduction to the *Phenomenology of Spirit*, we must understand it in this context. The struggle is to define a method of reflection that is completely open, in the sense that everything can in principle become an object of assessment or of reflection, as required by the demands of the investigation. In Kantian critique, there is something fixed, inaccessible to its critical assessment, determining it behind its back. The shape of Hegelian critique is determined by Hegel's attempt to engage in critical assessment, to reflect on our criteria, without presupposing, in this sense, anything at all.

5.2 THE PROBLEM OF THE CRITERION

Hegel introduces the problem of determining the method of the inquiry as follows:

It seems that this presentation, regarded as a *relating of science* to knowledge as it appears, and as the *investigation and testing of the reality of cognition*, cannot take place without some *criterion* [*Maßstab*], which can be laid at the basis as a presupposition. For the testing consists in the application of an assumed criterion; and in the decision of correctness or incorrectness based on the resulting agreement or disagreement with the criterion. The criterion in general, and likewise science, if it is the criterion, is thereby assumed as the *essence* or as the *in-itself*. But here, where science first comes on the scene, neither it, nor anything else, has yet justified itself as the essence or as the in-itself. And without something of the sort, it seems that no testing can take place. (PhG, 75–6/¶81)

Granted that the condition of our reflection on criteria is that nothing has yet justified itself as the criterion or as the in-itself, we are faced with the problem that we cannot assume criteria on the basis of which this prior, epistemological inquiry would itself be possible. Without assuming criteria for determining our criterion in reflection, how is any investigation at all possible? Hegel's problem here arises precisely given his attempt to complete Kantian critique. Kant's failure to pose this problem marks the failure of his critical reflection to be fully reflective.

The passage quoted may seem to present a couple of stumbling blocks to the line of interpretation I have been pursuing. First, if we regard this inquiry 'as a relating of science to knowledge as it appears and as an investigating and testing of the reality of cognition', in what sense is it an epistemological inquiry at all? I have represented this inquiry as a reflection on the standards of justification or of rationality in response to the recognition that these standards are not yet established or not yet shared. But if the inquiry consists in determining among various *appearances* of knowing which is *real* knowing, then it is more properly an investigation into the object (i.e., into what is true), than an investigation into the subject (that is, into the nature of cognition), it seems. What can the difference be, after all, between the questions 'what is true knowledge?' and 'what is true?'?

The second difficulty also concerns the respect in which this inquiry is epistemological. Hegel seems (here as elsewhere in these passages) to identify the criterion with the essence and the in-itself.[7] But this identification of criterion and in-itself seems to put into question the very motivation of the critical reflection, as I have presented it (or to put into question the interpretation of the inquiry as a critical reflection). As I have presented it, we reflect on the criteria of justification on the assumption that our inquiry can gain traction in this self-reflection, because, whatever may be true in itself, the justification of that which would make claim to our assent cannot escape our grasp, granted that judgment is our task. The criteria must be, in some sense, ours. If Hegel identifies the criterion and the in-itself, then what is the point of the reflective inquiry? Commentators who argue that Hegel rejects Kant's critical inquiry altogether (not just in a certain period of his development) might support their contention by appeal to this apparent identification of the criterion and the in-itself.

One can see that these supposed stumbling blocks pose no real obstacle to the line of interpretation I pursue, when one attends to the fact that Hegel remains in his return to critique fully sensitive to his fundamental objection to critique. This objection concerns the possibility of a prior, independent, epistemological inquiry; it concerns the independence of our epistemic criteria from the in-itself. Hegel's phenomenological inquiry is, with Kant's, epistemological and reflective in the following sense: our concern in this inquiry (our *immediate* concern, that is) is to determine the criteria on the basis of which to distinguish truth from falsity, rather than to determine what is true. The inquiry concerns immediately the nature of metaphysical knowledge, how and whether it is possible. We ask how *we tell* what is the truth rather than what the truth is (in the field of metaphysics). Hegel's inquiry is also, in a certain sense, prior. Hegel recognizes that the claims of metaphysics appear unjustified and even unintelligible, according to the criteria of ordinary consciousness, from its standpoint over against that of

---

[7] Hegel notes that, if we apply a criterion or a standard in this investigation, we must be assuming it as the essence or as the in-itself; and since nothing has yet justified itself as the essence or the in-itself, we can have, apparently, no criterion to employ in this investigation.

metaphysics, and he acknowledges as a crisis for metaphysics this general unintelligibility and unavailability of its claims and criteria to ordinary consciousness. He undertakes this inquiry in the recognition that only through the fulfillment of the demand of ordinary consciousness to have the criteria of metaphysics demonstrated *to ordinary consciousness* (beginning with its criteria of knowledge) can metaphysics be founded as a science.

However, Hegel, in undertaking this inquiry, remains suspicious of the presupposition that we can tell this—tell, that is, how *we tell* what is true—*independently* of an investigation into what is true (the in-itself). This presupposition determines Kant's reflection as subjectivism; that is, the presupposition that we can determine our criteria in a self-reflective inquiry, while bracketing our epistemic relation to the original object(s) of reason, essentially establishes empty self-reflection as the ultimate norm of judgment. Hence, Kant's conclusion that we can know things only as they are for us, not as they are in themselves is essentially a presupposition of his inquiry. I understand Hegel's identification of the criterion and the in-itself in this paragraph to betray only the assumption that, *if* the knowledge the possibility of which we reflect upon in this investigation is possible, then how *we tell* what is true (the criterion) must be responsive to what is true (the in-itself). We can know the in-itself only if our criterion for distinguishing true from false claims is responsive to the in-itself. As I understand it, this is not supposed to be a substantial claim. However, it is perhaps a pointed claim against the background of Hegel's suspicions regarding the relation of Kant's critical reflection to the Copernican revolution in epistemology. Hegel suspects that Kant's reflection on criteria in fact severs the criteria from the in-itself, and thus predetermines that objects must conform to our knowledge and the transcendence of the in-itself relative to our knowing. Hegel does not mean to presuppose here that knowledge of the in-itself (metaphysics) is possible for us; rather, he merely operates here on the assumption—which he considers naive, I assume—that, *if* this knowledge is possible, then our knowledge corresponds to the object, to the in-itself, and so our criteria are responsive to the in-itself. He means only to undertake the prior reflection on criteria without presupposing that such knowledge is *not* possible for us.

In the two paragraphs following that quoted above in which he raises the problem of the criterion, Hegel introduces terminology and then re-poses the problem in the terms introduced. It becomes clearer through this rephrasing how the problem of defining his critical method has as its background the *Auseinandersetzung* with Kantian critique and subjective idealism. Hegel claims that the abstract determinations of 'knowing' and 'truth' arise for consciousness as follows:

Consciousness *distinguishes* something from itself to which it at the same time *relates* itself; or, as this is expressed, something is *for consciousness*. And the particular side of the *relating*, or of the *being* of something *for a consciousness* is *knowing*. However, from this being-for-another we distinguish the being-in-itself. That which is related to knowing is at the same time distinguished from it and posited as *existing* as well outside this relation. The side of this *in-itself* is called *truth*. (PhG, 76/¶82)

Hegel can seem to be claiming here much more than he means to. For example, this way of determining knowing (as being-for-consciousness) and truth (as being-in-itself, i.e., being outside of its relation to the knowing subject) can seem to imply that we cannot know the in-itself. But, clearly, Hegel means to imply no such thing. He means only to define 'knowing' and 'truth' in an explicitly preliminary and tentative manner so that we can pose the problem of how we can know the in-itself—or rather, the problem of how we can question whether or how we can know the in-itself. These preliminary specifications of 'knowing' and 'truth' make clear that the problem of the possibility of metaphysics *and* the problem of the possibility of critique are, in the wake of Kant's subjectivism, problems concerning the immanence or transcendence of the object (the in-itself, the absolute) relative to the knowing subject or to consciousness.[8]

Then, in the next paragraph, Hegel re-poses the problem of the criterion, now in the terms of 'knowing' and 'truth', of immanence and transcendence relative to consciousness, and now as applied to our specific object: namely, knowing. He begins: 'If we investigate now the truth of knowing, then it appears that we investigate what it is *in-itself*.' It is very important to be mindful (as we will see below) that we are inquiring after the truth *of knowing*, rather than after truth itself (the in-itself). We reflect on the nature of knowledge, on how *we distinguish* between the true and the false. Although

---

[8] From the way Hegel finishes this paragraph, it is clear that he *means*, anyway, to be uncontroversial and to avoid making substantial claims in specifying these terms: 'Just what might be involved in these determinations is of no further concern to us here, for, since our object is knowledge as it appears, we also take up its determinations at first as they immediately present themselves; and they do present themselves very much as we have apprehended them.' I take this passage to be an important indication of Hegel's effort to determine his method without making substantial presuppositions; I take this passage to pose a problem for interpretations according to which Hegel complacently and self-consciously defines his method on the basis of substantial philosophical theses.

Hegel does not make this explicit in this passage, it is clear from other passages that this reflection is in response to a skeptical crisis; the possibility of our knowledge is at stake in this reflection. It is in the condition of fundamental disagreement on what counts as justification (hence as true) that we reflect on our knowing. However, in the rest of the paragraph, Hegel poses for this investigation of knowing the same problem that arises for the investigation of truth (namely, the problem of the criterion). So, as I interpret him, he raises the question implicitly of how this reflection is of any help to us. He writes:

But in this investigation it [knowing] is *our* object, it is *for us*; and the *in-itself* that would supposedly result from the investigation would rather be the being of knowledge *for us*. What we would claim as its essence would be not so much its truth as our knowledge of it. The essence or the criterion would fall within ourselves, and that which should be compared with it and about which there should be some decision through this comparison, need not recognize the validity of the criterion. (PhG, 76/¶83)

Hegel here is applying the general problem of the criterion to the specific case of the prior epistemological inquiry. The *general* problem is how we can test whether our knowledge claims are true without independent access to the true (the in-itself). What criterion can we employ in telling whether the object is or is not *in itself* as it is *for us*? As applied to the specific case of the epistemological inquiry, the case in which our object is knowing, not truth, the problem is how we can validate our claims regarding the nature of knowing without comparing *knowing* as it is in-itself with *knowing* as it is for us? We seem just as much confined to our own conceptions in the reflective, epistemological inquiry as in the objective, ontological inquiry. Or, how not? How does reflection help?

The problem Hegel poses here is the problem of the possibility of the inquiry into the nature of our knowledge, the problem of the possibility of *critique*. Kant does not pose this problem. The critical turn consists in posing the problem of the possibility of *metaphysics*—in these terms, the possibility of knowledge of the in-itself. Kant addresses this latter problem through stepping back from the original objects of inquiry and reflecting on our cognitive faculties, on knowing, on how and whether we can know these objects. But in failing to pose the problem of what constitutes our criterion in this prior inquiry, an inquiry that is prior just in the sense that it is to determine the criterion, Kant in effect presupposes that we already have the criterion in self-reflection itself. The object of knowledge is merely immanent to our cognition in the sense that it is the object as it is merely *for* our cognition, while the in-itself *transcends* our knowing. The problem of determining a method of critical reflection that doesn't already implicitly presuppose subjective idealism is the problem of finding a way to examine knowledge, to reflect on the possibility and nature of (metaphysical) knowing, without implicitly presupposing a standard or criterion for this prior investigation. How does one conduct an investigation (that is, employing what standards) that is exactly to yield the justified standard?

5.3 SELF-TRANSFORMATIONAL CRITICISM

In the following passage, Hegel gives the gist of his solution to the problem he has raised regarding the possibility of the prior epistemological inquiry:

But the nature of the object we investigate overcomes this separation, or this illusion of separation and presupposition. Consciousness provides its criterion from within itself, and the investigation is thereby a comparison of consciousness with itself; for the distinction made above falls within it. In consciousness, one thing exists *for another*, or consciousness contains in general the determinateness of the moment of knowing; at the same time, this other is to consciousness not only *for it*, but also outside of this relation, *in itself*: the moment of truth. Thus, in that which consciousness declares within itself as the *in-itself* or the *true*, we have the standard [*Maßstab*] consciousness itself establishes by which to measure its knowing. (PhG, 76–7/¶84)

We must understand Hegel's move here in order to understand his critique, his methodology of reflection. In order to understand this move, we must specify our object in this investigation, what its nature is, and how its nature solves the problem posed, according to Hegel. Our object is knowledge (*Wissen*), or more exactly, knowledge as it appears to consciousness (*das erscheinende Wissen*). Knowing for consciousness is *dual* in the sense that, on the one hand, consciousness knows *an object*, and on the other, consciousness employs a criterion or standard of justification in its knowledge claims; and the fact that claims to know presuppose (at least implicitly) standards of justification implies that *we*, as the inquirers into knowing, need not presuppose standards in criticizing consciousness's knowledge claims. We can merely observe while consciousness tests its knowledge claims according to *its own* criteria. But we must examine this supposed solution further.

It can seem that we are subject here to a sleight of hand, to another of the metaphysician's conjuring tricks. The difficulty is to see how this strategy of undertaking a prior epistemological inquiry, a prior reflection on our criteria of knowledge, enables us to gain traction or orientation within metaphysics without in effect presupposing subjectivity as the criterion.

A natural and common way of understanding Hegel's move here completely misses his aim, I think. According to this reading, Hegel claims in the above-quoted passage that the in-itself—that is, that which metaphysicians have traditionally sought to know—is (indeed *must be*) *immanent* to our consciousness; that is, the in-itself must (already) be *for us*. J. N. Findlay gives a brief formulation of this view in his 'Analysis of the Text' appended to the Miller translation of the *Phenomenology*. In explaining the passage quoted above, Findlay writes:

In reality ... both self-existent truth and the knowledge of it fall within consciousness; or, otherwise put, the object as it intrinsically is, its essence, on the one hand, and the object *as* an object of consciousness or a notion, on the other, both fall within consciousness, and the latter has to be made to conform to the former ... What objects 'in themselves' are is always more or less adequately there in and for consciousness, and in knowledge it has merely to replace an inadequate by a more adequate revelation.[9]

I will specify some factors that lead people to this reading, show how this reading nevertheless badly misses Hegel's ambition, and then substitute what I think is a better understanding of Hegel's move here.

The foremost reason readers are tempted by this interpretation is that it looks to be what Hegel's words say. 'In consciousness, one thing exists *for another*', Hegel writes, 'or consciousness contains in general the determinateness of the moment of knowing; at the same time, this other is to consciousness not only *for it* but also outside of this relation, *in-itself*: the moment of truth.' Does not Hegel simply claim here that the in-itself is also available to consciousness, for use in testing its claims to know? It can also be said in favor of this interpretation of Hegel's move that (supposing it is intelligible) it would amount to a solution to the problem of the criterion. If we can be assured in advance that that which we set out to know in metaphysics is available to consciousness, then we can be sure that consciousness has already a standard by which to measure its knowing in reflection.

Also, a historical consideration contributes to this interpretation, I believe. Debate arose immediately in the wake of Kant's transcendental idealism regarding how to understand Kant's references to things in themselves,

---

[9] Hegel, PhG, Miller translation, 506.

which according to Kant's idealism, we could think, but never know. Fichte prominently propounded the view that the thing in itself should be conceived of, not as something existing external to thinking, but as a product of thought instead; or, to put it in our terms, the thing in itself is immanent, not transcendent, to consciousness. The concept of the thing in itself is the product of the philosopher's theorizing about how our knowledge arises; it should not be understood as meant to refer to some real existent standing over against our thinking, determining it externally. According to this view, the thought of something that truly transcends thought (which is what the thought of the thing in itself is, according to some interpretations) is impossible or incoherent.[10] One can find passages in Hegel's writings in which he adopts this claim of Fichte's and adapts it to his own purposes (contrary to Fichte's purpose of *defending* Kantian idealism as true idealism).[11] Knowing that Hegel is prone to claiming in other contexts some version of the claim that the in-itself must be understood as immanent to our thought or consciousness makes it easier to understand him here as casually making a similar claim.

Of course, it is Hegel's view at the end of the day that the object of metaphysical pursuit is not transcendent to the knowing subject or to consciousness. But to see Hegel as casually claiming this in the outline of his method in the Introduction, to see Hegel making the method itself dependent on this claim, seriously misses his aim in the work. He aims here exactly to *demonstrate* immanence of the absolute to consciousness. The interpretation of Hegel as claiming here that the object of metaphysical pursuit must be understood as also present to consciousness, *as a condition* of the intelligibility of the method of this epistemological inquiry, conflicts with the interpretive claims argued above regarding the specific *work* of the *Phenomenology* and regarding the problem of knowledge to which it is addressed. As Hegel presents it in the Preface, the need to examine knowing critically (as it appears) arises from the fact that the standpoint of ordinary consciousness

---

[10] Fichte, 'Review of *Aenesidemus*', I, 2, 52–3/68. Also see Fichte's 'Second Introduction to the *Wissenschaftslehre*', I, 4, 232–44/64–76.

[11] Hegel writes the following in the *Encyclopedia Logic*, commenting on Kant's philosophy: 'The '*thing-in-itself*' (and under 'thing' is also understood spirit, God) expresses the object insofar as everything which is for consciousness ... is abstracted away. It is easy to see what remains: that which is *entirely abstract*, that which is completely *empty*, that which is determined only as *Beyond* .... The reflection is likewise easy that this *caput mortuum* is itself only *the product* of thinking .... One can be surprised, then, to read so repeatedly that one does not know what the 'thing-in-itself' is; there is nothing easier to know than this' (Hegel, EL, § 44A).

and that of metaphysics stand opposed, lacking shared criteria. This condition constitutes a crisis for metaphysics, since the possibility of metaphysics depends on satisfying the rightful demand of ordinary consciousness that the claims and criteria of metaphysics be made intelligible, further be justified, starting from its position, reflecting on its accepted criteria of knowledge. Thus the possibility of metaphysics, as scientific knowledge of the absolute, is *at stake* in this inquiry, in this attempt to arrive at absolute knowledge through critical reflection on the standards of knowledge, beginning from a standpoint (apparently) outside of and opposed to that of metaphysics. For all we know at the beginning, a skeptical conclusion regarding the knowledge in question, or a subjectivist conclusion according to which the in-itself transcends our knowing in this sense, is a possible outcome of the inquiry. According to the not uncommon reading of the above-quoted passage, however, this skepticism is not a live threat, there is no genuine crisis for metaphysics, since we can assure ourselves in advance through a simple analysis of the concept of knowledge that the in-itself is already present for consciousness, however obscurely.

Reading Hegel otherwise requires attending to what Hegel indeed emphasizes here: that *the object* of this investigation is *not* truth (not the in-itself) but *knowing*. So when Hegel claims here that the in-itself is also present in consciousness to serve as a standard by which to measure knowing, he means, not the object of metaphysics (the in-itself), but rather the object of this epistemological inquiry, namely, our knowing (or, knowing as it is in itself). He writes at the beginning of the previous paragraph: 'If we investigate now the truth of knowing, then it appears that we investigate what it is *in itself*.' It is this in-itself of knowing that we can be assured is present to our consciousness to employ in testing our claims to know. That Hegel means this is clear from the way he continues the passage quoted above (in which he seemed to claim that the object of metaphysics was available to serve as a standard). The whole passage reads as follows:

In consciousness one thing exists *for another*, or consciousness contains in general the determinateness of the moment of knowing; at the same time, this other is to consciousness not only *for it*, but also outside of this relation, *in itself*: the moment of truth. Thus, in that which consciousness declares within itself as the *in-itself* or the *true*, we have the standard consciousness itself establishes by which to measure its knowing.(PhG, 76–7/¶84)

Hegel explicitly notes here that what serves as consciousness's standard is that which consciousness itself *declares within itself* as the in-itself (that is, what consciousness itself claims to know). If we can be assured that both knowing and truth (being-for-us and being-in-itself) are immanent to consciousness, and hence, that they can be compared to test (phenomenal) knowing, this is not because we can simply presuppose as a condition of our inquiry that the traditional object of metaphysics is somehow there for consciousness, however obscurely, to serve as standard, but rather because our object in this inquiry is (immediately anyway) exactly *not* the object of metaphysics (the transcendence of which is an open question), but knowledge. Our object is the being-*for-us* of being. Because our object is knowledge, we can be assured that the criterion for testing is immanent. In answer to the question asked earlier, this is how reflection helps.

It is difficult to shake the sense that something mysterious has purportedly been accomplished here. Somehow we solve the problem of the criterion by taking as our object something immanent, knowing rather than truth? Granted that our object in this inquiry is the being-*for-us* of being, it is, nevertheless, the being-for-us *of being*. The knowing in question here is our knowledge directed at *the in-itself*, on some conception of it, or knowledge of the object(s) of metaphysics. So how exactly has the problem of the possible transcendence of the object, of the essence or the in-itself, hence of the criterion, ceased to plague us through the fact that we reflect, that we take as our object not the in-itself but our knowing of it? Moreover, Hegel's own objection to Kant's criticism contains the point that the reflective inquiry into knowing must not be detached from an inquiry into being, lest we simply presuppose subjectivism. If the interpretation is correct, how is Hegel here not making his own method subject to the same complaints that he levied against Kant's?

The important point to attend to is how *little* Hegel means to have accomplished with this move. The problem he means to have solved here is only the problem of *how to proceed* in this reflection on knowledge without *presupposing* in the method itself the answer to the question at issue (the possibility of metaphysics; the nature of the criterion of metaphysical knowledge). The problem he means to have solved is how to engage in critical reflection on our knowing, in order to determine how and whether metaphysics is possible, in a condition in which nothing has yet justified itself as the in-itself (hence in a condition without justified criteria). The problem of the possibility of the transcendence of the object of metaphysics relative to our knowing remains open, to be solved or not through this reflective inquiry; Hegel does not purport to have solved it as a condition of undertaking this investigation. But, against the background of Hegel's objection, the problem of the criterion *of this* prior investigation, has two aspects: not presupposing the object of metaphysics as the criterion (thereby begging the question of the critical inquiry from the standpoint of ordinary consciousness, which is skeptical regarding metaphysics); *and* not presupposing as ultimately valid the criteria of ordinary consciousness (thereby again foreclosing the question, though with an opposite answer).[12]

---

[12] Confusion arises here because of an ambiguous use of 'criterion' (*Maßstab*). On the one hand, the criterion is what we aim to arrive at *through* this reflective investigation—that is, the criterion on the basis of which metaphysical judgment is possible. In identifying the criterion with the in-itself, Hegel employs 'criterion' in this sense. On the other hand, when he claims that 'consciousness provides its criterion from within itself', he means the criterion on the basis of which, *not metaphysics*, but rather *the reflective, epistemological* inquiry is conducted. Missing this difference may mislead one to take Hegel to dispel the threat of the transcendence of the in-itself with a simple declaration in a sentence in the Introduction that the absolute is for consciousness. As I interpret Hegel, we labor along the path of the *Phenomenology* essentially under this threat, and dispel it only through the long labor of the dialectic.

In asserting the modesty of Hegel's ambitions in the Introduction relative to the traditional problem of the criterion, my interpretation differs from that of others who also interpret him to be responding there to that problem. Kenneth Westphal provides an interesting, detailed, and informative discussion of Hegel's paragraphs on method in the Introduction, which he also takes to be responsive to—indeed to solve—the problem of the criterion, particularly as articulated by Sextus Empiricus. (See *Hegel's Epistemological Realism*, chs. 6–8.) My interpretation conforms to his on some important points. Like him, I understand Hegel to strain to devise a method of epistemological inquiry that avoids presupposing subjectivism, and like him, I read this to require for Hegel that the method of the reflective inquiry be so devised that our conceptions be open to being transformed through the inquiry itself. But there are differences, at least in emphasis. The considerable complexities Westphal finds in Hegel's response to Sextus's problem of the criterion seem motivated only supposing that Hegel means to accomplish more in the paragraphs on method than I think he does. On my interpretation, Hegel finds in the fact that consciousness provides a criterion within itself for testing its knowledge claims a basis for proceeding in critical, epistemological inquiry while leaving *everything open* to be determined through the inquiry itself, including whether skepticism or subjective idealism are our plight. Though Westphal does note that the possibility of skepticism is open in Hegel's inquiry (137–8), his interpretation of Hegel as an epistemological realist leads him (by my lights) to underplay that threat and therefore also Hegel's conception of the nature of being as subject that belongs at the heart of his response to it. My interpretation points to Hegel's dynamic conception of being as what enables him to conceive the epistemological inquiry of the *Phenomenology* as a founding inquiry relative to metaphysics without presupposing subjectivism. That substance is understood also as subject, expressed in terms of the relation of epistemology to metaphysics, is that the *Phenomenology of Spirit* is the coming-to-be of science (*das Werden des Wissenschafts*)—hence neither a separate, prior inquiry, outside of science/metaphysics, nor an inquiry that presupposes science/metaphysics as already established. In calling Hegel an epistemological realist, Westphal takes him to be defending the view that 'we can know the way the world is, even though it is not dependent on our cognitive or linguistic activity' (1). Insofar as the denial of this 'realism' implies subjectivism, that is, the relativization of 'the way the world is' to the way it is 'for us', then I agree that Hegel is a realist in this sense. However, for Hegel, substance is to be understood as also subject; and this means, in part, that being is not independent of its self-conception, its knowledge of itself, and that being is inseparable from its coming to be what it is through transformations in its (hence our) self-conceptions. Hence, in coming to his characteristic conclusion, Hegel presents an idealism that

It will help to demystify Hegel's move if we illustrate it using more concrete terms than Hegel allows himself. I understand as follows the claim that 'consciousness provides its criterion from within itself', which is the claim that enables the investigation aimed at establishing the justified criterion for the first time to go forward. The subject's claim to know always carries with it, mostly implicitly, some conception of what the knowing subject goes on in making the claim, that is, an implicit conception of the criteria of justification. We must be able to reflect on the justificatory basis of our claims, for otherwise we make no claim at all. So, when Hegel writes: 'In that which consciousness declares within itself as the *in-itself* or the *true*, we have the standard consciousness itself establishes by which to measure its knowing,' he declares knowing to be essentially dual: we know *an object* according to *some justificatory basis* which is also present for us (at least implicitly). Since both elements are present to the knowing subject, the configuration of knowing can be tested internally, as it were, by comparing them with each other.

It may seem, at first, that these two elements will of course agree with one another, since the claim to know is founded on, or derived from, a particular conception of justification; it might also seem that the fact that they agree will prove nothing, since our configuration of knowing might be self-coherent and yet still deluded or illusory or false. As I understand him, Hegel does not mean to deny the possibility of a self-coherent, yet false, configuration of knowing either. Hegel does not simply plunk for a coherence theory of truth here, since here he means to define a method for questioning what counts as truth and as justification. Whether truth is to be understood in terms of coherence or in terms of correspondence or in some other terms must remain an open question to be determined through the inquiry. But Hegel does take metaphysical knowledge to be at stake in the reflection of ordinary consciousness on its criteria for knowledge. The path of the *Phenomenology* consists in consciousness's reflection on its criteria. Consciousness brings its criteria to bear in testing its knowledge claims. If these two elements fail to agree in the comparison, then both consciousness's criteria and its claims to know—the whole configuration—must change. Hegel puts the possibility of

is not only ontological, as Westphal maintains (141–5), but also epistemological—epistemological without being subjective. Since Westphal acknowledges that the ontological structure for Hegel 'has an historical teleology, namely, that the world-system develops towards full self-knowledge and freedom' (p. 145), and that this story of its becoming in relation to its self-knowledge belongs internally to the ontological account, I am not confident that this interpretive difference goes beyond a difference in emphasis.

metaphysics, of absolute knowledge, at stake in the question of whether this process of immanent critique of the knowledge (and criteria) of ordinary consciousness culminates in knowledge of the absolute or not, as a configuration in which concept (criterion) corresponds to object and object to concept.

To see how this comparison works and how the two elements of comparison can fail to be in agreement, it will be helpful to consider an example. Let's consider, then, an adapted and much-simplified version of Hegel's own dialectic of perception from the section on Consciousness in the *Phenomenology*.[13] Suppose, on being asked what I go on in making judgments or in discriminating the truth, I answer: perception. I perceive the truth. The first element in the comparison, my criterion, is perception. The second element consists in what I claim to know on the basis of this criterion. What do I perceive? What are the objects of perception? I perceive, say, things and their properties. I perceive, for example, that the sugar is white and sweet and cubical. So, corresponding to my criterion of knowledge, perception, there are the things I claim to know on the basis of this criterion, things and their properties; both are available to be compared in reflection.

The test consists in asking if the criterion is adequate to the knowledge I claim or if the knowledge is adequate to the criterion. So, in this case: is perception adequate as a basis for knowing things and their properties? Or is knowledge of things and their properties adequate to the conception of knowledge as arising through perception? Trouble begins when we press the question: do I actually perceive the thing? I seem to perceive the color, the taste, the shape of the sugar, etc.; but do I perceive the sugar itself? We may say that the thing, the sugar, is the unity of the various properties that we perceive (whiteness, sweetness, etc.); but we might describe this unity as 'underlying', thereby marking it as escaping our perception. It is clearly incoherent to say that we perceive the color, the taste, the shape, the position in space, etc., of the sugar, and then, in addition to this, the sugar itself.

Already it may seem that perception is not (or not alone, anyway) the adequate basis of what we claim to know. (Or do we begin to doubt that we have knowledge of *the sugar* at all?) However, the configuration of knowing that Hegel labels 'Perception' is not defeated through these bare considerations. There are various avenues of defense that Hegel pursues on behalf of

---

[13] Hegel, PhG, 93–107/¶¶111–31. I don't intend this as an interpretation of Hegel's actual reasoning in the Perception chapter. If we were to consider the details of Hegel's complicated and confusing moves in this chapter, we would defeat the purpose of this illustration, which is to clarify the methodological points, and to show how the method works *in concreto*.

the configuration of consciousness called 'Perception'. For our purposes of illustrating the general method, we will look only at the way in which this comparison or testing can, in breaking down one configuration of knowing, at the same time yield another.

If, according to our conception, we know the thing and its properties through perception, then we claim to individuate the thing through perception. For example, we distinguish the salt from the sugar by tasting each: the sugar is sweet, the salt is not. The sugar and the salt may, of course, share many perceptible properties: both may be white, cubical, etc. And, of course, the sugar might be some other shape than cubical without ceasing to be sugar. As Hegel puts it, the thing is 'indifferent' to some of its properties. But if we distinguish the sugar from the salt on the basis of perception (and granted that the thing itself, over and above its properties, is not perceptible), the sugar and the salt must not share all their perceptible properties. The sugar cube is the instance of the kind of thing it is only by virtue of *excluding* certain properties which belong to what is *not* it, in this case, the salt. And if knowing the sugar as sugar is a matter of knowing which properties it is 'indifferent' towards and which it 'excludes', can knowing the sugar plausibly be a matter of perception?

If not perception, then what? We begin with the conception that we know the thing and its properties through immediately perceiving the properties cohering together to constitute the thing. But through this comparison, we recognize that we can only distinguish the 'unity' of properties as the instance of the particular sort of thing it is by understanding how it stands in relation to other things which it is not, or by understanding how it excludes certain properties, while being indifferent to others. However, these relations between, for example, the sugar and its properties and the salt and its properties are not immediately perceptible; they are a function of the causal laws that determine these perceptible qualities. And the physical and chemical laws that determine the properties can only be known through the *understanding*.

Through this testing of perception by what we claim to know through it (and vice versa), we discover that perception is an inadequate criterion for knowing. Instead we know through the understanding. And with this change in criterion comes a change in the proper object of knowledge. Properly we know, not things and their properties, but (natural) laws. True knowledge occurs only at the level of the understanding of the physical and chemical laws, at which level the individual things of perception tend to disappear.

In this way, our configuration of knowing, our conception of both how and what we know, has changed.[14]

We need yet to specify exactly how this method of investigating knowledge in a prior inquiry improves on Kant's. How exactly does this response to the epistemological demands of critique avoid implicitly presupposing subjective idealism? How does this inquiry manage to leave *everything* to be determined through the investigation itself? It is not difficult to see wherein the improvement is supposed to consist: knowledge critiques *itself*, and because knowledge critiques itself, *we* need not presuppose criteria; the investigation can therefore be completely critical. Hegel continues the paragraph on method on the beginning of which we have commented above by noting that it is indifferent which of the two elements in the comparison we regard as truth or object and which we regard as knowing or concept. He completes the paragraph as follows:

> What is essential, however, is this: that we hold fast, through the entire investigation, that these two moments, *concept* and *object*, being-*for-another* and being-*in-itself*, both fall within the knowing that we investigate. Therefore we need not bring to the investigation criteria (*Maßstäbe*), nor apply *our* bright ideas and thoughts. Through leaving this aside, we achieve the goal of observing the matter as it is *in* and *for itself*. (PhG, 77/¶84)

We need to question how this leaving aside of our criteria and bright ideas manages to achieve genuine—as opposed to Kantian or subjective—critique. The key to the difference of Hegel's critical method, I think, is that the investigation into the criterion or into knowledge achieves dissociation not only from the 'object' of metaphysics (from the in-itself, the unconditioned, the absolute), but also from the standpoint of finite self-consciousness (from the criticizing subject) while not being severed from either—since, after all,

---

[14] It is interesting to compare Hegel's reasoning in the Perception chapter with Descartes's famous argument concerning the piece of wax towards the end of the Second Meditation. Descartes's argument arrives at a similar conclusion and may have served Hegel as a source for the dialectic of perception. Descartes argues against the claim that we know the piece of wax through the senses by showing that the perceptible qualities of the piece of wax may all change while the piece of wax itself remains. At the end of his reflection on the wax, the meditator says: 'I now know that even bodies are not strictly perceived by the senses or by the faculty of imagination but by the intellect alone, and that this perception derives not from their being touched or seen but from their being understood' (Descartes, AT, vol. 7, 34). Plausibly, Descartes's reflection leads, like Hegel's, to a change in conception not only of the *way* we know (through intellection and understanding, rather than through the senses), but also of *what* we know as well (the mathematical-dynamical laws of extension, rather than individual pieces of wax).

the criterion at which we aim is to be both *our* criterion and the criterion for knowledge *of the in-itself* or of knowledge of the absolute.

In dissociating the inquiry from the object, Hegel simply follows Kant. This dissociation from the object consists in the stepping back from the object (or objects) of metaphysics in order to examine critically (the possibility of) our knowledge of such objects. We gain orientation for our disoriented metaphysical inquiry by reflecting on our standards of justification. The *difference* from Kant's critique is marked by the dissociation of the inquiry *from us*, as the criticizing subjects. Hegel's distinctive critical inquiry requires achieving a sort of self-dissociation in the inquiry. As Hegel describes his method, knowledge criticizes itself according to its internal criterion, while *we* merely observe. Our part is restricted to 'pure observation' (*das reine Zusehen*) (PhG, 77/¶85). Thus, we achieve the aim that the examination be not only of the possibility of metaphysics but also the criteria of ordinary consciousness as well. To the problem Kant fails to pose (namely, how can we examine our criterion without presupposing implicitly further criteria), Hegel answers with this dissociation.

As I understand it, the self-dissociation ensures that the relation to the object is not completely severed in the reflection; it ensures that the reflective inquiry on criteria may be responsive to what is anyway the case. In Kant's transcendental critique, the standpoint of critique is independent of, or stands over against, that which is criticized. In Kant's method, *we* set ourselves up as critics of the possibility of metaphysics through our reflection on our cognitive capacities, in a standpoint conceived of as outside (over against) that of metaphysics. As argued above, we thereby implicitly presuppose that the ultimately authoritative standpoint is that of self-reflection; we implicitly presuppose as the ultimate criterion of our knowledge the formal criterion of our empty self-relating activity. Thus, there is no *genuine* testing or no genuine critique since the normative ground is already implicitly determined in the reflection, rather than being something genuinely open to be determined in the reflection. Transcendental critique already contains the assumption that objects must conform to our knowledge rather than our knowledge to objects. From this perspective, then, the failure of transcendental critique to be genuinely critical lies in the fact that the critical standpoint implicitly severs the relation to the original object of metaphysics, the in-itself, in the reflection on criteria.

Thus, the point of the fact that in Hegel's method *we* do not criticize is that our reflective investigation (the object of which is the criteria of justification in knowledge) may be responsive or open to the original object, the object of metaphysics, the in-itself. Our inquiry concerns what can *count for us* as knowledge of the absolute. Hegel's concern is that the object of metaphysics be allowed a say in this inquiry to determine our criteria. As Kant himself describes it, in the process of critique the possibility of metaphysics is tried before the tribunal of reason's self-reflection. In defining his distinctive method for essentially this process, Hegel undertakes to ensure that, rather than it being *we* who try this possibility, there is an independent prosecutor; he seeks to ensure that *our criteria* are themselves at stake in the reflection. This is required granted that the condition of critique is exactly that 'nothing has yet justified itself', everything is open to be determined through the inquiry. Granted that the aim of the critical inquiry is exactly to determine the criterion, and the criterion is itself the basis of judgment, the critical investigation must be one in which the criteria on the basis of which the inquiry is conducted can themselves be transformed as required by this investigation itself. If everything is at stake in this inquiry, then there can be no fixed standpoint from which critique occurs; rather the criteria of this investigation must be themselves open to transformation. As I understand it, by managing to put the criteria of the investigation at stake in this investigation through the dissociation of the inquiry from us, Hegel means to avoid the implicit presupposition of subjective idealism and to achieve genuine critique.

There is more than one way in which criteria of examination are at stake and transformed through Hegel's critical inquiry. The criteria of the consciousness we are examining in the phenomenological investigation are at stake and transformed through the inquiry; but, the point of the phenomenological investigation is to put *our* criteria at stake. First let me illustrate the former, by a look back at our example, and in the next section we will examine the latter. Hegel refers to each stage of the dialectic as *ein Gestalt des Bewußtseins*, which I translated above, in referring to the stage of perception, as a 'configuration of consciousness' or 'of knowing'. 'Formation' would perhaps better translate *Gestalt* than 'configuration'. By the use of this word *Gestalt*, Hegel indicates that the particular stage consists of a complex formation composed of specific elements: namely, a conception of the object, of *what* we know; a conception of the criterion, of *how* we know; *and* a conception of the subject, of the subject's role in knowing. In the *Gestalt* of perception, we know things and their properties on the basis of perception, and the perceiver conceives her role as consisting in passively taking up what presents itself to the senses. Perceiving consciousness takes itself to achieve knowledge by putting aside what it would bring to knowledge in order to take things up passively in perception as they really are.

If the *Gestalt* fails to withstand the internal testing, as in the case of perception, then the *whole complex* changes; there is a transformation, *eine Umgestaltung*. As we saw in the example above, not only does the criterion change from perception to the understanding, but the object changes from things and their properties to natural laws. Hegel explains why both elements must change as follows:

> If the comparison shows that these two moments do not correspond to one another, it would seem that consciousness must alter its knowledge to make it conform to the object. But, in fact, in the alteration of the knowledge, the object itself alters for it too, for the knowledge that was present was essentially a knowledge of the object: as the knowledge changes, so too does the object, for it essentially belonged to this knowledge. (PhG, 78/¶85)

Further, the conception of the subject and its role in knowing also alters. Whereas perceptual consciousness conceives itself as striving to be a purely passive receptacle of the truth, through the comparison and the transform-ation, consciousness comes to conceive itself as an active investigator who approaches nature with questions, hypotheses, and experiments, and who attempts to go beyond or below the surface of appearance in order to understand the inner essence of things.

The significance of the fact that the whole complex changes in such a transition—that the transition is, in this sense, a transformation—is clear in this context. Everything changes because everything is at stake; nothing has yet established itself as the ground upon which the investigation can take place. The critical investigation is exactly the one in which the criterion, and hence everything, is in question. Hegel has meant to define a method whereby our knowledge can criticize itself according to its own internal criterion. Through this critique, we can change our criteria of rationality—and, if the criteria, then the whole complex, the whole *Gestalt*—as required by reason itself.

5.4 THE PROBLEM OF THE 'WE'

But this is not the whole story. One would be right to deny that all elements do shift in the transition; one would rightly insist that there is a standpoint outside the configurations of consciousness that does not shift in the transformation from one configuration to the next. 'We' who observe this process do not change, but remain fixed in our spectator seats, while the drama of consciousness unfolds before us. Granted that the consciousness that we observe undergoes a complete transformation in the transition from one stage to the next along the path of the *Phenomenology*, our position is preserved from this change precisely because we have effected the dissociation of the object of our investigation, namely, knowledge or consciousness, *from us*. In effecting the dissociation of our position from the knowing we investigate, to the end that knowing may criticize itself, instead of *we* criticizing it—that is, rather than we applying, and hence, presupposing, our criteria—Hegel may solve the problem of the criterion, but only by raising at the same time what has been called in the scholarship on the *Phenomenology* 'the problem of the "we" '.

This problem is perhaps best expressed initially as a question. How are we to understand that distinctive and strange structural feature of Hegel's *Phenomenology* that it is presented as a sort of drama *for us*? Hegel periodically interrupts the progression of the argument in the *Phenomenology* in order to address us and to call our attention to something which 'we' see but which the knowing consciousness we observe cannot. Such passages remind us that we are not wholly immersed in the action, but occupy, structurally, a position outside of it as mere observers. But, then, who are we? And, in particular, what is the significance of this structural feature in Hegel's attempt to develop here a fully *critical* investigation?

Kenley Royce Dove claims that one's interpretation of the *Phenomenology* as a whole tends to govern or be governed by one's interpretation of the 'we'.[15] He supports this claim by briefly surveying what the most important commentators on the *Phenomenology* (in the first half of this century, anyway) have had to say about the 'we': commentators such as Marcuse, Lukács, Hartmann, Hyppolite, Kroner, and Heidegger. The interpretation of Hegel's method pursued here, according to which it arises from his attempt to meet the epistemological demand of Kantian critique without presupposing subjectivism, implies a distinctive interpretation of the place and the role of 'our' position in the methodology. According to the interpretation offered here, the role of the observing 'we' in the method is to allow for a fully critical procedure, which implies a procedure in which our criteria, our standpoint, as criticizing subjects, are at stake in the inquiry. This openness to transformation in turn enables us to avoid presupposing subjectivism.

---

[15] Kenley Royce Dove, 'Hegel's Phenomenological Method', 631. Dove compares Hegel's interruptions of the argument, in which he turns to address us, to the device of dramatists which Brecht called attention to and labelled the *Verfremdungseffekt* (627).

Most of the commentators Dove surveys assume 'that the "we" has some kind of privileged access to the absolute'.[16] As Marcuse baldly puts it, we, the readers of the *Phenomenology*, 'must already dwell in the element of philosophy'.[17] Thus, according to this interpretation, the task of the *Phenomenology* does not involve a genuine questioning of the possibility of knowledge of the absolute, since we investigators already occupy the standpoint of metaphysics or already possess knowledge of the absolute. It is only by virtue of the fact that we already occupy this standpoint or have this knowledge that we are able to *comprehend* the development of consciousness that we observe. Only because *we* are already at the end or telos of the path of consciousness's development can we grasp the transitions consciousness undergoes as necessary or as rational.

It will be clear already that I must depart from any such reading and how I must do so. To read Hegel in this way misses the respect in which the *Phenomenology* represents Hegel's return to critique. According to such interpretations, 'we' already possess the justified criterion. But, as I have argued, this avoids or evades the *criticism* of the *Phenomenology*, the respect in which it responds to a skeptical crisis regarding the possibility of metaphysics, a skeptical crisis Hegel belatedly comes to recognize through his coming to recognize the right of the subject to make the epistemological demand expressed in the critical inquiry.

In order to understand to whom Hegel refers when employing the methodological 'we' in the *Phenomenology*, we need to recall Hegel's staging of the scene of criticism, as discussed in the previous chapter. The scene of criticism is constituted by the opposition between the standpoints of individual (ordinary) self-consciousness and of philosophy or metaphysics. It is clear that Hegel thinks of himself as occupying the standpoint of philosophy in that scene, as occupying the standpoint according to which the principle of philosophy is the principle of identity (as against the standpoint of ordinary consciousness, according to which knowledge is achieved through conforming representations to objects (*Gegenstände*) standing over against consciousness and its representations). This supports the common view that Hegel means by the phenomenological 'we' those who share with him that knowing perspective, those who already dwell in the element of philosophy, constituted as it is by 'pure self-knowledge in absolute being other' (PhG, 29/¶26).

---

[16] Kenley Royce Dove, 'Hegel's Phenomenological Method', 635.
[17] H. Marcuse, *Reason and Revolution*, 94. Quoted in Dove, 630.

Even granted this reference for the 'we', it does not follow that the argument of the *Phenomenology* depends on 'our' bringing to bear in the investigation criteria for knowing that 'we' possess by virtue of occupying already the standpoint of philosophy. Nor does it follow that Hegel means to preclude a skeptical conclusion with respect to the possibility of rational knowledge from the beginning. As discussed in the previous chapter, Hegel already contends in the Introduction to the *Critical Journal of Philosophy* that, in the situation in which philosophy stands in a position of opposition with another point of view, a position characterized by lack of shared criteria, the philosopher must, in order to establish his truth over against that of his opponent, engage critically the position of the opposite number without presupposing as valid his criterion. Moreover, in the context of discussing the method of the *Phenomenology*, Hegel explicitly emphasizes that we must not bring to bear *our* criteria in the investigation. So, even if 'we' already occupy the standpoint of philosophy by virtue of possessing in some sense consciousness of the principle of identity as the principle of rational knowledge, it is nevertheless the case that the *validity* of our criterion, and hence of rational knowledge, depends on the open question of whether the self-criticism of the standpoint opposed to us, that of natural consciousness or of the individual self-consciousness, will arrive at this criterion as the stable end point of its process of self-criticism.

However, the interpretation that has the reference of the 'we' restricted to those who already accept the principle of philosophy cannot be right, I think. This draws the circle far too narrowly. As Dove points out, whoever else the 'we' of the *Phenomenology* are, we are the audience of the book, those who are to be taught whatever lessons it has to teach.[18] Presumably the text is addressed to a significantly broader audience than those who are already converts to the identity philosophy. Thus, while it seems hard to deny that Hegel assumes that our position is *relatively* knowing relative to the consciousness that we observe in the phenomenological investigation (at least for the first few steps of the dialectical progression), it also seems hard to deny that 'we' are meant to encompass a wide variety of philosophical positions, many of which are in sharp disagreement with identity philosophy.

In order to understand who we are and our role in the phenomenological investigation, we must see how the position of the 'we' emerges in the construction of the method, given its purposes. Granted the perspective I

---

[18] Dove, 'Hegel's Phenomenological Method', 632–8.

have attempted to develop, the standpoint of the 'we' emerges as required by the attempt to criticize rational knowledge without presupposing either its possibility or its impossibility for us. Since the investigation is to be critical, we must put everything at stake in the investigation; we must examine and test knowledge without presupposing *any criteria* as already established. According to Hegel's proposed solution to the problem of how such critique is possible, it requires *self-dissociation*; it requires our becoming observers of our own knowing. Whatever school of philosophy one belongs to, one is also, originally or in daily affairs, an ordinary or natural consciousness, an individual self-consciousness, relatively unreflective about one's standards of knowledge. The standpoint of Hegel's critical investigation is constituted through holding this consciousness, this ordinary standpoint of knowledge, at arm's length as it were, and observing it in its self-criticism. The standpoint of the 'we' is constituted by the self-detachment required by the critical investigation of knowledge, the critical investigation that is undertaken in the absence of any criteria that have yet justified themselves. Assuming that 'we' are the phenomenological inquirers, we are not constituted as a group through sharing criteria amongst ourselves; rather, we are those who have effected this position of self-detachment in order to observe the internal criticism of knowledge, beginning from the position of natural or ordinary consciousness.

Though the emphasis so far has been on what we must *refrain from contributing* to the critical examination of knowledge (namely, our own criteria and bright ideas, as Hegel explicitly says), Hegel also emphasizes that there is something essential that we do contribute by means of our mere observation, something not present for the object consciousness itself. Without the element that we contribute the investigation would not be rational. I noted that we achieve an inquiry in which the criterion itself—and if the criterion, then everything—is at stake only through dissociating the structure of knowing under investigation from us. We have seen how such an investigation may lead to a complete transformation in standpoint (insofar as the criterion itself changes), a transition in which all elements are reoriented and nothing remains fixed. Then we raised the objection, which we have not fully answered, that there *is* an element which remains fixed essentially throughout this process: namely, us, the observers, who hover securely above the fray, all-seeing but unseen. Thus, we have not managed to put *everything* at stake in the investigation after all. To this objection it can be responded immediately that 'we' struggle to be pure observers exactly to ensure that we do not provide, even against our intentions, a criterial basis for the investigation. However, insofar as 'our' position is in principle immune from transformation through the inquiry, there remains ground for suspicion. So how does it really stand with us? Are 'we' really secure from having our position undermined? Let us consider this issue by attending to Hegel's specific claims regarding what our mere observation essentially contributes.

Hegel claims that what is *for us*, but essentially not for the object consciousness, is that and how the succeeding stage of consciousness develops out of the breakdown of the preceding stage. Consciousness, in comparing its criterion with its claims to know (its objects), finds that they do not agree, and in its effort to make them agree, it finds itself with a different criterion and a correspondingly different object. The object consciousness *experiences* this change, it undergoes the transformation, but it does not comprehend it. The object consciousness does not occupy the perspective on this change from which it could grasp *how* it happens. But this is precisely the perspective we occupy through the dissociation; this is precisely 'our contribution' (*unsere Zutat*), as Hegel puts it (PhG, 79/¶87). Precisely because our position is dissociated from the object consciousness, and is not, therefore, relocated in the transformation, we are in a position to see that the succeeding configuration of knowing is not merely another, different configuration, but a result or a product of the failure of the preceding attempt. In seeing how the succeeding configuration of consciousness comes to be through the dialectic, we see it as something for which there is a reason. Our contribution is essential, insofar as we provide the perspective 'through which the series of experiences of consciousness elevates itself to a scientific process' (PhG, 79/¶87). It is through our contribution alone that the path along which we determine the criterion of rationality is itself rational. If Hegel would meet his ambition, it is obviously essential that we make this contribution through *merely observing* the emergence of the succeeding configuration through the breakdown of the preceding. We do not see the development as rational through applying criteria of rationality that we independently possess.[19]

---

[19] Hegel also describes our contribution as that of the *necessity* of the transitions: 'But it is just this necessity [of the progression] itself, or the *origination* of the new object that presents itself to consciousness, without its understanding how this happens, which proceeds for us, behind the back of consciousness, as it were' (PhG, 80/¶87). The question of how or whether we can understand the transitions of the *Phenomenology* as necessary has been much discussed in the commentary. Many commentators look dimly on the chances of making out Hegel's claim of necessity for the transitions. If the transitions can be understood as necessary, then this is only with the help, surely, of the knowledge with which we are already supplied by virtue of already occupying the standpoint of philosophy or of the absolute. However, I think there are resources for resisting

As Dove emphasizes, what follows from this is that what is required of 'us' as investigators, first of all, is the effort of self-restraint. We 'must strenuously avoid the temptation of interrupting the immanent development of the subject-matter by the introjection of interpretive models'.[20] While I agree with Dove's characterization of the effort required as that of a tremendous self-restraint by which we hold ourselves back from interfering with the autonomous development of the subject matter, I think he significantly underdescribes the structure of the method through failing to acknowledge that the particular subject matter, the autonomous development of which we are merely to describe or to observe, is *our own* consciousness. Independently of the fact that this observation is *self*-observation, independently of the fact that this investigation is self-investigation, the restraint required of us would not be so tremendously difficult—or at least, it would not be difficult in quite the same way. It is essential to the structure of Hegel's method, I think—both to the promise and to the difficulty of it—that that which we attempt to follow in its own autonomous development is *our own* activity of knowing. We dissociate ourselves from the structure of knowing so that it may genuinely be at stake in the inquiry; but, given that this structure of knowing is our own, 'we' are at stake in the fate of the consciousness we observe. To achieve putting our own position at stake with the possibility of metaphysics was the very point of this dissociation. If we find it tremendously difficult to refrain from constantly jumping in with our own bright ideas and criteria, this is because we desire to protect against the development or change or transformation that may be required *of us* through this investigation.[21]

---

this view in the fact that Hegel in this passage *equates* the necessity at issue with the origination of the new object. Whereas it is perhaps odd to imagine us as merely observing the necessity of the transition, it is not odd to imagine that this origination is something we can pick up on by mere observation. If, as Hegel suggests in this passage, the necessity of the progression just is this origination, not some further quality or feature, the origin of which must remain mysterious, then it is comprehensible how 'our contribution' is this necessity, despite the fact that we bring nothing to the investigation but our eyes. When we do the work of abstracting or of dissociating, whereby this activity of knowing, in which we are normally immersed unself-consciously, becomes an object which we try merely to observe in its own life, then we are able simply to see what normally must occur behind our backs: namely, *how* the object with which we find ourselves confronted comes to be through a process. To *see* this is perhaps all there is to grasping the rationality of the process.

    [20] Dove, 'Hegel's Phenomenological Method', 615.

    [21] I find it interesting to compare the structure of self-observation in the context of Hegel's phenomenological method and the structure of self-observation in the context of dream interpretation according to Freud. In *The Interpretation of Dreams*, Freud emphasizes that we must take a special, somewhat artificial, relation to our own mental life in order to interpret our own dreams. He calls this special stance 'self-observation', and contrasts it with the usual stance, which he calls,

I claimed above that the key to the difference of Hegel's critical inquiry is that it achieves dissociation both from the original object of metaphysics (the in-itself) and from us (us investigators), without severing the relation to either. I argued that the specific difference of Hegel's method from Kant's consists in the dissociation *from us*; and this dissociation of the knowing under investigation from us allows the investigation to be responsive to the demands of the original object of metaphysics, the in-itself or the absolute. Thus, this dissociation is in order to maintain, or not to sever, the relation to the in-itself in the reflection. Here I emphasize that the relation *to us* must also not be severed, as it would be if we failed to regard this investigation as a *self*-investigation, despite the dissociation (as Dove does, for example). We pursue self-knowledge in this inquiry, as distinct methodologically from knowledge of objects. That the critical inquiry is self-knowledge or self-reflection shows up primarily in the peculiar anxiety, in both the hope and the despair, of this inquiry.[22]

interestingly, 'critical'. Our critical faculty wants to reject or change parts of the dream, and so, in order both to describe the dream and to interpret it, we must somehow put our critical faculty to sleep. Although Freud does not characterize it this way, I think we may describe the structure as a sort of self-dissociation. (Hypnosis is a way to achieve this dissociation, and particular features of the psychoanalytic setting are designed to achieve it.) If, for some people in some contexts, successfully bringing about this dissociation is very difficult, as Freud notes, an important psychoanalytic explanation of this is resistance. (See Sigmund Freud, *The Interpretation of Dreams*, 132–5).

[22] The aspects of Hegel's method with which we are here concerned have an important source in Fichte's 'Two Introductions to the *Wissenschaftslehre*'. Fichte claims in those texts that an act of self-observation is necessary in order to elevate oneself to the standpoint of philosophy. Fichte emphasizes the need to let the object of our investigation—which is, since the investigation is reflective, the self itself—develop without intervention, in the following passage:

What the [*Wissenschaftslehre*] takes as the object of its thinking is not some dead concept ... Instead the object reflected upon within the *Wissenschaftslehre* is something vital and active, something that generates cognitions out of itself by means of itself, while the philosopher merely observes what happens. The task played by the philosopher in this process is no more than this: His task is to engage this living subject in purposeful activity, to observe this activity, to apprehend it, and to comprehend it as a single, unified activity .... [I]t is not for him to decide how the object should manifest itself. This is something determined by the object itself; and he would be working directly counter to his own goal were he not to subordinate himself to this object, and were he instead to take an active role in the development of what appears. (I, 4: 209–10/36–7)

Fichte claims that in order to elevate ourselves to the standpoint from which alone philosophy is possible, we must first gain insight into the self and freedom. In order to gain this insight, we must revert into ourselves, and *observe* how we do it. He writes: 'Think of yourself, construct the concept of yourself; and take note of how you do this. The philosopher maintains that everyone who does no more than this ... will find that in the thinking of this concept his activity as an intelligence reverts into itself and makes itself its own object' (Fichte, I, 4: 231/41). The reflecting self is supposed to observe that the self consists precisely in this activity of self-relating. Thus, the self is to perform itself, as it were, and through observing and thereby comprehending its self-re-enactment, rise to the standpoint of philosophy. Though in Fichte this self-re-enactment is an immediate reflection,

In the Introduction, Hegel characterizes the epistemological path of the *Phenomenology*, not only as a way of doubt (*Weg des Zweifels*), but 'more authentically as a way of despair' (*Weg der Verzweiflung*) (PhG, 72/¶78). This characterization is not ancillary, but fundamental to the nature and ambition of Hegel's epistemological project. On the interpretation I am offering, the path is a way of despair precisely owing to our openness to being transformed through the investigation. The openness to transformation through critique is, on Hegel's conception, what makes his method, as against Kant's, genuinely critical. Kant's method ends ineluctably in subjectivism or skepticism because *our* position is not staked in the inquiry with the possibility of metaphysics. Hence, the peculiar anxiety of this inquiry: we are directly at stake in it.

5.5 OUR TRANSFORMATION

I have argued that the purpose of Hegel's elaboration of the structure of Kantian critique is to enable our transformation, as required by the requirements of reason, objectively conceived. According to the interpretation advanced here, Kant's criticism just is subjective idealism because his self-reflective procedure implicitly presupposes that empty self-reflection is criterial (for us); hence it presupposes that objects must conform to our knowing and that the in-itself transcends the limits of our knowledge. Hegel struggles to ensure that we do not criticize or test, in order that it may be possible that our criteria, and hence our position, may be revolutionized through critique, as required by 'reason', objectively considered (or, as we put it above, as required by the object of metaphysics, the in-itself).

Though it is true of all of us (as readers of the *Phenomenology*) that our criteria (whatever they may be) must be at stake in the inquiry, since, as I have argued above, we do not share criteria (some of us are Schulzean skeptics, others Kantians, etc.), the nature of the transformation or transformations a given reader is subject to will depend on the particular criteria of reason

---

whereas in Hegel it is extended over the long, arduous path of the *Phenomenology*, the basic structure is the same in both philosophers: we attempt to dissociate ourselves from our reflection so that we may observe this activity of reflecting, and by observing it, grasp it, and by grasping it, rise to the standpoint from which alone philosophy is possible. Furthermore, Fichte also already insists upon the self-transformational aspect of this self-knowledge. To recognize one's selfhood and freedom through this act is to achieve or to realize both selfhood and freedom, according to Fichte. In the 'Two Introductions', Fichte attributes the common failure to recognize selfhood to a fear and an avoidance of selfhood and freedom.

that she recognizes. It belongs to Hegel's justification of rational knowledge (knowledge of the absolute) through the phenomenological inquiry that all candidate philosophical positions occupy a place in the series of configurations of consciousness that develop out of the process of consciousness's self-criticism in the *Phenomenology*. (In this way it is demonstrated that the standpoint of Hegel's science is the one self-consistent position, the one position not subject to negation through internal criticism, among alternative philosophical positions.)[23] This must imply that, whatever criteria to which one is committed prior to undertaking the inquiry, one will come across one's own in the course of the inquiry. At *each* stage of consciousness, there is a sense in which the consciousness one observes is one's own. Hegel claims that 'the series of configurations which consciousness goes through along this path is, in reality, the detailed history of the *education* [*Bildung*] of consciousness to the standpoint of Science' (PhG, 72/¶78). Though at a given stage of the dialectic, it may be the case that we *no longer* occupy the standpoint we are observing, it belongs to the history of our own development, and is in that sense not other to us. But there is a difference too, insofar as one does not accept—one *no longer* accepts—as valid the criteria at stake in the configuration. However, there must come a point in the itinerary in which the criteria at stake are indeed those to which one is currently committed. At that point, one's own criteria are immediately at stake in the investigation. The breakdown of the configuration is, as Hegel puts it, 'the loss of one's own truth'. The emergence of the ensuing configuration is one's own education; one is oneself *gebildet* or *umgestaltet* (transformed) through the transition. Even if one begins the inquiry already occupying the standpoint of absolute idealism, already possessing in some sense the criterion of metaphysical knowledge, one's criterion is still transformed by coming to see how it has its justification through coming to be through the dialectical development presented in the *Phenomenology*.

My claim is that the procedure of critical inquiry is so designed that the critic of knowing (us, however more precisely our individual standpoint is to be determined) may be transformed (or *gebildet*) through the process of critique, and that this feature is what enables the critical procedure to proceed without presupposing subjectivism. The procedure in this way requires that we conform our criteria to reason's demands. That this is Hegel's conception of the transformation that we must be open to in critique is indicated in Hegel's

---

[23] For discussion of this characterization of Hegel's demonstration of the standpoint of science, see Forster, *Hegel's Idea of a Phenomenology of Spirit*, ch. 3.

characterizations of Kant's procedure as fending against transformation—or rather, against what he calls *Bildung*. Whereas Hegel had earlier accused critique as such of fending against *philosophy* in order to save subjectivity, now, with his return to critique, he understands *Kant's* critical procedure to fend against *development* or *becoming* or *Bildung*, which is now understood by Hegel to be an essential feature of subjectivity, properly understood, in order to save the subject's conception of itself as self-standing or self-grounded. In the paragraph quoted above, Hegel distinguishes the 'way of doubting' from the 'way of despair' in order to distinguish the particular skeptical procedure which his *Phenomenology* presents. Other skeptical challenges, Hegel claims, implicitly presuppose that we (the skeptical challengers) already possess the criterion of truth and of justification. Such skeptical ways are, to that extent, hedged. It is in this context that Hegel describes his *Phenomenology* as 'self-completing skepticism' (*der sich-vollbringende Skeptizismus*):

This self-completing skepticism is therefore not that skepticism with which an earnest zeal for truth and science fancies it has prepared and equipped itself in their service: the *intention* [*Vorsatz*] not to give oneself over to the thoughts of others, upon mere authority, but rather to test everything oneself and to follow only one's own conviction, or better yet, to produce everything oneself, and to hold as true only one's own deed. (PhG, 72/¶78)

The reference to Kantian critique is especially suggested in the reference to the demand that we produce everything ourselves and hold as true only our own deed. The demand of Kantian critique can be represented as the demand that reason legislate for itself through self-reflection, or that it not be subject to an externally legislated constraint. As Hegel goes on to express his complaint against such skeptical ways, he claims that they presuppose that the work of *Bildung* is 'already over and done with', whereas the skeptical investigation that he presents actually undertakes the work of *Bildung* through the investigation itself.[24] Miller renders *Bildung* here as 'education', but it also connotes, importantly here, the idea of 'formation'. Such a procedure presupposes that we are already *gebildet*, or that we have already become what we ought to become. Hegel's procedure, in contrast, in staking our criteria with the possibility of metaphysics, opens us to a change of our criteria through this procedure, hence to *Bildung*, to formation and transformation.

---

[24] 'That zealous intention represents education [*Bildung*] simplistically as immediately over and done with in forming the intention; but this path is the actual performance, in contrast to the untruth of that view' (PhG, 72/¶78).

As I understand Hegel's view, in determining the criterion, we determine what we ought to become, and hence, at least partly, what we are.[25]

We may want a more concrete sense of the way in which we are at stake in the reflective inquiry into criteria. The critical question concerning the standards of rationality is ultimately a question regarding the nature and source of the law of my being. I am at stake in this questioning since I am (at least partly) determined through what I take as the law, or through what I take as ultimately authoritative for me. The law, whatever its nature and source, cannot simply determine me independently of *my* relating to it—that is, independently of my recognition of, and insight into, its authority. Through Hegel's belated recognition of this, he accepts the epistemological challenge that it implies. He recognizes the critical demand. Hegel concedes this much to 'our age of criticism'. As backed by the modern discovery of the immediate self-relation, we are licensed to demand that the law be validated in a reflection on our knowledge as a condition of our acceptance of its authority for us. But the fulfillment of this demand must not be such as simply to presuppose implicitly that self-reflection (over against the in-itself) *is* the ultimate law (for us). To avoid the subjective idealism of Kant's critique, Hegel insists that we must be open in the critical investigation to development and change in our conception of the ultimate nature and source of the law. Given that we are (at least partly) determined through *our relating* to the law (through our conception of what is ultimately authoritative), the change or development to which we must open ourselves is a change in who or what we are.[26]

[25] If we look again at the metaphor Hegel repeatedly uses when he objects against Kant's method, we see that it too expresses Hegel's view that, in Kant's procedure, the subject fends against surrendering its own stance as self-standing or as self-grounded. As we have seen, when objecting against Kant's method, Hegel tends to characterize it, cryptically, as the attempt to know before knowing, which he glosses as not wanting to go into the water before one has learned to swim. In Ch. 2, we showed how Kant's method can be seen to exemplify the attempt to know before knowing. Here we see the point of the specific metaphor Hegel chooses to describe this attempt. 'Going into the water' here implies surrendering one's independent grounding or standing on *terra firma*; in order to learn to swim, one must at some point take that apprehensive plunge. Hegel's procedure, in contrast, in putting our criteria at stake, opens our position, as self-standing, before or outside metaphysics, to transformation. Hegel's metaphor for the Kantian philosophy of not wanting to go into the water before one has learned to swim complements his representation of the procedure of truly free thinking: setting out into the open sea with nothing either above or below us, and where we exist in solitude with ourselves alone (Hegel, EL, § 31Z).

[26] Kant himself marks the existential stakes of the critical inquiry into the possibility of metaphysics when he introduces it. Kant notes that the common indifference to metaphysical questions that characterizes our critical age can only be 'feigned' since our interest in these questions is unavoidable. (See Ax.) The avoidance of these questions is just the common form in which our *interest* in them expresses itself in our critical age. The metaphysical questions are ultimately

5.6 HEGEL'S ALTERNATIVE MODEL: CRITICAL TRANSFORMATION AS SELF-REALIZATION

There is the following problem with the way I have been putting things. On the one hand, I express Hegel's objection to Kant's critique this way: the critical demand that the claims of metaphysics validate themselves in our prior and independent self-reflection presupposes this prior and independent self-reflection as ultimately authoritative for us. Hence subjective idealism is already implicit in the epistemological demand. But then, on the other hand, I express Hegel's return to critique, against his earlier rejection of it, as a reorientation to this epistemological demand: instead of rejecting it as inherently subjectivistic, he comes to acknowledge it. With this change the problem with Kant's critique is expressed this way: Kantian critique fails itself fully to *meet* this epistemological demand since it *presupposes* implicitly the ultimate authority (the criterion) of self-reflection. In recognizing the demand, Hegel recognizes that we find ourselves *before the beginning* of metaphysics, in the sense that the ultimate criterion, on which all rational judgments are ultimately founded, has not yet justified itself. In this critical condition, we reflect on our criteria in order to establish the justified ultimate criterion of rational judgment for the first time. Hence Hegel's critique is also a prior, self-reflective inquiry in which the possibility of metaphysics is at stake. But if the subjective idealism of Kant's critique just inheres in its being a prior, self-reflective inquiry in which the question of the possibility of metaphysics is resolved, how does Hegel's critique escape it? Do we not need to go back and revise our way of putting the problem with Kant's critique? Or do we perhaps need to modify the characterization of Hegel's critique as a prior self-reflection?

The inconsistency is shown to be merely apparent by seeing the difference made by allowing for the transformation of our critical standpoint over

---

directed to the ultimate end [*der letzte Zweck*] of our existence. (See A797–9/B825–7.) That we are free, rational beings implies that we have the *problem* of working out for ourselves our relation to the ultimate end of our existence. That is, we *must* ask the (*metaphysical*) question: what ought I to become? (The contrast is with a merely natural being, which becomes what it ought naturally, as it were. The end of a merely natural being is not self-posited, but posited by nature.) The *Phenomenology* is Hegel's presentation of the path along which the subject works out this problem. Of course, an important difference between Hegel and Kant is that Kant relegates this problem to pure *practical* reason, over against theoretical reason, whereas Hegel resists this Kantian division of pure reason.

against or before metaphysics. As shown in the previous chapter, Hegel retains through his return to critique his earlier conception of philosophy (and of reason) as essentially all-encompassing—that is, as essentially *unopposable*, with no coherent outside, as it were. *If* metaphysics is possible, then there cannot be a self-standing, evaluative standpoint prior to, or outside or independent of, metaphysics itself. On the strength of this conditional, the earlier Hegel rejects the epistemological project of critique in favor of metaphysics, since it seems that each precludes the possibility of the other. But with the return to critique, Hegel struggles to define a reflective, evaluative procedure that is genuinely open in the sense that neither of these possibilities (neither Kant's subjective idealism nor Hegel's own earlier objective idealism) is precluded. That the *criterion* is in question in this inquiry implies that *everything* is to be determined through it. But, given the background, what this particularly means for Hegel is that the standpoint of criticism of knowledge as self-standing opposite metaphysics must be equally at stake with the possibility of metaphysics. Granted the validity of the above conditional, and that metaphysics is indeed possible, then it must turn out through the critical reflection that our reflecting is *not prior to, or outside of, metaphysics after all*. A genuinely critical procedure must allow the position of reflection in relation to metaphysics genuinely to shift through the reflection.

Hegel clearly states that the investigation of 'phenomenal knowing' (*das erscheinendes Wissen*, 'knowing as it appears') which the *Phenomenology* presents is not just the necessary propaedeutic to metaphysics, but *already* metaphysics—in his terms, already 'science'. This assertion is often taken to show that Hegel continues with his *Phenomenology* to reject Kantian critique as the prior, foundational inquiry into the possibility of metaphysics. This way of taking this assertion sits well with the interpretation of the 'we' according to which we are already metaphysicians who can comprehend the process of reflection as scientific only by virtue of already occupying the position at the telos of this process. But it sits ill with the reading offered here. The conception of this inquiry as *prior* and founding with respect to metaphysics and the conception of it as *already* metaphysics are taken, naturally enough, to be contrary, incompatible conceptions. However, the interpretive choice with which this leaves us is not happy. On the one hand, if it is simply not true that nothing has yet justified itself as the criterion, if it is simply not true that, from the standpoint of the critical inquiry, metaphysics does not yet exist, then the inquiry does not represent a return to Kantian critique after all. On the other hand, if it is not true that the inquiry is already metaphysics, then Hegel must be renouncing a principle that is central to his idealism (and which we have taken to be central to his relation to Kant's critique): namely, that the science of metaphysics, if it be possible at all, cannot be grounded from a reflective standpoint outside or before it. Neither of these interpretive options satisfies.

However, this exclusive disjunction misses the possibility with which Hegel has provided himself through his recognition of subjectivity; the possibility that allows us to retain the truth in both of the above alternatives. It transpires that this inquiry is the *becoming* or the *realization* of metaphysics (*das Werden der Wissenschaft*) (PhG, 74/¶80). This disjunction excludes Hegel's concept of *Bildung*. On the one hand, metaphysics does not yet exist at the point at which we find ourselves lacking the common, shared, justified criteria in terms of which to assess its claims. Metaphysics comes to exist only through the process of arriving at these common terms. On the other hand, we come to understand its coming to be through this process such that the becoming belongs to metaphysics itself, in the way that the process of maturation of a human child belongs to that human being. In another sense, then, metaphysics does already exist, even at the beginning of critique; it exists in the form of *appearance*, in the form of what is not yet realized, as something private or inward, as a mere goal. As documented in the previous chapter, the becoming of science through the *Phenomenology* consists in the *articulation* (*die Ausbildung*) of the Idea through our coming to terms with metaphysics. Thus, *our* transformation and *Bildung* through the critical reflection is at the same time the realization of metaphysics. As Hegel figures it, our coming to terms with metaphysics in the critical inquiry is both *our Bildung* and self-realization and the *Bildung* and realization of the metaphysics at the same time.

There emerges from this struggle with Kant's criticism a distinctively Hegelian conception of subjectivity, a conception according to which the human subject is by its very nature critical. Although the topic of Hegel's conception of subjectivity, in contrast to Kant's, requires its own study, I would like to end this study with some remarks on it, since we are led into it at the end. The Hegelian conception of the subject that emerges is something like the following: we essentially *become* what we are (or fail to) through staking ourselves (or failing to) in the critical encounter with radically opposed others. What makes this encounter critical is exactly that we find that we do not share between us the normative terms governing our relation (the criterion is in question). Moreover, the encounter is critical in the sense that our being is at stake in the question of what constitutes the ultimate norm of our activity. The ultimate norms are constituted through the self-reflective process. Through the self-reflective process common terms are constituted, and thus, community is constituted out of the initial scene of opposition. However, this reconciliation, though it constitutes both our self-realization and the realization of the other, demands at the same time transformation. Thus our realization depends on our staking ourselves, hence on our opening ourselves to transformation in the encounter or confrontation with the other. Hegel is led to this conception of the subject through taking on the modern epistemological project of critique against the background of his earlier rejection of it.

Hegel's figure of the mutual transformation and realization of apparently opposed parties is meant, I believe, to be read in contrast to Kant's figure of a reversal or revolution in the conception of what must conform to what: the object to our knowing rather than knowing to the object. As I have presented it, Kant's critical reflection on criteria is intimately bound up with Kant's articulation of the standpoint of the subject. In order to understand ourselves as subjects, in the sense of authors of judgment, we must understand ourselves likewise as the source of the norms that ultimately govern our activity of judgment. Kant conceives the subject as a formal structure of self-legislation. Kant's critical reflection to determine the criterion essentially predetermines our self-reflection over against metaphysics as the ultimate criterion, in the sense that the opposed other must submit to the empty (formal), self-standing self-reflection in order to count as anything for us. That we relate to the other only as mediated by a prior (an *a priori*) self-relation, implies that the object of knowing is merely ours, whereas the other before which we initially reflect, the in-itself, becomes permanently other and transcendent relative to our reflection; our very activity of reflection separates us eternally from it. An authentic relation or encounter with the initially opposed other is permanently precluded by our subjectivity.

Hegel's return to the standpoint of Kantian critique consists in his recognition that being a subject in fact demands that we not be determined by laws or norms independently of our recognition of them (our insight into them as rational). The recognition that the scene of criticism, the scene in which we stand over against each other, lacking shared criteria or fundamental norms of reason in terms of which to resolve conflicts between claims, constitutes a *crisis* for metaphysics. Hegel recognizes this as a crisis for metaphysics in the sense that what metaphysics proclaims as 'the law' or the unconditioned can have validity for us only through the general recognition of its authority or rationality. If we are subjects, then the law cannot simply determine us independently of our reflection. Accordingly, metaphysics must submit to the critical reflection in which its possibility is at stake. So far, Hegel follows Kant.

The difference consists in Hegel's insistence that the crisis of metaphysics must be a crisis for us as well. In our reflection on criteria, we must submit 'the law', *as we take it* to be, as we determine ourselves with respect to it, to testing, and hence to a transformation as may be required by the in-itself or by reason, objectively considered. For Hegel, as I understand him, the human subject is *critical* in the sense that its self-determination implies a critical process through which it must lose its truth in order to recover it eventually in recognition of 'the rational'. I take Hegel to say this in the following passage from the Introduction:

Whatever is confined within the limits of natural life cannot by its own efforts go beyond its immediate existence; but it is driven beyond it by something else; and this uprooting entails its death. Consciousness, however, is for itself the concept of itself. Hence it is something that goes beyond limits, and since these limits are its own, it is something that goes beyond itself .... Thus consciousness suffers [] violence at its own hands; it spoils its own limited satisfaction. (PhG, 74/¶80)

That consciousness is for itself the concept of itself means, as I understand Hegel, that we must determine ourselves—or, that 'the law' can only determine us through our activity of relating to it. This implies that what we take as the law is subject to change through our reflection and experience. Each such change is a sort of death, since we are determined, or we determine ourselves, according to the law. But each such change is also a sort of birth, since it introduces us to a new world organized around the new principle. The series of such transformations presents a picture of the development or *Bildung* or becoming of a human life as it approaches and determines its end. The development of a human being in relation to its end is distinguished from that of a natural organism exactly through its being *critical*. Since the human subject must *relate itself* to its end—that is, must determine its own end—it must *submit itself* to the crisis, hence to self-loss and to transformation, as a condition of attaining its end.

This may seem a vision of hell rather than a vision of human freedom. However, the conception of our freedom (or of its discovery) as bringing with it a hell is an old idea which both Kant and Hegel preserve and express in their distinctive ways. The despair of this path is bound with its hope, which Hegel represents as the eventual reconciliation with the initially opposed other. The reconciliation consists in the identity of what *we take as* the Idea or the law and the Idea, objectively considered (in-itself). This point of reconciliation marks the realization of 'the Idea', of metaphysics, *and* of us. As discussed above, the Idea remains *merely an idea*, in the sense of something private and inward and unrealized, independently of the critical process. In this process, the Idea is articulated and determined (*ausgebildet*). This process is the embodiment of the Idea in the lives of individuals and, in that respect, its realization.

But this process is also our realization, in the sense that we realize our freedom only by making the Idea, objectively considered, our own. It is only when we take the Idea, as articulated through the critical process, as the law through which our being is determined, that we cease to be in any way determined by something 'other' to us. This reconciliation with the rational, the initially opposed other, renders us completely self-determined for the first time. Since our being consists in our freedom, we properly exist through the realization of our freedom in the recognition of the absolute.[27]

The story of this transformation and self-realization is the story of the *Phenomenology* itself, whereas here I have meant only to tell the story of its method. I have meant to show that this method requires, in order to be genuinely critical, the openness to transformation, according to Hegel; the fending off of transformation is the common failure of critique. We have been concerned with two common ways in which the criticism of the *Phenomenology* has been missed. First, according to those interpretations that represent us as already occupying the standpoint of metaphysics, Hegel does not even aspire to meet the demands of critique in this work. However, I have been more concerned with the second, subtler, increasingly more common way in which Hegel's criticism is missed: namely, the interpretation according to which Hegel is engaged here in Kantian, transcendental critique. If my argument has been convincing, then, as Hegel sees it, transcendental critique issues in subjective idealism because it fails to put our criteria genuinely at stake in the critical reflection. Consequently Hegel's effort to define the method of the *Phenomenology* takes the shape it does both against transcendental critique and against his own earlier rejection of the critical project itself. Hegel's effort to achieve genuine critique requires putting at stake both the possibility of metaphysics and our criteria, and this effort issues in his distinctive self-transformational procedure.

---

[27] The thought is never expressed as concisely and directly by Hegel, so far as I know, as it is by Emerson: 'We apprehend the absolute. As it were, for the first time, *we exist*' (Emerson, from 'Nature', in *Ralph Waldo Emerson: Essays and Lectures*, 37).

Bibliography

Allison, Henry, *Kant's Transcendental Idealism: An Interpretation and Defense* (New Haven: Yale University Press, 1983; second edition, revised and enlarged, 2004).

――― *Kant's Theory of Freedom* (Cambridge: Cambridge University Press, 1990).

――― *Idealism and Freedom* (Cambridge: Cambridge University Press, 1996).

Ameriks, Karl, 'Kant's Transcendental Deduction as a Regressive Argument', *Kant-Studien* 69 (1978), 273–87.

――― 'Hegel's Critique of Kant's Theoretical Philosophy', *Philosophy and Phenomenological Research* 45 (1985), 1–35.

――― 'Recent Work on Hegel: The Rehabilitation of an Epistemologist?', *Philosophy and Phenomenological Research* 52 (1992), 177–202.

――― *Kant and the Fate of Autonomy: Problems in the Appropriation of the Critical Philosophy* (Cambridge: Cambridge University Press, 2000).

――― (ed.), *The Cambridge Companion to German Idealism* (Cambridge: Cambridge University Press, 2000).

Austin, J. L., 'Other Minds', in id., *Philosophical Papers*, edited by J. O. Urmson and G. J. Warnock, third edition (Oxford: Clarendon, 1979).

Beiser, Frederick, *The Fate of Reason: German Philosophy from Kant to Fichte* (Cambridge, MA: Harvard University Press, 1987).

Beiser, Frederick, (ed.), *The Cambridge Companion to Hegel* (Cambridge: Cambridge University Press, 1993).

Beiser, Frederick, *German Idealism: The Struggle Against Subjectivism, 1781–1801* (Cambridge, MA: Harvard University Press, 2002).

――― *The Romantic Imperative: The Concept of Early German Romanticism* (Cambridge, MA: Harvard University Press, 2004).

Bird, Graham, *Kant's Theory of Knowledge* (London: Routledge and Kegan Paul, 1962).

――― 'Hegel's Account of Epistemology in the *Lectures on the History of Philosophy*', in Stephen Priest (ed.), *Hegel's Critique of Kant* (Oxford: Clarendon, 1987), 65–76.

Brandom, Robert, *Making It Explicit: Reasoning, Representing and Discursive Content* (Cambridge, MA: Harvard University Press, 1996).

――― *Articulating Reasons: An Introduction to Inferentialism* (Cambridge, MA: Harvard University Press, 2000).

Breazeale, Daniel, 'Fichte's *Aenesidemus* Review and the Transformation of German Idealism', *Review of Metaphysics* 34 (1981), 545–68.

Bristow, William, 'Are Kant's Categories Subjective?', *Review of Metaphysics* 55 (2002), 551–80.

_____ '*Bildung* and the Critique of Modern Skepticism in McDowell and Hegel', in Karl Ameriks and Jürgen Stolzenberg (eds.), *Internationales Jahrbuch des Deutschen Idealismus/International Yearbook of German Idealism*, 3 (Berlin: Walter de Gruyter, 2005), 179–207.

Burnyeat, M. F., 'Idealism and Greek Philosophy: What Descartes Saw and Berkeley Missed', *Philosophical Review* 91 (1982), 3–40.

_____ 'Can the Skeptic Live his Skepticism?', in id. (ed.), *The Skeptical Tradition* (Berkeley, CA: University of California Press, 1983), 117–48.

Cavell, Stanley, *The Claim of Reason* (Oxford: Clarendon, 1979).

_____ *Conditions Handsome and Unhandsome* (Chicago: University of Chicago Press, 1990).

Descartes, René, *The Philosophical Writings of Descartes*, vol. II, translated by John Cottingham, Robert Stoothoff, and Dugald Murdoch (Cambridge: Cambridge University Press, 1984). (I cite Descartes's text using the pagination from vol. VII of the edition of his writings edited by C. Adam and P. Tannery (abbreviated **AT**) for ease of reference.)

Dove, Kenley Royce, 'Hegel's Phenomenological Method', *Review of Metaphysics* 23 (1970), 615–41.

Emerson, R. W., *Ralph Waldo Emerson: Essays and Lectures*, edited by Joel Porte (New York: Library of America, 1983).

Fichte, J. G., *Grundlage der gesamten Wissenschaftslehre* (1794), in I. H. Fichte (ed.), *Johann Gottlieb Fichtes sämmtliche Werke*, vol. I (Berlin: Veit, 1845–6), 85–244. (This edition of Fichte's works is abbreviated **SW**.)

_____ *J. G. Fichte: Gesamtausgabe der Bayerischen Akademie der Wissenschaften*, edited by Reinhard Lauth, Hans Jacob and Hans Gliwitzky (Stuttgart-Bad Cannstatt: Frommann 1964). (This edition is divided into four parts, each with multiple volumes, so a citation to a work in vol. 4 of Part One will read: I, 4, page number.)

_____ *Fichte: Early Philosophical Writings*, translated and edited by Daniel Breazeale (Ithaca, NY: Cornell University Press, 1988). (Abbreviated **EPW**.)

_____ 'Review of *Aenesidemus*', published in *Fichte: Early Philosophical Writings* (**EPW**), 59–77. (When citing the review, I first give the citation to the German text in the *Gesamtausgabe*, followed by the page reference to this English translation.)

_____ *Introductions to the* Wissenschaftslehre, *And Other Writings*, edited and translated by Daniel Breazeale (Indianapolis: Hackett, 1994).

Forster, Michael, *Hegel and Skepticism* (Cambridge, MA: Harvard University Press, 1989).

_____ *Hegel's Idea of a Phenomenology of Spirit* (Chicago: University of Chicago Press, 1998).

Franks, Paul, *Kant and Hegel on the Esotericism of Philosophy*, Ph.D. thesis, Harvard University, 1993.

―――― *All or Nothing: Systematicity, Transcendental Arguments, and Skepticism in German Idealism* (Cambridge, MA: Harvard University Press, 2005).

Friedman, Michael, *Kant and the Exact Sciences* (Cambridge, MA: Harvard University Press, 1992).

Fulda, Hans-Friedrich, and Rolf-Peter Horstman (eds.), *Skeptizismus und spekulatives Denken in der Philosophie Hegels* (Stuttgart: Klett-Cotta, 1996).

Freud, Sigmund, *The Interpretation of Dreams*, translated and edited by James Strachey (New York: Avon Books, 1965).

Fulda, H. F., and D. Henrich (eds.), *Materialien zu Hegels* Phänomenologie des Geistes (Frankfurt am Main: Suhrkamp, 1973).

Guyer, Paul, *Kant and the Claims of Knowledge* (Cambridge: Cambridge University Press, 1987).

―――― 'Thought and Being: Hegel's Critique of Kant's Theoretical Philosophy', in Frederick Beiser (ed.), *The Cambridge Companion to Hegel* (Cambridge: Cambridge University Press, 1993), 171–210.

Harris, H. S., *Hegel's Development: Night Thoughts (Jena 1801–1806)* (Oxford: Clarendon Press, 1983).

Henrich, Dieter, 'The Proof-Structure of Kant's Transcendental Deduction', *Review of Metaphysics* 22 (1969), 640–59.

―――― 'Die Deduktion des Sittengesetzes: Über die Gründe der Dunkelheit des letzten Abschnittes von Kants *Grundlegung zur Metaphysik der Sitten*', in A. Schwan (ed.), *Denken im Schatten des Nihilismus* (Darmstadt: Wissenschaftliche Buchgesellschaft, 1975), 55–112.

―――― 'Fichte's Original Insight', translated by David R. Lachterman, in *Contemporary German Philosophy*, I (University Park, PA: Pennsylvania University Press, 1982), 15–53.

―――― 'Identity and Objectivity: An Inquiry into Kant's Transcendental Deduction', in id., *The Unity of Reason: Essays in Kant's Philosophy*, edited by Richard Velkley (Cambridge, MA: Harvard University Press, 1994), 123–208.

Hume, David, *A Treatise on Human Nature*, edited by L. A. Selby-Bigge, second edition, revised by P. H. Nidditch (Oxford: Oxford University Press, 1978).

―――― *Enquiries Concerning Human Understanding and Concerning the Principles of Morals*, reprinted from the 1777 edition with Introduction and Analytical Index by L. A. Selby-Bigge, third edition, with text revised and notes by P. H. Nidditch (Oxford: Clarendon Press, 1975).

Hyppolite, Jean, *Genesis and Structure of Hegel's* Phenomenology of Spirit, translated by S. Cherniak and R. Heckman (Evanston, IL: Northwestern University Press, 1974).

Jacobi, Friedrich Heinrich, *David Hume über den Glauben, oder Idealismus und Realismus. Ein Gespräch* (Breslau: Lowe, 1787). Reprinted with 1815 *Vorrede* (New York: Garland Publishing, 1983).

_____ *The Main Philosophical Writings and the Novel 'Allwill'*, translated and with an introductory study, note, and bibliography by George di Giovanni (Montreal: McGill-Queen's University Press, 1994).

Kierkegaard, Soren, *The Sickness Unto Death*, translated with an introduction and notes by Alastair Hannay (New York: Penguin Books, 1989).

Korsgaard, Christine, *Creating the Kingdom of Ends* (Cambridge: Cambridge University Press, 1996).

Maker, William, *Philosophy Without Foundations: Rethinking Hegel* (Albany, NY: SUNY Press, 1994).

Marcuse, H., *Reason and Revolution* (Boston: Beacon Press, 1941).

Marx, Werner, *Hegels* Phänomenologie des Geistes: *die Bestimmung ihrer Idee in 'Vorrede' und 'Einleitung'*, (Frankfurt am Main: Vittorio Klostermann, 1971).

McDowell, John. 'Knowledge and the Internal', *Philosophy and Phenomenological Research* 55 (1995), 877–93.

_____ *Mind and World* (Cambridge, MA: Harvard University Press, 1994).

Neuhouser, Frederick, *Fichte's Theory of Subjectivity* (Cambridge: Cambridge University Press, 1990).

Nietzsche, Friedrich. *On the Genealogy of Morals*, translated by Walter Kaufman and R. J. Hollingdale (New York: Vintage, 1967).

Norman, Richard, *Hegel's Phenomenology: A Philosophical Introduction* (New York: St Martin's Press, 1976).

O'Neill, Onora, *Constructions of Reason: Explorations of Kant's Practical Philosophy* (Cambridge: Cambridge University Press, 1989).

Pinkard, Terry, *Hegel's* Phenomenology: *The Sociality of Reason* (Cambridge: Cambridge University Press, 1996).

_____ *Hegel: A Biography* (Cambridge: Cambridge University Press, 2000).

Pippin, Robert, *Hegel's Idealism: The Satisfactions of Self-Consciousness* (Cambridge: Cambridge University Press, 1989).

Plato, *Republic*, translated by G. M. A. Grube, revised by C. D. C. Reeve (Indianapolis: Hackett, 1992).

Prauss, Gerold, *Erscheinung bei Kant* (Berlin: de Gruyter, 1971).

_____ *Kant und das Problem der Dinge an Sich* (Bonn: Bouvier, 1974).

Priest, Stephen (ed.), *Hegel's Critique of Kant*, (Oxford: Clarendon, 1987).

Quine, W. V. O., 'Epistemology Naturalized', in id., *Ontological Relativity and Other Essays* (New York: Columbia University Press, 1969), 69–90.

Reinhold, Karl Leonhard, *Beiträge zur Berichtigung bisheriger Mißverständnisse der Philosophien*, vol. 1 (Jena: Mauke, 1790).

Reinhold, Karl Leonhard, *The Foundation of Philosophical Knowledge*, excerpted from Reinhold's *Über das Fundament des philosophischen Wissens*, and translated by George di Giovanni, in di Giovanni and H. S. Harris (eds.), *Between Kant and Hegel: Texts in the Development of Post-Kantian Idealism* (abbreviated **BKH**) (Albany, NY: SUNY Press, 1985), 54–103.

Rockmore, Tom, *Hegel's Circular Epistemology* (Bloomington: Indiana University Press, 1986).

_____ *On Hegel's Epistemology and Contemporary Philosophy* (Atlantic Highlands, NJ: Humanities Press, 1996).

Rorty, Richard, *Philosophy and the Mirror of Nature* (Princeton, NJ: Princeton University Press, 1979).

Schelling, F. W. J., 'Of the I as Principle of Philosophy, or On the Unconditional in Human Knowledge', in id., *The Unconditional in Human Knowledge: Four Early Essays (1794–1796)*, translated and commentary by Fritz Marti (Lewisburg: Bucknell University Press, 1980), 63–149.

_____ *Fernere Darstellungen aus dem System der Philosophie*, in Manfred Schröter (ed.), *Schellings Werke*, Nach der Originalausgabe in neuer Anordnung, first supplemental volume, (Munich, 1956), 385–562.

Schulze, Gottlob Ernst, *Kritik der theoretischen Philosophie*, in two volumes (Hamburg: Carl Ernst Bohm, 1801). (Re-issued by Aetas Kantiana, 1973.)

_____ *Aenesidemus, oder Über die Fundamente der von dem Herrn Professor Reinhold in Jena gelieferten Elementarphilosophie*, edited by A. Liebert (Berlin: Reuther und Reichhard, 1912). An excerpt of this is translated and published in George di Giovanni and H. S. Harris (eds.), *Between Kant and Hegel: Texts in the Development of Post-Kantian Idealism* (abbreviated **BKH**) (Albany, NY: SUNY Press, 1985), 104–35.

Sedgwick, Sally, 'Hegel's Treatment of Transcendental Apperception in Kant', *The Owl of Minerva* 23 (1992), 151–63.

Sextus Empiricus, *Outlines of Scepticism*, edited by Julia Annas and Jonathan Barnes (Cambridge: Cambridge University Press, 2000).

Smit, Houston, 'The Role of Reflection in Kant's *Critique of Pure Reason*', *Pacific Philosophical Quarterly* 80 (1999), 203–23.

Smith, John E., 'Hegel's Critique of Kant', *Review of Metaphysics* 26 (1973), 438–60.

Stern, Robert, 'Going Beyond the Kantian Philosophy: On McDowell's Hegelian Critique of Kant', *European Journal of Philosophy* 7 (1999), 247–74.

Strawson, Peter, F. *The Bounds of Sense: An Essay on Kant's* Critique of Pure Reason (London: Methuen, 1966).

Taylor, Charles, *Hegel* (Cambridge: Cambridge University Press, 1977).

Westphal, Kenneth, *Hegel's Epistemological Realism* (Dordrecht: Kluwer, 1989).

_____ *Hegel's Epistemology: A Philosophical Introduction to the* Phenomenology of Spirit (Indianapolis: Hackett, 2003).

Winfield, Richard Dien, *Overcoming Foundations: Studies in Systematic Philosophy* (New York: Columbia University Press, 1989).

_____ *Autonomy and Normativity: Investigations of Truth, Right and Beauty* (Aldershot: Ashgate, 2001).

Index

absolute, the 13, 52, 99–102, 113, 120, 134, 139, 164, 181–2, 200, 207, 220, 232, 247
  justification of knowledge of 106
  presupposition of 118, 209, 212
  see also Idea, the; metaphysics, objects of; rational knowledge
Academic skepticism 123, 136, 157
  see also ancient skepticism; Pyrrhonist skepticism
Academy, the 111, 123, 136, 159
Acnesidemus 123, 136
agency:
  epistemic 5, 9–11, 19, 29–31, 33–5, 51, 70–3, 80–1, 83
  rational 71–3, 80–3, 190–1, 241 n. 26
Agrippa 136, 161–2
Allison, Henry 8, 21–2, 29 n. 15, 78 n. 38
Ameriks, Karl 2 n. 4, 24 n. 10, 38–9, 42–4, 48–9, 54 n. 6, 65 n. 25, 66 n. 27, 67 n. 28, 106 n. 3, 124 n. 10, 124 n. 11, 206 n. 1
analytic philosophy:
  Hegel's reception 1–2, 4–6, 108–10, 114
  Kant's reception 6–8, 54
ancient skepticism 135, 150, 151–2, 156–64, 176
  distinguished from modern 11–12, 107–8, 136–140, 155–6
  see also modern skepticism; Pyrrhonist skepticism
anti-foundationalism 65–6, 95, 206 n. 2
  see also foundationalism
appearances 47, 135, 188
  living according to 136–7, 158
  of philosophy 201–03, 244
  and things in themselves 27
apperception, Kant's principle of 7 n. 12, 10 n., 28–35, 71–3, 79–80, 81–4, 89, 96, 120, 128, 148 n., 191
  see also self-consciousness; subjectivity
Austin, J. L. 110 n.
autonomy 75, 91, 102, 129–30, 132–3, 168, 190–91, 245–6
  as structure of rational subject 9–10, 71

Beiser, Frederick 61 n. 21, 121 n. 6, 123, 124 n. 10
Berkeley, George 8–9, 20–1, 132
Bildung 70, 160, 187–88, 239–40, 244, 246

Bird, Graham 8 n. 14, 21 n. 3, 22
Boehm, Miren viii
Breazeale, Daniel 127 n., 128
Burnyeat, Myles 156–8

categorical imperative 70, 83, 89, 96
  see also reason, practical for Kant
categories:
  pure meaning of 42–44
  as rules for the understanding 37–8, 40–1, 47–9
  subjectivity of 38–49
  transcendental deduction of 7 n. 11, 9, 11, 35–6, 40, 65–6 n. 25, 81–3, 128
  see also concepts, pure
Cavell, Stanley vii, 172 n. 4, 183 n. 13
certainty 129–30, 150–55
cogito 129–30, 151, 152–3, 156–7, 189–90
cognition, *see* knowledge
concept, the (*der Begriff*) 69
concepts:
  intellectual 46
  and intuitions 25, 40–1
  in knowledge 10 n. 15, 25
  of an object in general, 45
  as representations 141–2
  of the understanding, pure 35–6, 82
consciousness 135, 216, 218, 224, 235
  configurations of 210, 225, 229–30
  fact of 125, 128–9, 135, 150–1, 154–5, 159, 163
  ordinary, *see ordinary consciousness*
  philosophical 13
  representational 124–5, 128, 142
  see also Principle of Consciousness
Copernican revolution in epistemology 26, 33, 35, 62–3, 96, 215, 245
  and Fichte 130–32
  two-fold enactment of 63
criterion:
  of critique 70, 118, 171–5, 239
  of knowledge 13, 218–19, 224–5
  of ordinary consciousness 111, 142, 144, 194, 215
  problem of the 213–18, 219, 221–23
  of pure reason (of rational knowledge) 58–61, 62, 74, 77–8, 106, 120, 142–3, 144, 167, 193, 198, 202, 215, 239
  see also principle